Edward Bellamy Writes Again

Edward Bellamy Writes Again

by Joseph R. Myers, P.E.

ISBN: 0-9657458-0-5
Library of Congress catalogue card number: 97-093135

To Mary, my wife,
who has been my companion for centuries.

To Edgar Cayce,
the soul to whom I owe the most,
other than to Jesus of Nazareth.

Contents

Preface

"Joe, you sound like Edward Bellamy. You must have read *Looking Backward.*"

"No, I don't think so." I paused to think a moment. "No, I haven't read *Looking Backward* and I've never heard of Bellamy."

"Well, you sure do sound like him. You'll have to get his book and read it."

That conversation with Merle Randle, an old friend, gave me the key that I had been looking for. He and I were talking about the country's political problems, especially with regard to the money system. Merle is about 15 years older than myself. While I had no knowledge of Bellamy's work, he had studied *Looking Backward* in one of his college courses because the book was still quite current in the middle 1930's. It was a Utopian novel in which economic equality was the basis for political equality and the money system was drastically altered.

That incident occurred in the early part of 1964. About six years earlier I had become intensely interested in the study of reincarnation. A series of experiences with dreams, meditation, intuitive flashes and a great deal of introspection had given me some detailed memories or possibly hallucinations about having lived before. Names, dates and places were not among those details but rather events that had had a great emotional impact upon me. Dying by suicide, by drowning, by tuberculosis, by pneumonia, by infanticide, and other death and dying experiences came in more clearly than anything else.

By carefully examining the faintest memories and filing them away, so to speak, I built up an elaborate picture of the processes involved in dying and being reborn. During one very unique experience in deep meditation I witnessed a series of faces appear before me, all of which I knew to be my own. It seemed to me that the first of them were nebulous, but they gradually took more and more definite characteristics. As the series progressed, I saw faces in sharply etched detail. Each tiny line, each proportion, each and every aspect of these faces instantly revealed a facet of the personality of the human being behind them. While the personalities varied widely on the surface—pirate, galley slave, alcoholic, cruel slave master, monk, nobleman, sailor, missionary, writer—there was an inner character that was also written in the face which changed very little over thousands of years.

Regardless of the circumstances of birth and life, I saw that the physical resemblance of the face was similar to a startling degree for a series of several consecutive lives and noticeably similar over many centuries, especially around the eyes.

At that time, I had never encountered this information from any of the wide range of material that I had read on the subject of reincarnation. Through introspection and observation, I had learned that sometimes in a conversation, or when looking at a picture, or perhaps getting a telephone number, I'd make a connection with a related detail in a former life. This procedure had been going on for several years. One set of memories suggested a life as a newspaper man and author who had lived between 1850 and 1898 and died of tuberculosis. Many personal feelings and character traits of this man I had found to be still near the surface in my present life.

A few days after my conversation with Merle Randle, I got a copy of *Looking Backward* from the public library. It was an old edition, had no biographical data, not even a date, except in its context. Before I'd read two chapters, I realized that I had written it. It was actually my own book and Bellamy was that writer and newspaper man I remembered having been. Since there are several biographies of Bellamy, very shortly I was able to confirm all the biographical data which I had remembered. The physical resemblance was so close that one acquaintance thought a picture of Bellamy that I'd had framed was actually one of me until informed otherwise. My son eventually read *Looking Backward* and afterwards said, "Dad, he sounds just like you!"

A few of the more unusual examples of similarities between myself and Bellamy may be worth mentioning because of the implications they have. While Bellamy spent his whole life as a writer, my own education included no college and only one semester in high school in journalism. My standing was near the bottom of the class. After practicing meditation for several years and awakening the memory of having been a newspaper man, I found I had a gift for writing in the style of a newsman and doing book reviews. (Book reviewing was a forte with Bellamy.) My first professional writing was a one hour news documentary about Unidentified Flying Objects for WBT Radio, America's third oldest radio station. The documentary was broadcast with no editing by the studio and won first prize in its class and the sweepstakes award for WBT of Charlotte, North Carolina, in 1964 in a statewide competition sponsored by the Associated Press.

Because of his obsession with the idea of economic equality, Bellamy had certain pet dislikes. It is on record that he disliked the use of diamonds as jewelry so strongly that he would not buy one for his wife's engagement ring. My own sentiments were the same. When we were engaged in 1964, I gave my wife an amethyst instead.

Bellamy was so fluent in Latin that his daughter said he could read it almost as easily as he read English. Almost without studying, I made straight "As" in school in Latin and wondered why anyone found it difficult.

Bellamy worked in the time when reporters signified the end of a story by the number -30-. As soon as I was old enough to do any sort of papers in grammar school, even spelling tests, I ended them with the reporter's -30-.

Bellamy was a good swimmer, but especially preferred salt water; the same is true of myself. He enjoyed skating a great deal as a boy and was a very good rifle marksman. There was no ice in Oakland, California, where I grew up, but I roller skated from one end of that city to the other, taking my lunch and leaving the house on Saturday mornings to skate all day long. In the Armed Services in WWII, I qualified as expert in every piece I fired; carbine, M1 rifle and automatic pistol.

Bellamy was able to study on his own, went to college for less than a year, and took no regular courses, but only a literature study program. He planned his own course with some guidance from the faculty. He acquired on his own the education to become an editor and became fluent in French, German, Latin and could read Italian. His family had available the resources to send him to college, but he was unwilling to accept financial support from anyone.

My own family lived quite close to the campus of the University of California and were glad to support me if I wished to go. The tuition for the University was very nominal at that time. My oldest brother had graduated there and my next oldest brother was attending when I got out of high school. However, I wished to pay my own board at home and be financially independent and so went to work in a ship building yard. (Bellamy took a keen interest in boats of his day.)

Two years later, in October of 1942, I enlisted in the Air Force to avoid being drafted into some other branch of service not of my choice. After my discharge four years later as an aircraft engineering officer, I was eligible for four years of college financed by the government but chose not to accept. In the ten years that followed, I studied engineering on my own and passed all the written examinations in the State of North Carolina to become a professional engineer. In more than twenty years since then, I have not learned of another registered engineer who passed the written examinations without first attending college.

Even before he was in his teens, Bellamy was intensely concerned with political inequality and social injustices and had written short essays on such things. At the same age, I can remember talking to friends about these conditions and how they might be corrected. During this age period both Bellamy and I had a deeply moving conversion experience and resolved to spend our lives in dedication to serve the cause of social justice.

Since there are excellent biographies of Edward Bellamy (and I have read them), there is little to be added by trying to list all of the countless parallels in our lives. It would be possible to fill an entire volume with the details about our similarities; but, the fact that I have become intimately familiar with Bellamy's life would seem to discount my ability to make an impartial evaluation of them. For me, the question of whether or not I am the rebirth of Bellamy no longer exists. Yet, there are many obvious differences in our personalities. The reality for me is that the inner man, the I Am, the underlying identity which I think of as my true self, is the same as for Bellamy.

Joseph R. Myers

Introduction

Imagine having the opportunity to read a book that you had written seventy-five years previously and a biography of your own life as an author which had ended sixty-five years before! Then, imagine trying to improve upon that book and that life. Could anyone possibly have such an experience?

Bellamy Writes Again is precisely the example of such an experience, in this author's opinion. Edward Bellamy's novel, *Looking Backward*, and its sequel, *Equality*, were written to offer a political philosophy which the author hoped would have a practical effect to improve the lot of posterity. In order to present his philosophy in a highly readable form, he wrote in the language and style to which he thought the public would respond. He gave it somewhat of a plot so that it could be classified as a Utopian romance, a work of fiction. But, behind it were years of thinking and concern with the problem of political inequality, injustice and poverty in America and throughout the world.

Bellamy's *Looking Backward* did not catch the public's attention until about a year after it was published, selling only ten thousand copies its first year. After that, it became the most popular new book in print and was the first work in America to equal the sales of *Uncle Tom's Cabin*.

In the year 1936, three outstanding personalities, Charles Beard, John Dewey, and Edward Weeks, independently making a list of the twenty-five most influential books published in the previous fifty years, all put Bellamy's work in first place for American authors and in second place internationally, Karl Marx's *Das Kapital* being first. A few years earlier, ideas from Bellamy's work were lifted directly by some of the

New Deal administrators under President Franklin D. Roosevelt. Because of the efforts and influence of Eleanor Roosevelt, they were crystallized into congressional acts in the depression years, one notable example being the Civilian Conservation Corps, the CCC camps.

This new work, *Bellamy Writes Again*, is an attempt to improve upon *Looking Backward*. In many ways, there will be only a slight resemblance between the two. Constructive influence though Bellamy's work has been (it is still in print), it seems now that key ideas were missing. Some of the thinking was impractical and hindered the work from accomplishing many things that Bellamy had hoped it might.

The objective of this new work is actually identical with Bellamy's. But, as a nation we are in a different stage of political development. We have proven to ourselves that the material circumstances of the common man, the rank and file of the nation, could be immeasurably improved and his level of education lifted far above what it was in Bellamy's time. Yet it has not altered the measure of disregard we have for our posterity. In fact, it has even hastened the destruction of our environment. Bellamy's dream of economic equality is even farther away, with something in the neighborhood of fifty percent of our nation's wealth now being owned by less than one percent of our population.

In Bellamy's time, there was no Federal Reserve Law to control banking practices. The manipulation of the value of money enabled financial organizations to strip the farmers of their land and to acquire great wealth through loaning money against various securities, such as real estate property. The money would be loaned during a period of manipulated inflation and become due when its value had been increased several times over by a severe depression.

A different but equally dishonest and equally honored and legal method of stripping the wealth of the land was inaugurated in the 1920's. The originally honest and democratic Federal Reserve Bank Law was amended to create an astonishingly undemocratic system that precipitated the financial crash of 1929. With more amendments, the unbelievably dishonest system was created that has enabled a small handful of people to legally gain control of the wealth of a great nation and generated the ever increasing inflation which steals the life savings of the working man. The money system's functioning is again examined in *Bellamy Writes Again*, but not at such great length as *Looking Backward* and *Equality*.

However, the main thrust of this work is not so much to deal with such questions directly, but with the source of the problem at a deeper level. While the objective of these two books is the same, that is, to make a contribution toward the establishment of a Utopian form of government, their approach is quite different. Both are a philosophical work thinly disguised as a work of fiction in the form of a Utopian romance. Bellamy deals with the idea that analyzing the problem and proposing practical solutions in the form of social and political action will bring improvements. Observing the failure of such an approach with the perspective of a man living almost a hundred years later has inspired a different approach to the whole question.

Our ancient struggle as a race has always been to create a better society, a society where each and every child is born into circumstances that offer an equal opportunity to develop its greatest potential in surroundings that are most conducive to such an achievement. This work is built upon the premise that first as individuals we must find the incentive to set the welfare of the whole race above our personal, family, community, and even national interests before we can hope to establish a Utopian society.

Bellamy Writes Again is a work of fiction; but every facet of the philosophical views that are portrayed as the teachings of a wiser future generation has been researched in ancient mystical writings, and in modern works on the subject, and is a part of the personal experience of the author on some level of consciousness. In other words, the philosophical ideas to be found in this book concerning the origin of man, his destiny, his experiences in after death states, his relationship with astrological influences, with angels and the mythological spirits guiding various forces and life forms in the earth, are all based on some personal experience of the author's which has persuaded him that they are a true reflection of the natural order of things. While it may be only the author's opinion that he is describing realities, the point being made here is that these things are not presented as merely figments of a lively imagination.

The advantage of presenting philosophical ideas by incorporating them in a work of fiction is that it makes them easier to encounter and examine. Hopefully, this book can be enjoyed simply as an imaginative work of fiction with a hero with which the reader can identify. It is the author's belief that the greater adventure to be found in this work will be in the challenging experience of meeting with new ideas on a broad range of subjects. For example, the suggestion that for good reasons there inevitably shall be a Utopian society on earth and that everyone shall have the chance to experience it could hardly fail to be an exciting idea.

It is not intended that there should be suspense or fast moving action bridging from one chapter to the next. Each chapter presents a particular idea by incorporating it in the action of that chapter. There will not be found even a hint that immorality is other than destructive to the individual, but this view will not be tiresome because it will not come through as the usual sin and guilt approach.

It was a truly delightful adventure to write this book. Years of searching for answers, perhaps lifetimes, have been summed up in its pages.

Ancient Atlantean Definition of
SOUL

*An individual entity of infinite potentiality
which forever retains its identity through the
changelessness of change; constantly evolving
a higher and a better manifestation and
expression of itself and of itself alone, by, with,
in and through matter; eternally operative in
the positive and negative, active and passive
principles of being and consciousness of its own
existence; ever seeking and striving for
at-one-ment with the ALL of souls.*

CHAPTER 1

Awakening

"God is our refuge and strength, a very present help in trouble. Therefore will not we fear, though the earth be removed and though the mountains be carried into the midst of the sea."

—Psalm 46

W here am I? How did I get here? Who are these people? Why can't I feel anything? Why can't I move? What's wrong with my body? My mind was racing from one thought to the next as I groped for some explanation of the state I was in.

The room was well lighted but there was no glare. It seemed as if the walls themselves and the ceiling were glowing. Five men were standing around me and I could tell that my body was resting on a small table, perhaps an operating table. I had just opened my eyes and I could roll them but had no sensation in any part of my body, as though my mind had been entirely disconnected from it.

One of the men spoke a few words with intense emotion, but I found I could barely hear them. It sounded like he said, "He's reviving…his eyes are open…amazing!" I couldn't tell what the other men were doing, except that they seemed to be working on me somehow. While it was plain that these were men of the medical profession, their manner of dress was different from anything I had seen in a hospital and the room was not like any hospital room I'd ever been in.

They worked over me in silence as I lay there feeling absolutely nothing and barely conscious. No more words were spoken after the first remarks that I heard. How long this activity went on I could not say; but each moment seemed a century, for my mind was in a state of shocked confusion. It might have been twenty minutes or perhaps an hour before the first trace of feeling began to creep up the back of my neck. It was a dull ache at first which gradually expanded into a splitting headache. This grew into a bursting sensation in the back of my head and then became an unbearable pain moving like hot lava around the upper part of my temples. I would have screamed out in

1

agony; but I had no sensation of having a throat or lungs and I could do nothing. Tears welled up in my eyes. As the pain increased still further, a red film seemed to darken my vision. I was mercifully relieved from further agony as I lapsed into unconsciousness again.

How much later it was when I awoke again I had no idea; however, I noticed that the surroundings were altogether different. I was now in a room that was elegant and yet unpretentious in its decoration. A girl, perhaps twenty years old, was sitting near the bed so that I saw her as soon as I opened my eyes. She was the very picture of physical health and lovely young womanhood. It was plain that she had been keeping a vigil at my side until my consciousness returned. Her compassion toward me, which I felt as I looked into her eyes, was startling and disarming.

"Who are you?" This time my vocal chords were functioning and the words sounded clearly, if somewhat weakly. The pain was gone from my head and I could feel the rest of my body. For the moment I had forgotten the agony and confusion of the last time I was conscious. I was weak, but I could feel. I could move a little and felt like I was in my body.

"Please be still and don't try to speak now." Her voice was soft and gentle. "You have undergone an experience that brought you near death, but you are through it now. You are weak, very weak; and you must rest peacefully until you are stronger. Please, don't ask about it now. We will tell you all that we know when you are a little stronger. Please rest quietly."

Her words were soothing and reassuring. I felt that there was nothing to fear. A sense of my extreme weakness began to register when the effort to focus my eyes and move my head almost caused me to faint. If I could not talk or ask questions, perhaps I could think back to events that preceded my present condition. What was the last thing that I could remember? What was I last doing before the sleep or unconsciousness or accident or whatever it was that put me into my present condition? The effort to think seemed to exhaust me and I sank gradually into a state of mental fatigue that must have soon become a deep slumber.

The next time that my consciousness returned, my first awareness came in response to some strange music that was filling the room. The music had a quality that was new to me for it seemed to be going right into my bones. Different parts of my body felt like they were vibrating in resonance with it as the melody and rhythm changed. Now my body felt stronger and my mind was more at peace. As I looked around, I realized that the girl I had seen earlier was no longer with me. Now there was an older man standing near a window on the far side of the room. He smiled slightly as he turned from the window to find me looking at him with what I am sure was a puzzled expression.

"I'm Alex Karoll, Dr. Karoll. You are in my home and it was my daughter, Alice, who was with you when you first regained consciousness three days ago." His voice was reassuring, but it also had a certain ring suggesting inner strength. "You are responding marvelously to our treatment and we expect that you will be on your feet in another five or six days. Please, don't exert yourself mentally or emotionally with questions until we feel that you have the stamina you need."

This man is an unusual person, I thought to myself, for he has the atmosphere of a learned person, but the physique of a fine athlete. Like his daughter, he had a disarming manner and made me feel that I had no cause to be concerned.

In the days that followed I underwent many unfamiliar treatments to nourish and strengthen me physically and to keep me undisturbed emotionally. It was two or three days after my second awakening in the doctor's home before I was given any kind of food. During that time my body was massaged several times each day with various delightful smelling liquids. Some of these were oily and some seemed to be soaked up by my skin like water is taken up by chamois. After each of these massages I had a pleasant sense of having been nourished and strengthened. At times, more of the unusual music was used to cause my body and mind to relax. At other times a panel in the ceiling glowed brilliantly with gradually changing fluorescent colors which had a soothing effect and gave me a sense of physical and mental wellbeing.

Fresh fruit juices were my first food, then in a few days, delicious purees from fresh raw fruits, nuts and sprouted grains were added. Each of these were given at separate times and I was cautioned to take them slowly. Gradually, I began to feel like a normally functioning human being. By the time that I was up and around I had been treated with special rays, colored lights, sound, with electrical therapy using discs and wires applied to various parts of my body, massage, osteopathic manipulations, oils and solutions which were rubbed into my skin, incenses, hydrotherapy, sun baths and herbal tonics. The hypodermic needles, pills, and other internal medicines I was familiar with were conspicuously absent.

During my first weakness and confusion I took all the attention given me for granted, but as strength returned to my body, I became more and more conscious of the efforts being spent in my behalf. I began to be overwhelmed by the gentleness and kindness being expressed toward me by everyone. Though a stranger to them all, this family was showering me with loving kindness equal to the care my mother gave to me when I was a small child.

The day soon came when the good doctor said that I was strong enough to ask the questions which he knew were crowding my mind. He suggested that I have dinner with his family and afterwards we would talk. The evening meal was to mark my first association with Dr. Karoll and his family as a social experience. As with all my other needs, the doctor had provided me with appropriate clothing. While I had never been especially concerned with clothing styles, I could not fail to notice many differences in the attire furnished me. The evening was expected to be an unusual occasion by all and I could feel the excitement in the air.

Several days previously I had been introduced to the doctor's wife as she helped attend my needs. I was impressed that she was a perfect counterpart in womanhood to match the caliber of the man. It all seemed too perfect and ideal to be a reality. Like Dr. Karoll, she had poise and vigorous physical health and, in addition, a feminine beauty that was both youthful and queenly. Their daughter, Alice, who was twenty-five, and their sixteen year old son, James, were both with them for the evening. James was home from school just for the occasion.

The dinner was simple in its preparation, a variety of tasty raw and lightly cooked vegetable sprouts and nuts with a dessert of stewed wild cherries. Mrs. Karoll served an appetizing hot drink about twenty minutes before dinner to prepare our digestive systems, just as one might use a light wine. The doctor asked a blessing movingly from his heart, setting an atmosphere of reverence and humility. The meal itself was partaken of as if it were an act of worship. I found myself carefully watching the manners of those around me to imitate them, for my usual way of eating, acceptable as it was at any formal gathering, would have seemed uncouth in their presence. I particularly noticed that no one partook of nearly the quantity of food that I would have called normal and there was no conversation during the meal. Lovely classical music, some that I recognized, some that I had never heard, accompanied the meal loud enough to listen to but softly.

After this, we all gathered in their spacious family room around the fireplace. The smell of burning cedar was in the air and the pleasant surroundings were relaxing. However, the prospect of learning something of how I arrived in my present situation naturally excited me.

CHAPTER 2

A Stranger

"Let's see, you've told us that your full name is David Alan Neuport," Dr. Karoll paused and then added, "and how old do you think you are, David?" There was a slight smile about the corners of the doctor's mouth as he asked me this and I sensed that he had some kind of surprise for me.

"Why, I'm fifty-four," I said slowly.

"Hmmm," Dr. Karoll hesitated. "David, this is the year 2103. You must be more than one hundred years older than you think."

I couldn't take in what Dr. Karoll meant. I couldn't see why he had made such an incomprehensible statement.

"What do you mean?" I was almost angry. I had not expected such a confusing turn in the conversation. "How could this be? Where am I?"

Seeing my reaction to his statement caused Dr. Karoll to be silent for a moment. Then, without showing that he had heard my questions, he began asking me how I felt and what I thought of the treatments given me. This distracted me and, as we discussed my health and how I liked the food, I calmed down and relaxed. Then, in the same tone that he had asked how I liked my dinner a few moments earlier, he asked, "Where did you live?" The doctor said this without realizing the implication of his question.

"What do you mean...where did I live? My home is in Asheville." I did not see a sign of familiarity with the city showing on anyone's face. "Asheville, North Carolina," I repeated, miffed by the apparent insignificance of my hometown to these obviously well educated people.

"Oh, yes! Of course...we're not far from there right now." The doctor's response came as though he was just remembering something that he should have known immediately.

"What part of Asheville?"

I felt like his question sounded patronizing…as though he hoped that showing an interest that implied a knowledge of the city would put me more at ease.

"Charlotte Street…about six blocks from the freeway." Being suspicious of the purpose of the question, I did not care to elaborate further.

Dr. Karoll sensed my feelings and he said nothing for a moment. Then he gently began asking questions that would lead me to talk about myself, my family, my work, my religion, hobbies, and the ambitions I had for myself. It was apparent to me that the family was sincerely interested in me. Though I was a total stranger, they wanted me to know that their friendship and the accommodation of their home was offered as if I were a member of the family. The treatment I had already received at their hands left no doubt in my mind about the good thoughts they entertained toward me. Still, there was a disturbing implication that I would continue to need their friendship even after my strength was restored, and this I did not understand. However, once I began to talk about myself I became so engrossed that I temporarily forgot the alarming questions churning in my mind. The rapt audience they gave me was flattering so I talked on and on. This released my tensions and I found myself giving my life history.

"I was born in Asheville and grew up there. My father and I never got very well acquainted because he was a traveling salesman and was away even on weekends about half of the time. My mother was conscientious about taking care of her four children, my two older brothers, my older sister and myself. She had strong feelings about the value of an education and influenced me to take advantage of my own opportunities for learning." I began my account this way, touching only the high points as I went along.

They all listened so attentively that I was soon encouraged to give a more elaborate account. I told them of my high school successes in sports and academics, of my interest in science, of my time in the military air service and how I had served as an aircraft maintenance engineering officer. I outlined how I had come up the hard way, working after hours since grammar school to buy my own clothing and bicycles, and then going to work full time at eighteen, first as an apprentice to a carpenter and, later, learning steel fabrication in Norfolk as a boiler-maker's apprentice. I recounted how I enjoyed the challenge and the satisfaction of accomplishment in learning trades. I learned shipfitting, lofting, structural steel and ornamental iron work, moved into office work to become a draftsman, steel estimator, sales engineer, structural design engineer, and, eventually, a freelance professional engineer.

As each member of the family showed such keen interest in my story and asked questions upon various details to persuade me to elaborate on them, I began to feel confident that my mind was functioning normally. It seemed to me that the evening was hardly well started before it was time to retire. I had learned little for I had done all the talking. The family was anxious to have me continue with my account the following evening if I felt strong enough. With the interest that each of them expressed in me, it did not enter my mind that I was a stranger interrupting the routine of their household.

The doctor asked my permission to invite one or two friends that he felt would like to hear me continue my story and his son, James, made the same request. Flattered for the moment, I said I should be glad to have them, but after we retired and I was lying quietly in the dark before going off to sleep, my thoughts took me back over the events of the evening and I began to see them from a more impersonal point of view. I thought about this family group; the father and mother and their obviously superior qualities by comparison with myself, Alice, with such maturity and intelligence, the sixteen year old son with such a remarkably developed body and mind and the way his questions about my work showed a comprehension of engineering principles beyond my own.

The events of the past few days began to race through my mind. What about the totally unfamiliar home conveniences that I'd seen, the lighting techniques, the approach to healing that they had used to cause my recovery? A mental conflict was growing in my mind. The questions that at first seemed impossibly farfetched were becoming plausible. My heart began to pound. Could I have caught the interest of these superior people because I was actually from a different culture— a culture that was current more than one hundred years in the past?

Why else should I interest them?

Why hadn't they all known immediately that we were near Asheville?

Was Dr. Karoll actually correct when he said that I was over one hundred years old?

What prompted him to ask, "Where did you live?" instead of asking, "Where do you live?"

Sleep was gone from my thoughts now, though I was exhausted. A kind of insecurity I'd never known before came over me...fear would not be the right word, for I had learned to condition my unconscious mind against fear. Before setting up the last experiment that Professor Darch and I were working on, I had learned self hypnosis. The details of those experiments and the events surrounding the last few days before I awakened under Dr. Karoll's care were coming back to me.

As these memories took shape, powerful emotions began to arise. I began to breathe slowly, deeply and evenly to help master them. With all the will power I could muster, I tried to hang on to my powers of reasoning.

CHAPTER 3

The Cave

"**W**ell, Bill, I think we have the chamber ready. The ceiling's high enough." I glanced up where I had just chipped away some rock. "Tomorrow we'll move everything in, check the ventilation again, and I'll get ready."

Professor William Darch, my companion, was an instructor in psychology at a privately endowed college in the same city where I made my own living as free lance engineer. Our mutual interest in psychical research brought us together several years before and we had become fast friends. We were making preparations to carry out a dangerous experiment with suspended animation deep inside a cave that had its entrance on the hillside behind Darch's mountain cabin.

"You don't need to worry about ventilation, Dave. Besides, you won't be needing much oxygen once your body gets down to the ambient temperature."

"I guess you're right...I don't like to think about that," I laughed and shivered a little as I thought about the coolness of the air.

Bill Darch wasn't enthusiastic about our experiment. He would not have been willing to help me had I not convinced him of my determination to go through with it, with or without his assistance. He was too good a friend not to help under those circumstances and so he decided to do his part to make it as safe as possible. My idea for it came from some well documented accounts of trance phenomena achieved in India. We both identified the strange powers of the Hindu Fakirs with their capacity to self induce a deep hypnotic trance. Investigations carried on by psychical researchers in India had proven that some Fakirs could survive being totally submerged in cold water for thirty days without ill effects.

I didn't have the faith to risk my life with a try of even thirty minutes immersed in cold water, but lying unconscious in a cool cave did not seem so dangerous to me. At least there was nothing to entirely stop my breathing. I used a brain wave indicator to train myself and had learned to go into a deep trance that was very near death. I had gradually worked up to a full week of suspended animation. The more Bill and I investigated what could be done with hypnosis, the more unlimited its potential appeared. Miraculous healings, which included perfect knitting of bones only moments after a compound fracture, seemed to depend on the acceptance of a powerful hypnotic suggestion. There was no question about the genuiness of the healings but the many techniques used to administer an effective hypnotic suggestion to the patient varied from magic rites of African medicine men to priestly incantations at The Shrine of Lourdes. We hypothesized a Superconscious Mind for each individual which has miracle working power to control and alter both the physical body and conditions surrounding it. Hypnotically implanted requests from the unconscious mind, we theorized, released and directed this power. The research work of Max Freedom Long upon the magic performed by Hawaiian Hunas was one of the influences upon our thinking.

"We're through with the air hammer, Dave. Disconnect the hose and take out the tools and I'll clean up the debris." Bill picked up the broom and began to sweep the dust and stone chips toward the farther end of the chamber. The rough stone floor was fairly level now and we had enough head room to walk around without stooping. The chamber itself was about two hundred feet in from the cave mouth, which was only fifty feet away from the back porch of Bill's cabin. We had pulled a gasoline driven air compressor into his driveway and connected up enough hose to reach back to the chamber we wanted to enlarge.

"Three months is going to take us into the middle of September, Dave," commented Bill as we made our way toward the mouth of the cave. "Why don't you put this thing off until maybe the first of the year and enjoy one more summer?"

"What do you mean...enjoy one more summer, Bill?" I said, half jokingly. "I'm surely not planning on missing next year's!"

"You know darned well that isn't what I meant, Dave," Bill objected, and then added thoughtfully, "but since you put it that way, I am beginning to wonder why I've been willing to help you set up an experiment upon yourself that I couldn't be persuaded to undergo."

I paused for a moment before answering and then suggested, "Suppose we plan to have Walt and Milo and John here next Sunday. That will give me a week to get ready. By then I'll have three days on grape juice and three days of fasting. I'd like to check out the tape recorder running it for several days, too."

Intellectually I was convinced that hypnosis could release the power of mind over matter. I could expect my body to be preserved perfectly for an indefinite period and protected from injury of any nature. In fact, I believed that if my three month experiment left me with no harmful effects, it would prove one could spend years in suspended animation.

The tape recorder was going to repeat carefully worded suggestions to my unconscious mind at intervals during my first ten days of trance. These instructions would direct my unconscious to lower the body temperature to that of the surrounding air, to suspend all the life processes, to allow no destructive influences or changes to affect a single cell of my body and to draw directly from the air whatever was required to preserve and sustain it. We had prepared a casket-like box with perfectly fitted support for my body. The support was of stainless steel mesh and my body itself would be enclosed in a coarsely woven linen shroud. The box was well ventilated at both ends with fine mesh screens.

Bill Darch was terribly concerned for me but I knew that I could depend upon him. While I could set up the experiment entirely without his assistance, I was very grateful to have him work with me on it.

In answer to my suggestion that we begin the following Sunday, Bill pleaded with me to shorten the time.

"All right, David," he said, "if you insist that you want to hibernate through the summer instead of waiting until winter, then how about letting me wake you in the middle of August so that you can enjoy Autumn this year? Two months ought to be long enough to prove your point."

"Three months, Bill," I insisted, "a full three months."

CHAPTER 4

The Year 2103

*"I know not what the future has
of marvel or surprise,
Assured alone that life and death
His mercy underlies."*
—*Pawnee Indian Prayer*

Where should I start? As I lay in the dark, I went back over each of the troublesome questions the doctor had raised in my mind. Surely it was necessary for me to assume that Dr. Karoll was sincere. It would be little short of insane to imagine that a hoax was being played upon me to drive me mad. My reason quickly denied the possibility that the kindliness shown me during my weakness could be combined with some diabolical plan to shatter my mind. No, that would be irrational. But what could Dr. Karoll have meant when he told me that I was probably more than a hundred years older than I thought? "This is the year 2103," he had said…just as simply as that.

Here was the necessary starting point to work from. I set myself to carefully reviewing all my recent experiences. I was sure that I could find the logical consistency in the circumstances and events that would exist if I were actually alive in the year 2103. The doctor had unconsciously asked me where did I live instead of where do you live. None of the family had shown familiarity with the name of a good sized and very well known city, but later agreed that we were close to its geographical location. After I went over the evening's conversation, I thought about the unusual medical treatments given me, the interior of the home I was in, the many conveniences that were new to me, the interest shown in an ordinary person like myself by these people to whom I was a total stranger. Then there was the offer, which seemed quite sincere, for me to feel that their home was my own. These things would be appropriate if I were a person who had been transported some one hundred or so years into the future.

Difficult as the question was, I would have to consider the possibility that I was indeed living in the year 2103. Unless I could do this,

13

my mind would be cut off from further rational thought. Later on I could think about how to fully satisfy myself upon this question.

The next question was: How could I have regained consciousness a hundred years later than Professor Darch and I had planned? I was beginning to remember the events which preceded my entry into suspended animation. The cave entrance above Bill's summer cabin overlooked a green valley about ten miles west of Asheville. We had made such careful preparations that there seemed not the remotest possibility anything could go awry. My concern that nothing should disturb my entranced sleep bordered on obsession. We had taken elaborate steps to conceal our activity and to prevent accidental discovery of the cave opening by hunters or any others. However, we had also taken three personal friends into our confidence so that we would have witnesses to the experiment and to insure that, should anything happen to Bill Darch, I would still be properly awakened after three months. Considering these precautions, it seemed impossible that a catastrophe could have overtaken Bill and the three friends as well, so that no one was left to awaken me. This was as far as my thinking could take me. I gave up at four a.m., said a prayer, then sank into a deep dreamless sleep.

CHAPTER 5

Shift of the Poles

> *"There will be upheavals in the Arctic and in the Antarctic that will make for the eruption of volcanoes in the torrid areas, and there will be a shifting then of the poles—so that where there have been those of a frigid or semi-tropical will become the more tropical, and moss and fern will grow. And these will begin in those periods in '58 to '98, when these will be proclaimed as the periods when His Light will be seen again in the clouds."*
> —Edgar Cayce Reading (3976-15)

It was afternoon the following day by the time I had dressed and finished a late breakfast of fresh cantaloupe and orange blossom honey. Like all the food offered to me, I found these simple dishes more delicious and satisfying than any of the foods that I had been accustomed to. The doctor's son, James, had already shown me their herb and vegetable garden and pointed out the fruit and nut trees which provided all the food for the household. He said that the quality of the soil which produced the food one ate was considered a crucially important factor. In striving to maintain normal health and blood condition for normal functioning of the mind, the part played by fresh raw foods was vital. I already knew that "normal" to James meant very superior in my terms. The taste of the food was, according to James, the test for the quality and mineral content. The quality of their food, he said, was the result of years of carefully planned effort toward properly conditioning the soil. I was thinking about these things while I relaxed in the early afternoon sunshine. Even the porch chair under me had caught my attention because it was comfortable and yet designed to hold one in excellent sitting posture. About this time, Dr. Karoll came out and sat down beside me as though he had nothing more important to do than to make conversation with me.

"How are you feeling today, David?"

"Stronger, but I've been going through a terrible mental struggle."

"Perhaps you would like to tell me about it, David."

"After we retired last night I couldn't sleep. I kept going over the questions you raised in my mind. It seems to me that I may be experiencing a strange dream which I cannot distinguish from reality. Last night I felt I was going mad...as though my mind had created an illusion that had overpowered all my normal senses. Sitting here in the sunlight with your delicious food under my belt is forcing me to think my impossible delusions are real. I can't convince myself that I'm experiencing an hallucination and my logic denies that a terrible hoax is being played on me...you're too kind and considerate to me for that, and you have surely saved my life, even if I don't understand the circumstances."

Dr. Karoll looked seriously at me for a moment. "I'm sorry I didn't have the judgment to speak more carefully to you about your age, David. It's difficult to place oneself in another's shoes. I've been trying to imagine the impact of my words had I been in your position and I'm beginning to appreciate what a stable and strong personality you are to have gone through last evening as you did."

I looked at the doctor's face very closely to see his expression. "I'm glad to hear you make that comment for it gives me more confidence in my sanity." With this remark I began asking questions to clear away some of the inconsistencies which were troubling me.

"Dr. Karoll, how can it be that we are located close to Asheville, yet the climate is semi-tropical? The vegetation includes types of plants like your citrus trees which could only survive a mild winter."

"Why, I'd forgotten about the climate change since your times. It is no wonder that you couldn't accept my statement about our proximity to Asheville without skepticism."

"Climate change? I don't understand how that could take place."

"Well, David, you see, there was a cataclysmic change in earth around the turn of the century which altered our coastline and made North America fall into the semi-tropical zone. The thin outer crust of the earth shifted upon the inner core, much as the skin of an orange broken loose from the inner portion might slip out of position. The axis of the poles of the earth remained in line with the North Star, but the outer shell moved so that the geographical location of the poles is different."

"Shift of the poles! Incredible!"

"Yes...yes, it was."

"No wonder I couldn't recognize these mountains!"

"Again, let me apologize, David, for my failure to realize that you would see these changes and, also, for underestimating your faculties for logical thinking. We, today, are inclined to think that the people who were your contemporaries must have been exceedingly dull of mind. Such a prejudiced point of view on my part put me off guard." He paused thoughtfully, "You were apparently offended when I asked where you lived. Of course, I was trying to ease your mind about my ignorance of Asheville's location. Now I see why you felt that your answer could have no meaning to me. Asheville is uninhabited and still an area which is blighted with concrete, brick, asphalt and steel. The abused land where the city stood hasn't been restored but that's a project to be undertaken by our people."

"Hmmm!...blighted is the right word." I paused as visions of its slums, highways, business areas and polluted streams came to mind, then spoke again, "Perhaps, Dr. Karoll, you can clear up another question and help me to shake this suspicion of an overpowering hallucination, for I well know that a powerful hypnotic suggestion can produce all the sensory experiences to go with the illusion suggested. Can you recall any historical event which would explain how three men living in three different cities could have been prevented from awakening me from my suspended animation trance? They had agreed to remain apart until three months were up. Then, whether they had heard from Bill Darch or not, they were to come to the mountain chamber to release me themselves, if necessary. This was to prevent the unlikely chance that a freak accident could overtake all four of them when they were together. I wanted to eliminate the remotest possibility that my suspended animation trance might be indefinitely extended."

The doctor was silent for a few moments. I hoped that he was a good scholar of history for we were speaking of an event which would have taken place in 1985, a hundred and eighteen years before. I thought I might help him to remember by mentioning some of the things that would be recorded in a history of that time.

"Was there a nuclear war?" I asked.

"No, not then."

"Was there some great natural catastrophe?"

"Nothing to affect this area."

"Could there have been some kind of plague or germ warfare?"

"Not at that time. However, let me think; the year was 1984, wasn't it?"

"Yes, it would have been the fall of the year that I should have been released."

"Yes, yes, of course...that was several months after the American

17

government had called in the silver from the people...all silver...tableware...everything...anyone who did not turn in their silver possessions was accused of hoarding, a criminal offense."

"Why, that's true, but what could that have to do with the question?"

CHAPTER 6

The Money Failure

"The heads thereof judge for reward and the priests thereof teach for hire, and the prophets thereof divine for money: yet will they lean upon the Lord, and say, is not the Lord among us? None evil can come upon us."

—*Micah*

"Well, I imagine that only a handful of people in the entire country suspected what calling in the silver was going to mean or what had caused this measure to be taken."

"I certainly don't see how it could possibly be connected with my being abandoned in a cave by four good friends. Nothing short of losing their lives would have prevented any of them from releasing me."

"It very certainly could be, David, but you will have to listen carefully to understand how it came about. This misuse of the Federal Reserve Bank system was the source of America's international money problems. Calling in the silver preceded by about six months the event which brought chaos to America."

"Are you trying to tell me that America's money problems somehow could have caused my friends to lose their lives while I was asleep? It will be hard for me to imagine that!"

"Yes, David, along with millions of other Americans."

"Impossible!"

"Would you like to know how it happened?"

"Very much."

"All right. Many people, certainly your bankers and political leaders, knew that America's inflation was causing the disruption of international exchange but very few understood what had gone wrong."

"Well, now that's true."

"Of course, there was a tiny minority who understood exactly where the trouble lay but they were party to it and carefully concealed what they knew."

"Did the Common Market countries, the European Economic Community have something to do with it?"

"By all means."

"Did they cause it?"

"Oh, no! Rather you could say that the drawing together of the European nations and Japan into an economic coalition was forced by the conditions that America's bankers and great conglomerate corporations created."

"Why do you say that?"

"Because it was a matter of necessity for them which was so compelling that they were able to set aside centuries of differences to do it. All of Europe would have been drained and their economy devastated if they had not joined together to stop America's abuse of the world's economic systems."

"How could our Federal Reserve bank laws have permitted us to do that?"

"The Federal Reserve system was originally intended to generate sound currency backed by any useful commodity rather than only one particular commodity, gold. This was to free currency issue from the abuses that resulted when small groups gained control over the supply of gold."

"I don't see how you could possibly know such details on a subject like this, especially since you say it is history of some two hundred years ago."

"When you learn how we teach history, David, you will easily understand how I can know these things and many other subjects equally obscure to you now."

"I never did know much about banking. Can you give me a better picture of what you just said by using different words?"

"After the Federal Reserve Bank law was enacted, actual products, wheat, barley, automobiles, shoes, or any legitimate commodity became the basis for issuing money. The Federal Reserve Bank was established for the purpose of relating the issue of money to actual commodities in general instead of its being backed only with gold or silver."

"How was that a change?"

"Until then, only a producer of gold had the legal right to have his commodity, gold, minted directly into money or to get paper money in exchange for its gold."

"Hmmm! I seem to remember some history about free silver minting and the political controversy over silver and gold. But how did the new law change things?"

"Previously, a farmer mortgaged his farm against the money he hoped to get from his crops in order to pay the expenses of harvesting. Manufacturers had to mortgage their facilities when they had a large contract in order to pay their labor and material costs before they received payment for goods which they had delivered."

"What was wrong with that?"

"It was more than just unfair. The whole money system in America was privately owned and operated. This meant that small groups were constantly vying with each other for control of the nation's money supply. The value of the currency could be manipulated up and down by the faction currently dominating the market. A farmer who borrowed currency of a certain value might be required to pay back currency of a much higher value and, being unable to pay, lose his land."

"Just a moment! What do you mean; the money system was privately owned?"

"Oh, it was still privately owned after the Federal Reserve Bank law was enacted, just as it was before. The only difference was that it would be government supervised to keep it an honest and fair business."

"The Federal Reserve Bank was privately owned? You must be mistaken. That doesn't seem possible. I can hardly believe that."

"Very few people understood the money system in your time, David. Even among newspaper editors and key figures in government there was little understanding of how it was owned and operated. The name 'Federal Reserve Bank,' led people to assume that it was a branch of the government rather than a privately owned bank system."

"Well," I said, "I can see that I certainly knew next to nothing about our money system."

"Few people did, David."

"If a privately owned bank could manipulate the value of the money it loaned, I can see how vulnerable the farmer or manufacturer who mortgaged his property was," I said.

"The Federal Reserve Bank law was specifically intended to change that. The idea behind the original Federal Reserve Bank law of 1914 was to set up a wonderfully fair and honest system which used a currency that had no value in itself. In the same way that paper money had been issued as a gold certificate, the new money was a commodity value certificate. While they still called paper money "gold certificates" to maintain public confidence and for the benefit of international trading, yet the principle had been altered. Only a small percentage of gold was to be held for a reserve to satisfy any demand for gold in exchange for gold certificates."

"You mean that the Federal Reserve Bank system was intended to create a form of valueless paper money to replace money that actually had value like gold?"

"Well, of course, gold certificates had no value in themselves either, but were redeemable in gold."

"And you say this was a good idea?"

"A great advancement."

"Why?"

"Well, first let's put the new paper money and the gold certificates on par with each other. They were both paper and equally valueless in themselves."

"Yes, but one could get gold for the gold certificates, so it was not valueless."

"In the same way, one could get potatoes, shoes or machinery for the new paper money, so it was not valueless either. And they still called them gold and silver certificates, so the public never even knew there was any difference. They were still redeemable in precious metal for anyone who wanted it."

"All right, but why was this an advancement?"

"With the old system, a small group could gain control over the supply of gold, and then manipulate its value upward and downward. As individuals and businesses and governments borrowed money from those who had control of it, they were manipulated out of all they owned. By this means the common people were kept in a state of impoverished peasantry, great fortunes became the heritage of the few, and even the government became subservient to those few."

"Well, I'm not sure that I understand all that you are saying, but you mean that the Federal Reserve Bank law set out to correct a great injustice with its new kind of worthless paper money. And, then somehow failed miserably?"

"The principle upon which it was based was not the cause of the failure."

"Doesn't paper money always bring inflation?"

"Not if the system is honest. The new paper currency was intended to provide a media of exchange whose face value was solidly based on actual production. Instead of inflation, this currency would have been increased in its buying power with every improvement in production methods. The wages of the working people would have been increased by the deflation of the value of all commodities including gold in relation to their currency. With every advance of technology which reduced the number of man hours to produce an item, the wage earner's money would have gained in value."

"Well, I guess it worked wonderfully well in America at first. Tell me how the law so improved things."

"All right. The basic idea was that money should be issued in an amount that represented the value of some produced goods. The goods were given the same status as gold as a form of wealth."

"But gold doesn't wear out or get used up like food," I said in surprise, "so how could money be issued against things that are used up?"

"The new law took this into account in a manner that was very simple and practical. If a manufacturer or a farmer had a contract to deliver a certain amount of goods for a set price to be paid within sixty to ninety days after he delivered them, he could have the money issued which the goods were worth simply by furnishing the receipts to show he had delivered the goods and assigning the contract for the payment owed him to the bank in exchange for credit or currency. As soon as the goods were paid for by the customer, then the producer's liability was cleared for the money that was issued against his produce for his temporary use. This way the money was taken right back out of circulation as soon as it had served the purpose of paying cash to workers and meeting production expenses."

"You mean that the original Federal Reserve Bank law made it unnecessary for manufacturers to borrow money that someone else owned to pay their bills because provision had been made to issue currency against the value of their goods so they could get it immediately?"

"Yes, but not one hundred percent of it. Producers could get this currency only after they had delivered the goods and had commercial paper, that is, the receipts and contracts to show they had delivered the goods. They signed over to the bank their contracts and received cash."

"Well, David, you just must understand that we are talking about two separate banks. The Federal Reserve Bank was the banker's bank. It was set up like a corporation and owned by the banking industry through stocks. It issued the money to them for a low service charge, not interest. When the money was issued to a customer, the local bank's service charge was deducted as well as the Federal Reserve Bank charge and the banks called this 'discounting the note.' When the Federal Reserve Bank accepted the commercial paper collected by the local banks and issued currency against them, it was called rediscounting. The difference between the local bank discount rate and the lower rediscount rate of the central bank was the margin for profit for the local bank."

"They shouldn't have called the charges 'interest.'"

"The intent, as far as the inaugerators of the Federal Reserve Bank Act was concerned, was that only a small legally established charge or rediscount rate should have been required simply to defray expenses. This banker's bank was not for profit making. And the charges were to pay for the clerical help and maintain the organization, not as interest at all in the former sense. The new law had been carefully thought out by some brilliant and eminently fair minded men. They had set out to free the farmers and all producers of goods from enslavement and subservience to the money manipulators. Competition between local banks was supposed to determine that there would be only a minimum service charge rate that a customer would be required to pay for having money issued to him against his Commercial Paper. This system for issuing money was originally conceived and set up by Alexander Hamilton. The system that Hamilton originally established was destroyed by Andrew Jackson because of the political corruption which led to its use to influence elections."

"Well, when you start talking about service charges and interest, I'm sure the public never knew there was any difference. The money system has always been so encased in puzzling terms that I'm sure few people have ever really understood it. You are making it sound like a good system and yet say it caused the wholesale devastation of America. What happened?"

"The Federal Reserve Bank law was amended. The specific portion of it dealing with the issue of money was changed to furnish capital for speculation. Soon it had become so corrupt that you might say that America's privately owned central banking system, misleadingly named "The Federal Reserve Bank," was given license to counterfeit money."

"But where does the Treasury Department come into the picture. Doesn't the government print the money and mint the coins?"

"The Treasury Department was only a servant to the privately owned Federal Reserve Bank System just like the post office served the public according to its rules and regulations. It issued currency to the Federal Reserve System when they prepared the paperwork properly to show that they had been assigned the securities."

"Then how could you call it counterfeit?"

"It was the same as counterfeit because it was an issue of money that represented no production of goods."

CHAPTER 7

Calling in the Silver

"I certainly never expected this kind of dissertation on the money system today. I guess its good for me to try to understand."

"Would you like for me to go on, David?"

"Yes, please do. All of us knew something was terribly wrong but things were better in America than in other countries, even with our inflation and depressions."

"Perhaps you would like to think about what we have already said and ask a few questions," said Dr. Karoll.

"Yes...yes, I would," I said simply. We both were silent while I turned his words over in my mind.

"Well," I said slowly, "the whole business about rediscount rates, gold reserves, commercial paper, going off the gold standard, the Bretton Woods Agreement and news stories using these terms were like Greek to me. I hardly know how to ask a question. Is there some simple way that you could tell where this wonderful new approach to issuing money went so wrong that it turned the whole world against us?"

Dr. Karoll was silent for some time, "Of course, David, there is no simple answer to such a question. The seed was sown for the destruction of the new system almost before the ink was dry on the original bill."

"How was that?"

"The amendment of a key paragraph in such a way that it undermined the very principle on which the law was founded."

"The amendment of one paragraph could do that?" I asked in astonishment.

"Yes," spoke Dr. Karoll thoughtfully. "It was only necessary to change a few words to destroy the sound principles of the original law."

"What was the change?"

"That money could also be issued against wealth of longstanding instead of just against newly created wealth in the form of commodities which actually changed hands and were under contract to be paid for in not more than four months."

"I don't see why that would make any difference."

"Neither did your lawmakers. They were not bankers but were dealing with a long and complex law which outlined the entire setting up of the Federal Reserve Bank system. They never imagined that this minor change introduced an unsound principle and that their error would cause the crash of 1929, and later, the great devastation of America in 1985."

"Well," I said, "I'm so little informed about the money system that I'm not sure I understand very much of what you've said. Please tell me the way this change made the whole law unsound. Just what did it do?"

"Well, you might say that it opened up Pandora's box, could you see how it allowed greed to consume the lives of men and destroy a great part of earth's natural environment."

I was beginning to feel impatient and frustrated with my ignorance of how our money system had worked. Dr. Karoll's last comment was too much for me. "Dr. Karoll, I thought I was understanding you when you described what a great thing America had in the Federal Reserve Bank law. Now, I'm feeling that I must be very dull, since I can't imagine how a little change, which hardly even seems like a change, could make a monstrous fraud of such a fine law. What did the change do?"

"It allowed the Federal Reserve Bank to issue the money for the purchase of stocks, bonds and real estate, using those very stocks, bonds and real estate purchases as the security for the money issued."

"But," I said, "the Treasury Department actually issued the money, didn't it?"

"Technically, yes, but the bankers were actually running the operation and the Treasury Department simply carried out their instructions. The Federal Reserve Board appointees were all bankers and their appointments were for such an extended period that no president could change the character of the Board."

"Well, what was wrong with using stocks and real estate as security for loans?"

"Ordinarily, there would be no harm in this but you have used the wrong term. This was not the loan of existing money but the issue of new money. If it were the loan of existing money, there would have been no inflation."

"You make it sound simple but I still don't see why it was wrong. Wasn't the stock buyer risking his money and wasn't it right and good for companies to raise money to expand by selling stocks?"

"There would have been no real harm and much benefit if stocks were bought with actual savings but they were not. Of course, there were many honest working people who earned their savings and invested them but these people did not cause the crash of 1929. You wouldn't remember the stock market failure of 1929 but surely there was some discussion of it in your time, David?"

"Oh, yes, certainly! The crash of twenty-nine...I was born right in the midst of the depression...terrible times."

"Well, then, surely you know what caused the stock market crash?"

"That's odd," I hesitated, "now that I think about it, as much talk about it as there was, I really can't say I've ever listened to a clear explanation. I do remember an old gentleman who had worked in the shipyards during World War I...1914 to 1918," I added, "and he told me about investing money in stocks. Let me think about this to see if I can recall his story."

Dr. Karoll waited as I strained my memory about the old shipfitter I worked with as an apprentice in Norfolk's Navy yard. "He said it hardly took any money to buy stocks. Everybody was doing it...carpenters, painters, working men...everybody! They kept going up...you borrowed the money on the stock and never saw it...the bank held it...bought stocks on the margin he said...whatever that meant."

"That's a good description, David, very good. It took only a small percentage of cash, the stock was security to borrow ninety percent of the money. When it increased in dollar value, the increase was treated as cash to allow the purchase of more stock. Actually, by the terms of the Federal Reserve Bank law, as it was amended, the money was not loaned but issued against the value of the real estate, productive facilities and other assets of the corporation that the stock was assumed to represent."

"Well," I said in surprise, "I never would have imagined that! You mean money was issued to pay for a stock certificate which represented the corporation assets...but what difference did it make, just so long as the money was issued against a real value?"

"The money was issued, David, to pay for a stock certificate representing previously earned wealth. The money was not earned by the buyer. In making the purchase, the buyer was spending dishonest money, a false issue of currency which was not based on productivity at all. The stock certificate's value was based upon speculation of future activities of a business, as well as actual assets, and was an equivalent of honestly issued money in part. But to issue money against it, as if it were a commodity, was like issuing two dollars for one."

"But it was still wealth in terms of actual property, so why did it matter?"

"It caused the banking system to furnish money for speculation. The language of the banking industry concealed what was actually going on. Few knew what the implications were when money was furnished by the Federal Reserve Bank system using stocks as the security for rediscounting. This term 'rediscounting' was a most confusing word for the general public to understand. The public had no idea that it made reference to the actual issue, rather than the loan, of money against securities."

"What was wrong with that?"

"Nothing at first, that is, as securities against which money would be issued were originally defined by the Federal Reserve law. After the amendment to the law, there was issued a mixture of honest money and dishonest money."

"What do you call 'dishonest' money?"

"Money which was issued against previously earned wealth, such as stocks, bonds, deeds to property and similar instruments. If existing money had been loaned against them as security, there would have been no problem; but, new money was being put into circulation."

"Was that why stocks kept going up in 1929?"

"Well, David, not only did it take only a small percentage of cash to buy the stock, the ever increasing amount of money being issued was reducing the value of all money in circulation. Only things that had actual substance retained their value; and, they did this by going up in dollar price. Stocks were deeds, in effect, to something that had actual substance."

"What did 'buying on the margin' mean?"

"It meant that as a stock went up in dollar cost, the difference between what had been paid for it and the higher price could be used just like cash to have more money issued to buy eight or nine times the amount of the increase in more stock."

"This is too confusing for me. I do not follow how such an insane sounding system could possibly have been in effect in America. And I still don't see why money issued against gold or farm produce was all right but money issued against a house or farm was all wrong. You make it sound like money was being printed and given away just because it was issued against previously earned wealth."

"You are illustrating how easily one can be deceived by abstract terms. The effect of this minor seeming change of a few words in the law would be very obvious if you could see the whole fiasco acted out in three dimensions, David. The issue of new money, unrelated to productivity, is the equivalent of counterfeit currency. This kind of money was put into circulation in unlimited quantities and competed in purchasing goods with money earned by people who worked. To imagine that such a dishonest system could function very long seems childish."

I was silent for a moment and not inclined to pursue the money issue any further. "I know that you are leading up to the answer to my question about what could have happened to my four close friends. The crash of 1929, which we have been talking about, brought a banking reform. That crash was surely a terrible thing, but it would not explain anything like the chaos you say took millions of lives in America."

"In the crash of 1985 your money suddenly became valueless, David, just the opposite of 1929."

The effort to follow this conversation was beginning to be too much for my nerves. "Wait just a moment, please!" I interrupted. "All that I asked was how could calling in the silver by our government have anything to do with my three friends and Dr. Darch simultaneously meeting with some kind of disaster, and you have been giving me a dissertation on the banking system before the crash of 1929! I understand that you said the Federal Reserve Bank was privately owned but it was government regulated. The whole business about rediscount rates, gold reserves and devaluation of currencies was not clear to me because I didn't know exactly what the terms meant, nor did anyone else I knew, for that matter. In the last of the 1970's and the early 80's there were waves of news about runaway inflation and what the newspapers called an 'Attack on the Dollar' by the Europeans. I never did hear anyone give an intelligent reason why the dollar was subject to attack. You'll have to start back again with the silver being called in and tell me from there just what actually happened and how it could have affected four men who were responsible to awaken me in 1984."

"All right, David. We'll talk about why the collapse of '84 happened at another time; but, here is what took place. European governments and Japan demanded that America take immediate steps to hold up the value of American currency. First, the country's stock pile of valuable metals were offered, tin, zinc, copper, titanium and similar metals, to act as bullion to redeem our currency. They were sold below current world prices in relation to the exchange rates between United States currency and those of other nations. This allowed other countries to exchange their fast depreciating dollars for something which would retain its value. Temporarily, this measure prevented further inflation. When these metals were gone, the inflation continued again. Several years later the government began to auction off its gold reserves, then after silver had increased to more than the old price of gold, it called in all the silver in the hands of the public, silverware, serving pieces, everything made of silver, so that it could be melted down into bullion to redeem our currency."

"That should've stopped the inflation indefinitely," I commented.

"No, David, there were billions of dollars in cash in Europe to redeem. Within six months after the silver was first called in it became exhausted. The nations of Europe and Japan were forced to take a drastic measure. America had entirely depleted its stock pile of valuable metals and its inflation was progressing so rapidly that immediate action was necessary. All of Europe had formed a coalition in order to correct the conditions created by America's abuse of the currency system. When America could no longer make the needed corrections, then, to prevent the inflation of the American dollar from bringing financial ruin upon the world, the major financial powers refused to honor American currency. Once Europe refused American money, there was a total collapse in the value of currency in the United States. Without even silver to use for money, the nation was reduced to barter alone. There were no means to continue normal business activity. Law and order broke down in the cities. The people panicked. There was no way for them to continue on their jobs after the money failed. Without labor, all public utilities, such as water and electricity, were discontinued. Without water, the great cities became stench filled death traps. There was a mad exodus from metropolitan areas by the frantic masses. Millions of Americans perished in the months that followed."

"Impossible," I gasped in shock.

"David, this did happen. It occurred with such suddenness that one can easily visualize how your three friends and the professor may all have lost their lives. They evidently were rendered incapable of returning to awaken you from your unconscious state. In as well concealed a chamber in the mountains as we found you, it is certainly no wonder that you were not discovered until now."

My emotions were in a precarious state. This idea of my whole world having vanished with all the people I knew was at last becoming terribly real to me. As I thought about the people who were close to me, the gentle friends and many good people I knew, my blood relations, all these gone forever, an overwhelming sense of grief came upon me. As I dwelt upon Dr. Karoll's last words, the whole picture began to become an actuality in my mind. The tragic scene became intensely personal. As this sentiment welled up, I completely lost control of my emotions.

I was sobbing convulsively when the good doctor led me to my room and suggested that I might want to lie down. He said that he would put off our plans for the evening until another time.

CHAPTER 8

The Air Car

"Error came into existence before the earth, the heavens or space were created. Using free will, expressing selfish desire, spiritual beings separated themselves from a consciousness of Oneness with creative Will. Life, in material bodies, is the reflection of this separation in this state of consciousness."
—*Edgar Cayce Reading*

I guess that I sobbed myself to sleep like a child, lying with my face downward and buried in the crook of one arm. It must have been several hours later when I was awakened by the voice of Dr. Karoll's daughter speaking my name softly.

"David...David...Are you awake?"

I rolled over. Someone had placed a blanket over me to prevent my taking a chill. I looked around and felt the strange sensation of not recognizing my surroundings. For a moment I wondered where I was and sat up rather suddenly.

"Everything's all right, David. Please don't be distressed. All of the people you knew so well and who meant so much to you are truly not lost and gone. You will see."

I didn't understand what she was referring to. The grief of a few hours was completely out of my mind for the moment and I smiled at Alice.

"Father sent me in to cheer you up. He says that you ought not to think about the past until you have learned more about your present circumstances. When you understand some of the wonderful improvements in our society, you will see why you need not be despondent over the seemingly tragic events of the past."

"Your father expects too much of me, I think." I was beginning to remember the conversation with Dr. Karoll. The nap had helped to soften the shock. Still, I could not shake the feeling that I was having some strange kind of dream. "How can I be unemotional about losing every human acquaintance that I ever knew, even if you say the loss took place a hundred years ago?"

"David, perhaps you would like to shower and rest. And after

33

dinner I would like to take you for an evening ride in father's air car." Alice motioned toward some clothing that had been set out for me for such an occasion. "It's a beautiful evening to see the sunset from an air car."

I felt that the warmth and friendliness Alice expressed toward me were genuine and it flattered me, in spite of my keen sense of dejection. If I looked pathetic because of my state of mind, Alice showed no sign of noticing it.

"Yes, yes, I think I would like that...what's an air car?"

Alice couldn't resist smiling. My answer was like that of an injured child being offered some kind of surprise dessert if it would stop crying. She said, "Wait and see!"

The evening meal was excellent, but I took very little food because the family ate so sparingly and I felt obliged to imitate their ways to keep from appearing ill mannered. They ate in silence and, as with each previous meal, it was almost like participating in a religious ceremony. I noticed that everyone in the household had perfect teeth and they masticated their food with care. Anyone familiar with the literature of health faddists would know something of the way it was prepared. Their plainest and commonest of vegetables had superior flavor and required no seasonings, and, for the most part, were eaten uncooked or the freshly extracted raw juice was taken. I was beginning to learn to appreciate each for its own unique qualities. For example, I found that the flavor of fresh carrots was so delicate and satisfying that I realized I had never before eaten a truly good carrot. They had always been a tasteless vegetable to me when eaten raw and only palatable with plenty of dressing and chopped raisins.

When the meal was over Dr. Karoll walked with Alice and myself to a low mound shaped rise in the ground with shrubs and flowers growing upon it. It was located about fifty feet from the house and the entire area around it was landscaped. This was apparently a partly submerged enclosure housing the air car. When we came closer, I noticed that one end of the mound had bi-parting doors and, in a moment, when the doors were rolled back, I found myself viewing a craft which would have delighted a science fiction writer. It had the contour of a stubby cigar with needle points smoothly drawn out from each end. The length of the main body was about twenty-five feet and the diameter was six and one-half feet. The craft had four telescoping supports which were retracted and it floated a few inches above the ground as Alice maneuvered it up out of its chamber. Dr. Karoll took no notice of my astonishment at the air care. Putting his hand on my shoulder, he said, "Alice will thoroughly enjoy showing you some of the beautiful sights that can be observed from this little craft. And you couldn't be in safer hands with her at the controls."

As I looked at the strange ship with no wings or visible means of propulsion, then at the controls and the control panel with its various indicators, I began to wonder what I had let myself in for, and I wasn't sure I wanted to ride in such a craft. Both Dr. Karoll and Alice seemed to catch my thoughts and they could not restrain themselves from laughing at my apprehension.

"Oh, David, flying is so different today than it was in your time! Your scientists were just beginning to wonder if their theories about gravity were correct. The errors in their theories were found and now flying is as safe as walking...you will see in a moment why this is so."

The understanding smile that Alice gave me as she spoke left me no further compunctions about entering the craft. There was comfortable seating for six people and superior equivalents to the kind of conveniences one would expect in the finest of the motorized family travel units that I was familiar with. With a few deft movements, Alice put the machinery into operation that made the door close behind me and caused the craft to gently rise a few feet farther above the ground. The only sound I could hear was an almost unnoticeable vibration, such as fine record player might give out when no music was being played. It was more like sensing electronic equipment in operation than hearing mechanical equipment with moving parts. Alice waved to her father through the crystal clear vision panel before she turned to give her full attention to the controls.

After a few more adjustments of the knobs on the control pedestal before her, Alice turned toward me. Pointing to a vertical wheel which reminded me of a ship's steering wheel, except that it was turned sideways, she said, "This is the only control that is operated by a direct mechanical linkage. You see, this is the control that adjusts the balance of the forces of gravity and levitation that act upon the craft. The principle is parallel to the operation of an undersea craft which uses air chambers to balance the weight of the submarine with the surrounding water, except that we are working with ether. This craft has a tank that allows us to use the true vacuum, that is, a vacuum of ether as well as air, to overcome gravity in a manner precisely parallel to that of the submarine's air chambers."

My own familiarity with aircraft and the technology associated with flight made me keenly interested in anything that Alice could tell me of the principles behind this craft. She said the key to this method to control gravity lay in the discovery of how to create a metal from helium which was dense enough to contain, or rather to exclude, ether through which gravity operated.

As Alice turned the wheel she had just referred to, we began to rise vertically...slowly at first but with a gradually more noticeable acceleration which I could sense by the increased downward pressure of my body in the seat. The craft retained its horizontal orientation so that it was as though we were comfortably seated in an elevator making a vertical ascent.

The evening sky was red and a beautiful sunset spread before us in ever vaster proportions as we rose higher and higher. When Alice brought the craft to a standstill, the upper surface of the clouds was far below. It extended in all directions like a great pink and white sea with an occasional dark mountain top island projecting above its surface in the distance. The motionless craft was without vibration, for Alice had turned off whatever mechanism had produced the electronic hum I had sensed on the way up. The wonder of such vastness and beauty absorbed me so completely that I became unconscious of everything else. For perhaps ten minutes or more I sat entranced. Without any conscious effort to pull my thoughts away from the personal upheaval within, my mind had turned to contemplation of eternal values. There seemed to be a quieting influence upon my spirit flowing into me from the silent beauty of the sunset. A peaceful and relaxed calm gradually filled my whole being like water pouring into a jug until it overflowed. Along with this came a reverence for the Creator, a deeper reverence than I had ever known. I half imagined that some kind of mental communication was taking place above the level of consciousness between Alice and myself and this was working in me to influence my feelings. Almost without thinking I found myself saying, "Alice, tell me about your belief in God."

She turned to me with a look of tender understanding and joy so that I almost thought I saw a halo begin to glow around her head.

"Oh, David, I'm so glad that you should ask me that question. You lived in a time when people so needed to believe and have faith in God. And though there was much that seemed tragic and hopeless in those times, still we are amazed and wonder now that just observing nature wasn't enough to make people very conscious of their Creator. Of course, history makes it clear that this was not so."

"It's easy to agree that observing the earth from an air car ought to make anyone a believer," I said with awe.

"The earth was so very lovely when you were born into it, David. Many of its beauties and wonders in your time are gone forever; many species of life are extinct; even many forms of plant life will never be seen again."

"Hmmmm!" I mused thoughtfully, "There was a lot of speculation that we were on the verge of making ourselves and all life on earth extinct."

Alice was quiet for a moment and I could see that her feelings of sympathy were deeply stirred. "Oh," she said, "nothing was more painful to me during my early school days than to learn of the horror of the great wars, of how humans in your time devoted their best talents to destroying each other, to poisoning and crushing the life in nature at a time when earth was so exquisitely lovely and there was such abundance."

"Well," I said, beginning to feel a little defensive, "I guess we felt pretty much the same way about the treatment our ancestors of a hundred years before gave the Indians and what they did to the great forests and herds of wild animals and birds of America."

"But, David, that seemed different because then most people were uneducated. The leaders of the nation did not have the means to communicate with the masses and guide them. But history about your own time tells how the people of highly educated and technically developed nations had so little faith in the teachings of their Holy Scriptures that they could actually enjoy the pleasures of their prosperity while the greater majority of the earth's population suffered miserably in poverty and ignorance and fear. Even in America there was untold misery among the poorer classes. Children were brought into the world to experience the ugliness and uncleanness of crowded cities, so that their tender spirits became warped and stunted."

"Why, Alice, I can see that our normal way of life looks to you like a painful tragedy. Can things be so different now?"

"Oh, yes, they are different, altogether different. We do wonder how knowledgeable people could live with themselves in your day."

"Well now, poverty and ignorance have been part of human society throughout all history. Hardly anyone imagined that this could really be changed. Why, the more the government tried to give help to the underprivileged classes, the worse things seemed to get. As welfare programs were expanded, the riots and crimes increased. Besides, Alice, there has never been much connection between social conditions and belief in God. All through history we have had the rich and the poor...and churches for them both."

"Oh, surely you are speaking out of character. Were you also unfeeling like so many of your day...did you not agonize over the injustice, the inhuman wars, the poverty, disease and hopelessness of the under-privileged peoples of the earth?"

"Well, to tell you the truth, I did. I suppose that my willingness to risk my life with an experiment in suspended animation was partly the result of my frustration with our society and its calloused attitude toward worldwide social injustice."

"It must have been very difficult for anyone who saw it that way to live then," Alice said with tenderness.

"I did feel that things were terribly wrong when the government of a great nation like America seemed helpless to put its own Constitution into practice. It could not create order and peace even in its capitol city, much less throughout the land. Why, it seemed that the good people stood by and watched while the commercial interests were causing ghastly pollution of every body of pure water in the land. The land itself was being contaminated with insecticides, the atmosphere with industrial fumes, and the precious tidal swamps rendered sterile by poisonous wastes. The nation had billions of dollars to spend on munitions and space flights, but was not able to build adequate sewage treatment facilities or control air pollution or build suitable school facilities or plan recreation areas for the city people, much less clear the slums and build suitable residential districts. It was like living in a gigantic insane asylum. At a time when the National Budget allowed twenty-five cents per person for library materials to serve the needs of rural communities, the nation was spending several thousand dollars per person for ammunition being used to destroy a small Asiatic country of illiterates. Driven by the lust for power and wealth, individuals and corporations showed inhuman disregard for their fellowman, for posterity or for their natural environment. Through all this, the ministers preached on and eagerly cultivated the favor of their wealthiest church members and staunchly defended the Christian virtue of the youths who patriotically defended democracy by murdering primitive Asiatics ten thousand miles away."

"David, I didn't mean to bring our conversation to such a turn when you asked about my belief in God. You do share my feelings about your times. To have lived in them must be different than I can imagine for I simply do not see how people stood it."

"Yes," was all that I could answer for the moment. The thoughts of earth being so polluted and exploited were still very much before me and my new circumstances could hardly change my mental set from the accumulation of years of exposure to such times. All the grandeur of the fading sunset was lost to me as I thought about the world conditions I knew.

"I'm sorry, David," Alice said simply.

We descended just as we had risen. I took note of the instrument panel while we were returning. There were lighted navigation screens which showed the location of our ship and also any other craft in the vicinity. The electronic screen indicated our position with regard to altitude, latitude and longitude, and the direction in which the craft was moving. It was apparent that the ship could be guided to any point on the globe with ease and safety from the information plainly showing on the glowing screens before us. Alice noticed my interest in the panel and answered a question arising in my mind before I spoke. I was wondering about the fuel requirements for a long flight. She informed me that the craft required no fuel, but received energy that was broadcast from various points on the globe. It was always tuned in to the power supply stations in a manner parallel to a radio receiver being tuned in to a transmitter wave length. After the rediscovery of the power source of ancient Atlantis, the world had available the limitless and ever present energy from cosmic rays which were converted into a useful form by gigantic crystals. She said that the cosmic energy conversion process was similar in principle to the way high voltage electricity is reduced to low voltage by means of a transformer coil.

We were back in Dr. Karoll's home in a few moments. The family noticed that I looked excited and nervous and suggested that I needed a rest. I retired early for a long and refreshing rest and had pleasant dreams which I couldn't remember very distinctly but seemed, nevertheless, to give me a deeper understanding of the events I was experiencing.

CHAPTER 9

Fame

"He who receives a benefit with gratitude repays the first installment of it. If we only feel as we ought, our thankfulness will be shown in our countenances."

—*Anon.*

The next day following the flight with Alice was a day of rest and recreation for me. Dr. Karoll was a tennis enthusiast and had a fine court on the grounds near his home. He was pleasantly surprised to find that I had developed a pretty fair game of tennis and although I did not have the stamina to go more than one set, he found my service was a challenge to his control and agility. When I wondered how he could take time from his normal routine to be with me, Dr. Karoll pointed out that I was probably unaware of my status in relation to his family and society in general. This statement naturally stimulated my curiosity.

"What do you mean, Dr. Karoll?"

"Well, David, can you visualize what would have taken place in your day if someone who had been unconscious for more than one hundred years was brought back to life?"

"Well, sir, I guess that I'm hardly able to believe fully that this is my status. However, if it had happened in America in the 1970's, why, yes, I certainly can. There would have been so much publicity given the incident that every school boy in the nation would have known about it. The man's name would have become a household word to the millions of families that watched television and listened to radio. Why, it probably would have been difficult for such a man to survive the strain of the publicity that he would have been subjected to. His opinion would have been solicited upon all kinds of things and the commercial interests would've vied with each other to have him endorse their products. As long as his story held interest as a news item, there would've been pictures and interviews to the limit of his endurance. Perhaps the lack of this treatment of myself is one reason

41

that I hardly can believe what you say has happened to me."

"Yes, that could be true, David. Our approach, you see, is different, for while your discovery and revival to life has been given international notice, your personal welfare as a fellow human being is also given every consideration. Your care has been assigned to me as a sacred charge, you might say, and you will suffer no exploitation for private gain or for curiosity or as a news item. Your survival of suspended animation is regarded as an important event to the scientific world. As soon as you were discovered, a consultation was held among our leaders so that immediate steps would be taken to provide suitable care and surroundings for you. My family was selected for these purposes and we will be devoting our time to aid you to make the adjustment to our society. You are considered a valuable person who can help us acquire a better understanding of your times and you are thought of as a scientific pioneer worthy to receive the finest care we can offer. In due time you will be highly honored for your courage and initiative in a public ceremony."

"You mean to tell me that the story of my experience has been broadcast throughout the world and that you and your family were chosen to devote your time just to taking care of me?"

"Yes, David, and we feel privileged to have been given this opportunity," Dr. Karoll answered.

"This is very humbling for me to think about," I said self-consciously.

"The last details of my release from regular duties have been cleared and I shall spend much of my time with you until you are physically and mentally prepared for exposure to the various scientific groups that will want to study your case. Eventually, we expect you to become a competent member of our society."

"I am beginning to appreciate what it means, Dr. Karoll, to have been taken into your household. Your family has already shown me the kind of thoughtful consideration and affection that one could not take for granted even from his closest relatives. It will be a small thing upon my part to cooperate with you and your family and any group, scientific or otherwise, that is interested in my story."

"We were sure you would feel that way, David."

"Where do we start," I said, feeling thankful that I might offer some useful service in return for the kindness being shown to me.

"There's no hurry, David. Your physical and mental health will be our first concern for some time. If it suits you, we will spend the next five days at outdoor sports and hiking, with plenty of time allowed for rest. Then we will plan to have another evening of discussion in our home on the sixth day, which will be the coming Saturday. For your benefit as well as theirs, we will arrange to have some scholars versed in several different areas of study to be present for this gathering."

I agreed enthusiastically to Dr. Karoll's suggestion and felt much enlightened about my status with his family. It wasn't difficult for me to imagine that if I had been unconscious so long my case would be very unique. On this basis I could easily see that a person like Dr. Karoll would be selected to give me his full attention and would take me into his family. I was still trying to adjust to the idea that I had actually survived a hundred and twenty years of suspended animation. Regardless of the circumstances, it was only logical for me to accept gratefully the wonderful treatment and interest shown in me by these superior people. However, my ego had so responded to Alice's attention that it was deflating for me to imagine that I might only be an object of academic interest or, perhaps, of pity to her, rather than someone she responded to in a personal way.

Five days of hiking, rest and recreation in beautiful mountain country went quickly. I observed many changes in the types of trees and shrubbery in the area which gave clear evidence of warmer climate. Brilliant colors of autumn were just beginning to touch the highest peaks of the surrounding Great Smokies. Mountain streams, with that crystal clearness characteristic of them during early Fall, and the invigorating coolness in the morning air made camping out a delightful experience. It reminded me of some long hikes in Hawaii through the mountains on the big island. I enjoyed the thrill of watching the sunrise from a mountain top campsite and we had unforgettable evenings of story telling in front of our campfires. Dr. Karoll's yarns sounded like science fiction I read in my teens.

I liked the lighter and simpler camping equipment. Dr. Karoll easily carried our tent, which was entirely contained in a small, light pack, and he was able to set it up in seconds because its design eliminated all ropes or poles. Its shape was something like an elongated igloo and the fabric was a fine weave cloth as light and flexible as silk. The seams contained the supporting mechanism which was a series of bead-like segments strung upon highly flexible braided glass cables. When the cables were drawn tight by a small winder, the seams became rigid and the tent took form; but, when it was relaxed, the tent folded into a small package.

On our way back from the camping trip, Dr. Karoll asked me about the discussion he had planned to see if I thought I was equal to the occasion. He was so natural in the way he treated me, like a member of his own family, that I began to feel he had adopted me as a son into his heart.

"Yes, Dr. Karoll, I feel fine," I responded. "However, the instability of my emotions in the past few weeks forces me to question my own judgement in the matter. I'm sure that you will stop any discussion, if need be, so that I won't make a fool of myself by becoming over emotional."

"Of course, David. Of course, I will."

"Uh...will...will Alice be there?" I was trying not to reveal any feelings by my words or by the tone of my voice.

"Oh, yes. She's taking her work with you quite seriously and has her own data to prepare."

The doctor answered matter-of-factly but I caught the slightly quizzical look on his face at the manner in which I asked about Alice. His answer raised further questions in my mind about the personal interest which I thought Alice had shown in me.

CHAPTER 10

Space Brothers

"The old idea was that the earth, like the `ever-lasting hills' upon it, had always been. But life is not ever the same; it is ascending. Man is not ever the same; at happy junctures new races have been born. History need not always repeat itself. Dowered with reason and social feeling, man has within him the possibility of indefinite advance. It is in the make of things that the possibilities of progress lie. Why is not, then, a world-state in which all are brothers, a 'Kingdom of God,' conceivable?"
—William M. Salter

"You say you come from an island a thousand miles west of here?"

"Yes."

"But there are no islands only a thousand miles west. It's all dry land, very dry."

The four professors had arrived a little before dinner and we had just finished our meal and gathered in the family room for the evening of discussion that Dr. Karoll had planned. I had directed this question to Dr. Daren to follow up some earlier remarks. This professor had been introduced to me as Dr. George Daren who was engaged in medical research at an institute of learning called the University of Utah Isle.

The professor was a man like Dr. Karoll in many respects. He had the manner of a self-confident and cultured person and the physiognomy of a gymnastic instructor. A particular difference in his physical make-up intrigued me. Dr. Daren was like a well proportioned Greek athlete who had been evenly elongated from head to toe. He stood six feet eight inches tall and appeared to weigh not more than one hundred and seventy-five pounds. The shape of his head reminded me of President Woodrow Wilson.

Dr. Daren looked thoughtfully around the room for a moment until his eyes fell upon a globe showing the configurations of oceans and continents of the earth. He turned to Dr. Karoll and asked if we might set it upon the low table near our chairs.

"Lucky for you that you were in these mountains to make your experiment with suspended animation, for much land throughout the earth has been submerged since your time. There have been extensive geological changes since the shifting of the poles."

45

"Why, I didn't realize the coast line was changed when the poles shifted. Dr. Karoll mentioned the shift to me. He said it was like the skin of an orange slipping loose and moving its position relative to the inner part."

"A good illustration, David. This caused extensive changes in the coast line. During the earlier upheavals there were some changes in the west coast. The greater changes came when the poles were relocated and much of the western part of the United States was submerged in the Pacific Ocean. The present west coast of this continent is at the edge of Nebraska. Some of the higher ground further west still projects above the open water to form islands such as our Utah Isle. Take a look at the globe and you'll see how extensive these changes are."

I inspected the finely detailed globe. Many of the changes were so drastic that it was difficult for me to become oriented. Geography never had been one of my interests so I was not able to tell just what had taken place in many of the areas. I mentioned my weakness in geography and then Dr. Karoll reached over and pressed a small button on the supporting stand of the globe. Immediately the globe lit up from the inside so that a dark profile of the continents as I had known them was outlined under the new geography of the world. Now it was apparent at a glance how extensive the changes were in the earth.

"What a terrible loss of life must have resulted!"

"This was needful, David, as you will soon understand." These were Dr. Karoll's words and I turned toward him in shocked surprise.

"Needful! What do you mean?"

"Is it not true, David, that there was beginning to be widespread interest in psychical research in the last of the 1970's?"

"Yes...yes, of course, I was interested in the subject myself. In fact, most persons who thought for themselves were becoming intensely interested in the subject. But how is this subject related to a tragedy of such proportions...the loss of millions and millions of people?"

"David, suppose we set this question aside for a time and go back to an unanswered question which you posed some few days ago to Alice while you were watching a sunset from the air car."

"You mean about religion...about belief in God?"

"Yes."

"Why should we change the subject. It's difficult for me to carry on a conversation when someone makes a statement that seems so inconsistent with the ideals of decent people. It sounds inhuman to speak of the extermination of millions of innocent people as being needful. God knows, we had enough inhumanity in the earth in my time. Mankind could not survive much more of it than we had then."

"Please, David, don't allow yourself to imagine that Alex could express an inhuman thought. You will be so wrong to do so and will only cause yourself shame and confusion." Mrs. Karoll spoke gently, but I could almost have gone through the floor in humiliation, for I recognized the implication of my words to Dr. Karoll.

"I am very sorry, Dr. Karoll. I'm not thinking clearly and I apologize to you. Self-righteousness is one of my failings. There seemed to be so much apathy toward injustice and cruelty in my time that those of us who were painfully concerned felt themselves to be different."

"Thank you, David. I accept your apology. I can easily understand your feelings. But let's look at this question of religion to help you understand our attitudes."

"All right, sir. My interest in psychical research stemmed partly from the impasse that I had with religion, that is, the form of religion that was being taught in the churches. They presented ideas of God that were altogether unacceptable to me. At least, psychical researchers seemed to be making some kind of an examination of spiritual questions. The church authorities refused to recognize that any modern man could contact the same sources of information which they claimed gave them their holy scriptures."

At this point Dr. Karoll turned to another of the visitors who, like the medical scientist, had the appearance of being in remarkable physical health as well as having the mien of a competent scholar. A marked difference distinguished him from the others. He was a shade darker in coloring than the olive complexion of a southern Italian and his physical proportions were a cross between those of Dr. Karoll and Dr. Daren. He had been introduced to me earlier as Professor Arthur Hilliard whose primary field of research was political science.

"Arthur, perhaps you would like to make some comment on the status of religion in today's society. You have what may seem to David to be very personal reasons for being able to comment upon certain aspects of religious thinking that could have been a stumbling block to David."

"I gather, Dr. Karoll, you refer to my mixed blood. I'm inclined to question if David is able to absorb ideas of such startling nature just now. We all know how earth people first reacted to the peaceful invasion of the new race after the shift of the poles. However, he is open-minded. He must have a very unusual mind for his time or he could not have conceived the courageous experiment that has placed him among us today." Dr. Hilliard turned to me. "David, the most beautiful of the tenets of all the great religions of the world might be summed up by the simple saying, 'all men are brothers under the skin.' This has become a universal truth among people of earth. It is no more questioned among us now than did people question if the world was round in your time. My own blood is three-quarters what earth people first called the 'long heads.' These were the celestial immigrants, who came from a far distant solar system. I am one-quarter Hindu."

"Many people talked about brotherhood in your time, but not many acted as if they believed that the backward peoples of the earth were their brothers. Selfishness and ignorance dominated your world. Spiritual values were nebulous in the minds of religious leaders. They thought that science had proven religious teachings to be only superstitious tales from the past."

My impatience to question Dr. Hilliard before he said any more was showing. Dr. Karoll raised his hand to stop the political scientist from proceeding and nodded at me. "Perhaps, Arthur, you have already brought up a point that's disturbing David. Suppose we let him bring you back to the thoughts which he wants you to clarify." With this all eyes turned toward me as the gathering silently waited for me to form my question.

"Dr. Hilliard, do I really...," I paused, choked with emotion and began again. "The planet isn't ours anymore? We were invaded by a superior race from outer space? You are one of these?" I could hardly conceal my shock at the very idea. "David...please, you can't possibly realize how wrong you are to feel as you do." Alice spoke without a trace of criticism but it seemed to me that her words both pleaded with me and shamed me. "We all know how violence, fear, greed and hatred ruled the earth in your day. We know that you've been immersed in an atmosphere of such thoughts. No matter how you may have tried to prevent it, your mind would be contaminated with them just as your body is still contaminated with poisons." Alice paused a moment while I painfully studied the floor in front of me.

"Couldn't the brotherhood of man extend beyond our little earth...don't you see?"

"David, the mothers of the nation in the twentieth century were not equipped either with an understanding of their responsibility or with the knowledge to carry it out," Mrs. Karoll spoke quietly. "We can give you some idea of the handicaps you will be helped to overcome."

Mrs. Karoll began to carefully reason with me about the influences of my earliest childhood, my home environment, my schooling, and how these had conditioned my thinking to be narrow, earth centered, nationalistic, favoring international white supremacy, capitalism, private ownership of natural resources and generally revolving around short-sighted materialistic self interest. She described how I was conditioned to hate the peoples of some nations and feel superior to those of others, how my desires and emotions were manipulated by advertising techniques which generated responses from deep within the unconscious mind. She pointed out how the air, food and water, contaminated with trace poisons in the form of insecticide residues, lead, cadmium, fluorides, and spoilage retardants, further dulled the people's compassion and damaged the linkage of the conscious mind with the intuitive faculties which normally keep man in touch with the Great Race Mind, called the Christ Consciousness by the western world.

I was relieved by her explanations but still astonished with the realization of my arrogance.

The group fell silent as they all waited for me to speak.

"I'm sorry, Dr. Hilliard, I guess that maybe my thinking really is knotted and twisted with suspicion and prejudice, criticism and anger. These feelings came to the surface in an instant. All my life I've tried to oppose these thoughts in a world that seemed to be ruled by them. It's hard for me to realize that the world is so different now. My thinking, which I thought was liberal and broadminded, must be far in the other extreme now. I know you are very understanding and tolerant of me." I was silent again and for a moment no one spoke. I could feel their sympathy. I was suffering embarrassment like a person who suddenly realizes that he is in a gathering for which his clothing is exceedingly inappropriate. It was difficult at best for me to retain my self assurance in this group and now having revealed such uncharitable thoughts I felt humiliated. However, their understanding and freedom from criticism or sense of superiority helped me get over this embarrassment. Just the same, my ego was suffering. I was accustomed to feeling myself to be more charitably disposed than most anyone in my acquaintance. Now I was humiliated beyond words to learn that my imagined broadmindedness and tolerance appeared rather to be on a childish level.

It was Alice who broke the silence again. Even as she spoke, a new awareness came over me of how the human voice could mirror understanding, kinship and tolerance. I needed so to feel these just then. "Don't be critical of yourself, David, please. Surely you can sense our feelings toward you." Words, of themselves, were inadequate to encourage me. However, in the way Alice spoke them they overcame their shortcoming.

Dr. Karoll suggested that we should take some time to refresh ourselves and stimulate our blood circulation with a breath of outside mountain air. Mrs. Karoll had left the room unnoticed by me a little earlier and was just returning with a tray of some delicious combination of hot herb tea and fruit juices. A tingling effect from head to toe went through me from this stimulating drink.

We walked out into the garden for a few moments to enjoy the autumn evening. The night sky was strewn with an infinite number of pinpoints of light. I looked up to see if I could pick out the big dipper and the North Star. Dr. Karoll seemed to read my mind at times. He quietly mentioned that the heavens must look a bit different to me because the latitude of the Great Smokies had changed considerably.

CHAPTER 11

Evolution

"When a scientist gets beyond his observations, he enters the realm of speculations, and speculation is not science. When he imagines that the universe originated in some 'chance' spontaneous movement in the depth of space, that all the 'laws' and 'order' we can see at work in it were 'self produced' and so on, he ceases to be scientific, and soon finds himself lost in absurdities, impossibilities, and assumptions that are flatly contradictory to the very basic principles of science."
—The Unknown God
Fred J. Mayers

When we were again settled about the glowing fireplace, I felt anew the atmosphere of beauty and human dignity that Dr. Karoll and his wife had created in their home. I wondered to myself what could have possessed me to ascribe to them, or to their guests, the kind of motives that had caused me to speak as I had a little earlier. While I felt that my indignant and self-righteous attitude had made me look like a fool, their freedom from anything but loving understanding enabled them to convey to me, without the use of words, their assurance that the incident was forgotten. Dr. Hilliard spoke first confirming this.

"David, you probably know that Alex and myself have talked at some length concerning you, and so, much of your background of study and your interests are familiar to me. Your interest in the entire study of psychical research came a little in advance of the great surge of public interest. You will probably have seemed like a fool because of your intense interest in the phenomena of the UFO...the Flying Saucers. We know that you must have had many questions about the position of science concerning the UFO and psychic phenomena. You must have done some thinking that was unusual among your contemporaries. Perhaps an age old question occupied your mind," he paused, "with a new twist. Tell us about your theory for the origin of man on the earth, if you will, please."

"Have you assumed, Dr. Hilliard, that it would be reasonable for me to associate visitations from outer space with the origins of man on earth?"

"This is logical, isn't it David?"

"Yes, and you are altogether correct, Dr. Hilliard, for it was logic that led me to construct an hypothesis that would provide a more suitable explanation of man's existence in the earth than either the religious or current scientific approach. My thinking in this area began before my interest in psychical research. I had been looking for answers to the riddle of man's origin by studying the reports of archaeologists and anthropologists. The theory of evolution of species that was laid out so well by Charles Darwin contained the very reasoning which seemed to make his theory invalid with regard to the evolution of man on earth."

With my last statement, I sensed that I had stimulated a sharpened interest from everyone in the room. It gave me a distinct lift to realize that these highly educated men were listening to me so carefully. I knew that they, like Dr. Karoll with his understanding of the money system, would be fully knowledgeable upon Charles Darwin's work. His work was much alluded to when I grew up but few people had actually studied his writing to know how thoroughly he had researched his subject and how keen an intellect he exercised in developing his theories.

As I paused a moment, Professor Riley Knudsen, who had been introduced to me as an anthropologist, indicated that he would like to speak. Professor Knudsen was a huge man. He was not overweight, but he was large, weighing perhaps two hundred seventy pounds, having large bones, broad in the shoulders, a muscular torso, broad hips and powerful thighs. He stood about six feet four inches and had the same faultless bearing as the other members of the group. He had high cheek bones, deepset eyes, a nose that was prominent and straight, but close to his face. His mouth was sensitive and well formed with lips that were neither over large nor thin. His chin and jaws were strong with more than the usual distance between the mouth and the lower part of the chin. His large hands were well formed with prominent thumbs and long fingers. When he was introduced to me, I thought to myself that this man must represent some unusual mixture of blood. His face had a flatness that reminded me of the features of the Eskimo. There was a tinge of red coloring to his skin. His bony structure reminded me of the huge Swedish men, who had manned the logging camps in the early nineteen hundreds. This was a man that you would like to have at your back in any kind of a fight, I thought to myself.

"Do you mean that you feel the principle of evolution through survival of the fittest does not apply to man?" asked Dr. Knudsen.

This man had a voice that reflected his powerful appearance, yet there was a refinement about it, perhaps like the base tone of a fine stringed instrument. His diction was precise. His tone showed keen interest and the question was not asked as though it was the opener for an educational discourse by him. I eyed his powerful frame thoughtfully and then I couldn't help but smile at the question. With his physique he was pretty well equipped to insure the prolonging of his species, if brute strength and physical prowess were the criteria.

"Yes, that is what I mean, Dr. Knudsen," I said. A ripple of humor showed all around the circle with Dr. Karoll chuckling audibly. "You see," I went on, "if survival of the fittest had ruled with regard to man here on earth, the findings of our archaeologists and anthropologists would have shown a different pattern of development. As it is, we sometimes find, for example, beautifully done pictures of prehistoric animals in caves believed to have been inhabited by men of several million years ago. The equal of the mentality and physical dexterity indicated by this kind of artistic workmanship was not yet widespread even in my time. Yet these people also provide us with good indications that they were having difficulty surviving the physical hardships entailed in their primitive way of life. Such artistic skills represent very complex mental processes. In a primitive world, they have little or no survival value and could hardly have evolved through the chance sorting out of fortunate combinations of genes when brute survival is uppermost."

"There is nothing very conclusive as evidence in that statement, David," Dr. Knudsen spoke without impatience, and rather, I think, to stimulate me to clarify my reasoning.

"Well," I said, "there are many things about man's history from the records of archaeology and anthropology that support this kind of reasoning. One of our great thinkers, an anthropologist and a contemporary of Charles Darwin, said that from all the evidence of early man's natural abilities that had been unearthed, he was led to believe that the earliest of our ancestors had highly developed capacities. The evidence indicated, he said, that one of them could have written the symphonies of Beethoven if he had grown up with the cultural background of Beethoven."

"Yes, David," Dr. Karoll was speaking, "it was Thomas Henry Huxley who said that. History has a way of weeding out all but those who make valid contributions when deciding whom it honors, based on the truth they added to human society. T.H. Huxley is believed to have stimulated Charles Darwin himself to assume there was a very logical reason for the absence of any evidence that man had made a gradual ascent from an inferior form to a superior form, such as he had discovered to be the case in the animal kingdom."

"The talk of a missing link in the evidence of man's evolution," proceeded Dr. Knudsen, "seems childish to us now. There was a long, long chain that was missing, instead of just a link. Irrefutable evidence was unearthed to indicate that vastly superior use of the mind was made by men some 12,000 years before the industrial revolution of the twentieth century. Anthropologists had found many inferior forms of man in various places on earth at different times, but these findings represented a falling away, reverse evolution, by small groups. The inferior men existed at much later times in history than was represented by the fossils of earliest man. In your time, it was known that a group of people with sharply defined peculiarities and inferior qualities can be created in as little as two hundred years, simply by isolation that protects them but limits their number, forcing inbreeding. This can occur when the number of persons in the group is limited to less than three hundred and no new blood is introduced. These are probably the circumstances which created the inferior Siamese man once alluded to as a missing link."

"Thank you, Dr. Knudsen," I said. "You truly express my thoughts. You can see, for example, why my logic compelled me to deny that the musical talent of the child, Mozart, composing at three and displaying amazing virtuosity at six, could be an evolutionary product of brute survival of the fittest. So-called scientists were able to rationalize away such things with talk about fortunate combinations of genes. The outcropping of towering genius was not given a suitable explanation by our anthropologists."

"The stage is pretty well set for you to present your own version of man's origin in the earth, David. I think that we have all followed your reasoning well enough." It was Professor Clarence Weidenhouse who spoke thus. He had been introduced to me as a philosopher. Dr. Karoll felt it was needful to qualify this introduction by stating that the importance and subject matter of philosophy had expanded. I would have to become more familiar with the thinking of the times before this field of study would be clear to me, he said.

Professor Weidenhouse seemed the least unusual of the group in physical appearance. He had excellent posture and a deep chest, but stood only around five feet ten inches tall, like myself, and appeared to be full-blooded German. He had blond hair and large, almost baby blue eyes. They especially caught one's attention, for this was the most unique characteristic about Dr. Weidenhouse. I would have judged him to be under thirty. His movements had the grace and coordination of a panther. There was an aura of radiant physical health and strength about him, so that I guessed that he would be an outstanding athlete. I surmised that he was actively participating in some vigorous sport as well as academics. His forehead was wide and high, a bit squarish, unlined, prominent cheek bones, a chin that was strong, almost jutting. He was a fine appearing example of an intellectual Nordic with a superior racial heritage. His beautifully formed teeth were even and shining like those seen in the toothpaste advertisements I remembered. They were often displayed for he smiled easily and broadly.

"This conversation is a new experience for me," I said. "All of you follow my thoughts easily despite my limited ability to express myself. I wonder if you are not staying a jump ahead of me by reading my mind. To give you my own theory for the origin of man on earth is passé now. Since you have anticipated that I would believe that man arrived on earth through a pioneering adventure in space travel by an advanced race from another planet, I know you have anticipated the general outline of my theory. It was original thinking on my part when it first came to me and I felt quite pleased with myself for arriving at an intellectually acceptable concept. It was compatible with the evidence that man was a creature of superior capacity for long ages before he had achieved a degree of civilization. I could understand the blossoming of art and technology overnight in such a light, whereas the theory of evolution was hopelessly inadequate to explain it."

"Why do you say that?" asked Professor Weidenhouse.

"A small group of the most educated of my contemporaries, no matter how well they understood science, would be helpless to preserve their knowledge if they were suddenly transplanted without tools to a world inhabited only by wild animals. They would hardly have the practical skills to survive, much less to develop the equipment of civilization to make paper and preserve their technical knowledge. Why, in a thousand years their offspring would probably be living like primitives and the knowledge of their origins would be lost or only faintly preserved in some kind of mythology. This theory explained man's capacity, in defiance to the law of evolution, to make starling progress in a few centuries as soon as he developed satisfactory methods to preserve records. My theory explained the incredible inventive genius displayed by Nicola Tesla with his photographic memory and ability to solve advanced mathematical equations in his mind. Unique figures like Tesla, Newton, Mozart, Lincoln, Edgar Cayce, and the founders of the world's great religions seemed to me to be a throw-back to our vastly superior ancestry rather than the product of some kind of fortunate accident in time and space. A haphazard brute 'survival of the fittest' kind of evolution could not produce these superior minds by chance, in my opinion."

"Well, David," Dr. Karoll nodded his approval as he spoke, "you have done some unusual thinking. You even justified the Biblical story of the fall of man, in a certain sense. However, David, you will undoubtedly be fascinated to learn what we, today, believe about man's origins and how we arrived at our views."

Mrs. Karoll and Alice had not participated in the discussion very much but I felt that either of them had the background to have done so equally as well as the professors, particularly in dealing with my very limited capacities and knowledge. The doctor's wife suggested that it was time to have their usual family devotion together and retire for the evening.

CHAPTER 12

"I could not love thee half so well, loved I not honor more."

—*Richard Lovelace*

Caleb

I wonder what time it is? I thought to myself, as I started to roll over and go back to sleep. Hmmm, I thought, I'm not really sleepy...so...I think I'll just get up before the family, enjoy an early walk and watch the sun come up.

I dressed quietly in warm clothing, put on some high top walking shoes, slipped a small but powerful flashlight in my pocket and silently let myself out the door onto the porch. As I looked over the area that I could see from Dr. Karoll's porch, I thought to myself that I would like to see one of the communal living areas of those who had not yet attained the standing of men like Dr. Karoll. I remembered that Alice had pointed to a hill about two miles distant and told me that it was five miles from the house in a straight line to a community on the other side of that hill. After a moment's consideration, I stepped back inside, wrote a short note to explain my absence, picked up for a precaution the belt with a two edged six inch blade sheath knife that Dr. Karoll had given me to carry during our camping trip, and started out for my destination.

The sky was getting light in the east as I reached the crest of the hill and I took time out to experience the break of dawn in silence. Looking on ahead from my vantage point, I saw that lights were visible from the community. It was another hour before I reached the edge of a beautifully landscaped quadrangle of multiple dwelling units with a park and recreation buildings in the enclosure. The area immediately surrounding the community was cultivated but in a manner quite unlike any farm I had seen. I resolved to ask about it when I got back.

"Good morning, sir. We are grateful and honored to have you visit us." A young man of good appearance with a girl beside him had turned aside from his direction toward one of the buildings and approached me.

"Why, uh, good morning to you," I said in surprise at this kind of greeting from a stranger.

"Will you have breakfast with us in our com-house?" The girl asked this and I looked directly into her eyes as she spoke. It seemed to me that there was a mixture of admiration and anxiety in them. How I could be the source of these feelings was beyond me.

"Well," I hesitated in some confusion, "well, yes, I'll be glad to."

"Thank God you have come, sir, thank God!" the girl spoke intensely.

"Please, Marie, say no more until after devotions and breakfast," the young man gently admonished her.

Now I was mystified and could not conceive how I was precipitating the emotions displayed. We walked together silently after that and entered a large dining hall along with several hundred other people whose ages appeared to range from twenty to thirty-five. They were not of the same make-up as Dr. Karoll's family or anyone that I met in association with him. It was my impression that they represented a less refined class and there did not appear to be a great amount of difference between the least and the best of them. This is not to say they were inferior people but only that they were not striking for their fine physiques nor did they noticeably appear to have the same qualities of leadership or educational background of the people I had met thus far.

In a few moments, we took our places at one of the tables for four which were scattered throughout the hall amongst the larger ones, seating perhaps twenty people each. After all were seated and quiet, a great bronze gong was sounded three times, sending out a pleasing note which vibrated through my body and gave me a thrilling sensation in my spine. Following this, all sat in deep silence for a space of about eight minutes. A choir of twenty or thirty voices then sang something that reminded me of a Gregorian chant. The great gong sounded once more, and then all stood with bowed heads. A prayer for guidance through the day, thanksgiving for the gifts of life and provision for all the needs of body and soul was spoken by two voices in unison, a deep male and a mature female voice. It was for me a soul stirring experience.

Waiters then took orders quickly and breakfast was before us in only minutes. We ate in silence except for beautifully orchestrated music

with melody and rhythm similar to the popular songs which were peren-
nial favorites that I remembered. When breakfast was over, the people
at the larger tables filed out, while many who sat at the smaller tables
delayed leaving and became engaged in conversations. Everyone who
had not left the hall seemed to have noticed me. Their reactions were
puzzling. My presence had definite implications of something momen-
tous for the community from the way it affected them. I was not
dressed differently to any noticeable extent and the only way I could
easily have been picked out from among them was by the harness belt
over my chest with the inlaid silver Crusader's Cross. It held Dr.
Karoll's knife sheath a little forward of my left arm pit and just above my
waist at a forty-five degree angle. The knife belt was designed so that
the knife could be withdrawn easily and quickly with the right hand.
The knife itself was double edged, razor sharp and the handle had fin-
ger grip grooves. It had a striking appearance for the fine workmanship
on it and the sheath and belt were of matching qualities.

"All right, Marie," the young man said, "now our Noble-Con
should be given your story and the reason why we have not been able
to put things in order without waiting for his visit."

I would have spoken then to ask about the title given me and the
meaning of his words, but before I could frame my questions the girl
began in an earnest tone, "Sir, I do not wish to say more about the incident other than that I give you my word before God that I gave him no
indication in any way that I admired him or would care to have his atten-
tions. He persuaded me to go with him alone away from our quadrangle with a story that he was sent by a close friend of mine. He said that
he was walking with her and that she had discovered an unusual herb
growing in the woods for which she knew I had been searching."

The emotions that arose as she told me this were too much for her
to contain. She paused to regain some control of herself. The young
man touched her hand lightly and after she had dried the tears that had
begun to roll down her cheeks, she began again. "The child I bore only
a month ago was put to death according to law, but as you know, it is
necessary that the man should have the choice either to meet his
accuser on The Rock or whoever stands in their place or else confess.
He will not confess and no one here is able to meet him on The Rock.
Jonathan," she nodded toward the young man, "would do it but the
match would be hopelessly uneven and I have begged him not to. No

one else in our Com will offer, especially since the first Noble-Con was killed. I and others now walk in fear and disgrace."

Before she had finished speaking a small gathering had quietly formed all around our table. All looked solemn and expectant and I felt they showed a certain awe and respect toward me from their manner. I hardly knew what to say in response to what had just been told me. I was silent for a moment as I tried to fathom why I had been accosted and then given such an account as though it were some duty of mine to correct it. Just then another person joined the group and spoke directly to me but for all to hear.

"Caleb has been informed that you are here and he is on his way over with his con-blade on."

These words had the effect of putting an electrical charge in the air. No one spoke further but the group began to disperse and convey some information to those still in the hall as they departed. It appeared to me that they were telling something important from the reactions I could see from those nearby.

"Come, we must go to the Rock for you to meet him." The girl stood as she spoke and took my hand. I found myself being lead into a central area of the quadrangle that was laid out like a park with winding walks, trees, shrubs, benches, and a clearing in the center where there was a round platform about ten feet in diameter. It was quite flat and appeared to be cut from solid granite. The clearing was about a hundred and twenty feet across and a number of persons had already begun to gather as though there was something about to transpire on the platform.

I was bewildered now, for it was obvious that my presence had stimulated all the activity that was taking place. I could not restrain my desire to know what was happening any more. Observing and listening to the conversation had not enlightened me as to what was going on. My first question amazed the young man and the girl.

"Why did you refer to me as a Noble-Con?" I asked the young man.

"But, sir, no one but a Noble-Con would dare enter a strange community wearing a contender's knife and the symbol of the order. Surely you know that you must fight Caleb until one of you has been killed. All know the custom. A Noble-Contender must fight when he finds there is someone to be confronted. All know about Caleb and Marie. You must fight! You will be forced to by the people now. Don't you know this?"

"My God! I didn't know. This is Dr. Karoll's knife, not my own. I was just out for a morning walk through the woods. I only took it for protection. He didn't tell me about it." I blurted this out in short disconnected sentences aghast at the idea of a knife fight to the finish.

"You're not a Noble-Con?" both said at once in a stunned whisper. Then the girl began to cry silently and the young man was utterly downcast.

"Oh, I can't stand to see another man killed because of me. Oh! I just can't. Oh, Jonathan! Can't you stop it somehow?"

Jonathan didn't speak but looked shattered. Then his face took on a strong set. They were both silent for a space of about fifteen seconds, then he took a long slow breath and said, "I'll face him, give me your knife."

At this the girl let out a moan and began sobbing quietly.

Now the picture was clearing up. My mind was racing to assemble the bits of information I had into something rational. The girl and the young man were clearly in love and she had been taken advantage of by Caleb. There was evidently a medieval-like custom which allowed such injustice to go uncorrected unless some man was willing to publicly make the accusation. But once accused, the wrong doer had the right to confess and accept the established penalty for his wrong or face his accuser in a hand to hand battle to death with the regulation weapon, the fighting knife I had ignorantly strapped on my chest as I left the Karoll home a few hours earlier.

I did not see how the term 'Noble-Con' applied but it was evident that my wearing Dr. Karoll's knife and belt into the community was the sign that I was one. This meant that I would accept, if need be, the task of standing up for a local citizen. Now I found myself, by happenstance, expected to act for Marie as the accuser and to face Caleb on The Rock, unless, of course, my appearance should intimidate him into choosing to confess rather than to fight. I had no choice but to accept my role or else see Jonathan save me from it in a battle that he plainly considered to be sure death for himself. There was no way for me to allow that and live with myself, or face Alice, or anyone, for that matter. After a long moment of painful silence, I spoke softly but decisively.

"No, Jonathan, it's my battle." I was silent and thoughtful and, as the two of them turned toward me, I asked, "Tell me anything you can about Caleb that may help me." As I said this, I lost all concern for my own safety. A certain sense of joy at having made a man's choice filled me and I began to feel a righteous indignation with the human weakness that had so terribly hurt Marie and humiliated Jonathan. Now that I looked at it like a man, my thoughts were clearer and I began to plan my strategy.

Several others had gathered in close to us during this conversation, and I noticed Marie was gaining command of herself, although she was being supported on either arm by a friend. Jonathan had shown himself a hero in the eyes of all who had witnessed the incident. For an instant, I wondered if I had any reason to be more optimistic about the outcome than Jonathan. This idea I quickly dismissed and turned my thoughts to what my approach should be when Caleb did arrive.

"Caleb is a big man," Jonathan answered my question. "He may not be as quick as some but his size and his long arms give him an overpowering advantage. He has always used his size and strength to assert himself."

"Why, that's a coward's way," I commented. Then, after a moment's thought, "How does he hold his knife?"

"Right straight in front of him...he points it at a man's throat and with his legs apart, his knees bent and his toes pointing out, he slowly walks toward him, holding his left arm outstretched to the side as if to keep a man from trying to dodge around him. Even in this position he stands half a head taller than an ordinary man.

About this time someone handed me a rolled sheet of heavy paper with a red cord tied around it and a large ink marking pen.

"Here is the confession scroll, sir. We swear it to be accurate."

I unrolled it and read the large clear print down to the place for Caleb's signature. I could understand why Caleb was inclined to fight rather than sign the scroll. It described his act briefly and outlined his acceptance of the penalty, which included seven years of intensive training in mental and physical disciplines and his submission to an operation that would make him incapable of repeating his crime or fathering a child. A lot better than the electric chair or the gas chamber or life imprisonment, but still a difficult correction to accept, I thought. I turned to Jonathan and asked, "How do I confront him?"

"You and Caleb stand at opposite sides of The Rock and one of us carries the scroll from you to him. After he reads it, you ask him to sign it and bring it to you or meet you in mortal combat upon The Rock." Jonathan and the others were plainly confused when they saw that I was not familiar with the proceedings.

About that time I saw Caleb a full head above the crowd, making his way toward the other side of The Rock. He probably weighed over two hundred eighty pounds and I could see that he was able to easily over-power most men with his strength. But I also saw he had a good appearance except that the cast of his features was that of a man with undisciplined emotions. To look upon his face gave me a pang of sympathy. His inability to earn the friendship and love of his fellows had brought the frustration that caused him to use his powerful frame aggressively. It saddened me to fight a man with childish emotions but there was little choice now. I could see the wisdom in the penalty designated by the scroll. How incredible to find myself in such a predicament, I thought.

The crowd backed away and gave Caleb a path ten feet wide as he approached. When he stepped directly on the other side The Rock, he stood glaring with, I felt, a certain apprehension. As he began to look me over, his face showed relief and then an unpleasant smile. There was little question that he was confident of the outcome of an encounter with an opponent as unimposing in appearance as myself.

Without commenting, I handed the scroll to Jonathan. He carried it over the Caleb and held it out toward him. Caleb whipped out his knife and struck the scroll from his hand, partly cutting it in two. Then he turned and grinned at me. Speaking not a word, I slowly detached my knife harness without removing the knife from its sheath and I stripped to the waist. Pausing a moment to add impact to my strategy, I carefully removed the knife from its sheath and laid it upon the surface of the stone in front of me. Looking straight in Caleb's eyes, I reached over deliberately, picked up the knife, and held it pointed at an angle over my left shoulder and then drew it down slowly, bringing the razor sharp edge against my bare chest just below the collar bone. The edge sliced into the layer of flesh over my rib cage, giving me a bloody but harmless gash about six inches long. My action was not anticipated and several people gasped. Then I spoke softly and sincerely.

"Caleb, I deeply regret that I must kill you."

With that I leaped up upon the rough stone platform and waited at the center for Caleb to approach me. The smile and all semblance of cocky self assurance faded from his face when he saw me standing above him with blood running down my chest. Directly, he mounted the stone and was moving toward me just as Jonathan had described. It was painful to me to see the emotions upon his face as he got closer. I felt like I was about to kill an emotionally erratic person whose failure was that he lacked self control rather than being of a wilfully criminal nature.

I held my ground in the stance of a boxer. The knife in my right hand was drawn back to my shoulder like I cocked my right fist when I had boxed. My left was extended forward with an open hand to grasp for Caleb's right wrist to stop his knife, if need be. As he moved in closer I weaved my upper body in a feint forward to the right, danced back a short step, and went into a crouch with my left hand held up toward his knife hand. He moved forward as I did this and I leaped one step to the right, sprang toward him in a low crouch, straightened up in close, and shooting my left hand out to grasp his knife arm, I threw a knife blow with my right to his midriff, like I would throw a body punch.

Caleb let out a cry of shocked surprise, put his left hand over the wound, dropped his knife arm to his side and let the knife slide from his fingers and then began to cry like child, begging me not to kill him.

I stood back not knowing what to do and feeling like a bully who just won a contest in which the other party had not had a fair chance.

"Please, don't kill him, sir. Let him sign now, please let him sign now," Marie spoke in a strained voice.

"I'll sign," Caleb sobbed.

"He needs a doctor," I said. "He needs one quickly or he'll die." My knife had gone in to the hilt and I knew he was bleeding internally. As I spoke these words, I suddenly felt the strain of what I had just gone through. My normal strength was still far from being fully restored since Dr. Karoll had been working with me. The loss of some blood, the great emotional stress, the exertion of the fight, and the shock of delivering a severe knife injury to a fellow human all at once became overwhelming; and I felt my legs buckling under me as I fainted dead away.

In what seemed only a momentary lapse into unconsciousness to me, I was apparently picked up and delivered by air ambulance to Dr. Karoll's home, for when I opened my eyes again I found myself in my own room with both Alice and Dr. Karoll standing anxiously beside my bed.

"Oh, Father? He's opening his eyes. I know he'll be all right. I know he will!" Alice's voice was full of concern.

"Of course, he will, dear. There is nothing to worry about at all. There is no injury but the shallow cut on his chest and that will heal easily."

I was surprised to find myself in bed for I hardly realized that I had been unconscious at all. I reached first to feel my chest to see if there was a gash. My hand encountered a dressing cloth held in place with surgical tape. Then my senses began to clear some.

"Alice! Dr. Karoll! Am I glad to see you! I thought I had seen my last of you or anyone! What a mistake I made!" Then after a pause, I said, "How is Caleb? Will he live?"

"Caleb will live, David. He was taken immediately to a skilled surgeon and his wound treated to prevent his death," Dr. Karoll answered me softly.

"You were wonderful, David. Marie told me all about it. We're so grateful that you were able to act as you did and yet not be harmed." There was no mistaking that what I had done was worthy of admiration and respect in Alice's eyes.

At this moment, Louise, Dr. Karoll's wife came in bringing me some hot broth. She set it down on the table beside me, and taking charge in a manner that seemed natural and becoming to her, she told me that Dr. Karoll said I had no serious injury but, nevertheless, she wanted me to take the broth and be left alone to rest.

"Please, Mrs. Karoll," I asked earnestly, "I would like to have Dr. Karoll explain to me what happened and why. I'm sure I couldn't rest for wondering how everything came about to put me in such a predicament."

Dr. and Mrs. Karoll talked this question over and he convinced her that no harm would come of my sitting up in bed to learn about my experience.

CHAPTER 13

Noble
Contenders

The right to responsibility is the outstanding right of the citizen. In the absence of it, all his own `rights' amount to nothing.
—The Right to Responsibility
L.P. Jacks

"First of all, Dr. Karoll," I asked, "I'd like to know what Jonathan meant by referring to me as a Noble-Con?"

"This term," began Dr. Karoll, "is short for Noble Contender. All who aspire to serve in a high position of authority in our government must prove themselves by spending two years among the common people as a defender of the rights of individuals, a righter of wrongs on the order of the Knights of the Round Table and King Arthur's Court. This is the way that we maintain a society where the spirit of the law is upheld in the unprogressive, as well as in the most advanced of our communities."

"Knights of the Round Table! Why, that was mythology, sir. There is no evidence they ever existed," I said with a laugh. "As for justice, how can you have any kind of justice by settling differences with knives?"

"The Order of Noble Contenders, David, is the very cornerstone of our method of preserving individual freedom and rights, the ideals upon which America was founded," said Dr Karoll seriously. "A Noble Contender may challenge any man in the nation, even including a member of the World Government Council if he believes the rights of an individual are being infringed. He is obliged to challenge a man like Caleb on any occasion that he is asked, unless he has reason to believe that the projected wrong has not been committed. In such an event, he is obliged to ascertain who is in the wrong and take the action necessary to bring justice."

"I venture to say that a Noble Contender leads a dangerous life," I commented.

"Only one out of three survives," said Dr. Karoll softly.

"Then who is willing, or rather, gets forced into this job?"

"It is not a job, David. It is the highest aspiration of our finest youth to be accepted as a Noble Contender. Those who survive have proven their dedication to serve the needs of the race without concern for their own personal welfare."

I was silent for a few minutes as I thought over the experience I had just been through. Dr. Karoll waited quietly for me to bring up my next question.

"Dr. Karoll...the knife and harness belt...they were yours...you were a Noble Contender!"

"Yes, David."

"You spent two years visiting communities like the one I was in this morning?" I asked, amazed at the idea that Dr. Karoll had survived the experience of a Noble Contender.

"Well, yes, David. Some were made up of more highly evolved people and some were less progressed. As a nation, we are so organized that we generally limit the range of difference in individual abilities of the members of each community. This promotes competitive spirit and generates self confidence among their members."

"Can anyone challenge another?" I asked, thinking about the way a bully might wreck havoc in a community.

"If a man believes that another person who is unable to defend himself has been wronged or if he becomes aware of an incident that is insulting to a woman or has been present when a man has shown disrespect for womanhood by using obscene language or by any suggestive act, then this man presents himself to his community council and asks for a decree scroll outlining the offense, the punishment, the confession required and the demand for the named party's signature. The case is investigated by the council sufficiently to check the details for accuracy. No one may challenge a man for an infringement of his own rights but only on the behalf of another."

"But can the council possibly know they have the facts, especially in such matters as you just mentioned?"

"This, David, is one of the areas where our society has made a great step forward. We recognize the use of intuitive faculties by developed psychics. We have refined tools developed by scientists to establish the recognition of individuals for their abilities and to back up their findings, if need be. No man dares to perjure himself before the council for he will unquestionably be exposed immediately and meet severe consequences. We tolerate no lying under any circumstances. Crimes arising from the failure to achieve self control are understandable and are dealt with in a constructive way but lying is a premeditated crime against the race and creates endless confusions."

"Well, now," I said, "that does put things in a different light."

"Yes, it does. It takes the settling of differences between individuals back to ancient times, such as in the days when some of the Pharaohs were great psychics. They could not be lied to by any man. Of course, they were limited to settling only a few of the problems among the commoners."

"I must say you are stretching my mind." I paused, and then wondered, "A man cannot challenge another for a wrong to himself, only if he is defending the rights of someone else?"

"By this means we assure that a challenger is defending human rights and is risking his life for a noble cause. Without this measure, a skilled fighter could terrorize a community and serve base personal ends."

"If every man in the community can challenge a wrong doer and demand a confession, why do you need a Noble Contender?"

"Your experience this morning gives you part of the answer to that question," said Dr. Karoll. "However, there is much more reason than that. A Noble Contender has a far more highly developed sense of values than the racial average. He is advanced in his understanding of the principles that bring progress to the race. Our scientific methods for the testing and evaluation of character are used upon those who aspire to the Order of the Noble Contenders. This assures the nation that only pure-minded and sincerely dedicated men will attain a position of high political authority. No one may be considered for election to a high office who has not fully demonstrated his willingness to die to preserve the rights of the nation's humblest member."

"It is still difficult for me to see how violence can possibly be the foundation for justice," I mused. "I thought that when we had peace on earth that the lion would lie down with the lamb, that we would no longer tolerate bloodshed...besides it is unChristian."

"In your times, the police force used violence to maintain order, David. Would anyone suggest that a police force made up of the most honorable men in the land, themselves personally responsible for their actions, could represent an evil use of violence to preserve order? And who but a Noble contender could force the hand of an unjust judge or a corrupt police chief or a brutal police officer? Does it not seem more appropriate that every able bodied man in the nation who honors the Constitution has the role of police officer and that no man, regardless of his status, is above being brought to justice by a special police force made up of the noblest men of the land, if his actions deprive even one other person of his rights? An obscene word, the mistreatment of a child, the pollution of a stream, cruelty to an animal, any such offense may require a man to confess his error, accept a just penalty, and desist from such action or possibly meet death at the hand of a fellow citizen who is willing to defend the rights of others with his own life."

"A nation of honor bound policemen...hmmm," I answered thoughtfully, "I'm sure there are more details involved than you've given me to making such a system operate."

"The entire principle lies in the idea of individual dedication to service to the highest good of the race, and the provision for this individual dedication to express itself, David."

"Those are beautiful words, Dr. Karoll, but we had the same kind of beautiful words from our politicians, our ministers, our college presidents, and the heads of large corporations. Yes these same men were in authority when private interests clear cut great national forests and raped every natural source of life and beauty in America because of their greed. I don't see why more of the same kind of beautiful words should make any difference."

"They wouldn't have in your day, David."

"Then how do they now?"

"We have made use of the channels of communication to generate lofty ideals."

"Sounds like brainwashing."

"No, David. Just accurate knowledge of the facts of life and the purpose for human life on earth."

I was beginning to feel the strain of the emotions that our conversation was bringing to the surface. Alice evidently noticed.

"I believe David is satisfied and can rest now, Father. Don't you think he should?"

Dr. Karoll and Alice left quietly, leaving me to wonder about all that had happened.

"A society where every man of honor has the privilege...no...the obligation to act responsibly...even to lay down his own life to challenge evil...what an exciting idea!" I thought to myself.

CHAPTER 14

Desperate
Times

"Let not this house be desecrated by a religion of show. Let it not degenerate into a place of forms. Let not your pews be occupied by lifeless machines. Do not come here to take part in lethargic repetitions of sacred words. Do not come from a sense of duty, to quiet conscience with the thought of having paid a debt to God. Do not come to perform a present task to insure a future in heaven. Come to find heaven now, to anticipate the happiness of that better world by breathing its spirit, to bind your souls indissolubly to your Maker."
—William Ellery Channing

I rested well and awoke the next morning fully refreshed but as I thought about the previous day, the excitement of the knife battle and the discussion that had followed, my mind was stimulated into a philosophical train of thought. While there was a feeling of emptiness that crept over me from time to time when my thoughts strayed back to the loved ones I had left in the past, yet the adventure of being with such remarkable people kept me from dwelling upon such things. Each day brought me in contact with so many new ideas that these longings were temporarily checked. Now breakfast was over and the sun was shining brightly on a beautiful Sunday morning. I was going to be alone with my thoughts for awhile as Dr. Karoll's family was preparing to attend a worship service that would entail their leaving the mountain home for about three hours.

Dr. Karoll explained that it would probably be better for me not to accompany them until I understood more about their beliefs and why their worship service took the form that it did. As they left, I could see that there evidently were some changes in Sunday morning worship. The entire family was wearing nicely tailored but loose fitting coverall-like garments with a hood hanging from their collars. In their hands each was carrying a pair of knitted slippers. Their clothing was of a soft, unreflecting, pearl gray material with a series of small royal blue and bright red religious symbols along the hems, around the cuffs and over the hood. Seeing the family leave this way sharpened my already keen desire to know more about their idea of religion.

Responding to a suggestion by Louise Karoll, I walked slowly to the stone walled enclosure in the garden that had been prepared as a secluded spot for meditation. It was far enough away so activities

71

around the house and tennis court would not disturb a person who wanted to be alone with his thoughts. A comfortable wooden bench and a low flat table were placed within the carefully kept area. Inside, it was about fourteen feet in diameter. A small cabinet built into the wall contained cushions and a soft warm blanket. Dr. Karoll often used this spot for meditation himself, sitting in the full lotus position of the yogi on the low table amidst the lovely flowers, Mrs. Karoll had told me.

As I sat quietly studying the various flowers that were in bloom, I noticed there were a number of delicately colored and perfumed blossoming plants which I didn't recall ever having seen before. I wondered if there were not many new plants and vegetables and trees developed since the times with which I was familiar. This led me to think about Luther Burbank, the great American genius in horticulture and his psychic ability to select the plants that were superior and those which should be culled, when both were little more than sprouts with no visible sign to distinguish them. His personal journals indicated that he was a deeply religious person, very humble and served God by serving people. I also knew of the achievements in medicine and science by men of similarly deep religious convictions, such as Pasteur, Paracelsus, Hippocrates, Helmholtz, Tesla, Steinmetz and many, many others. They were all men who used their great intelligence to make practical application of the understanding of natural laws which they had arrived at through inner experiences in meditation.

Then, as my still roaming thoughts reviewed the early beginning of the industrial age, I moved along in time toward the years of my own youth and how I saw the highly accelerating development of industry through modern science. The novels of Jules Verne were still popular but his more farfetched visions were fast becoming realities. It was a time when philosophers realized that the common man no longer needed to live and die in ignorance, a slave to long hours of toil to furnish bare necessities for his family. Mass production methods, science, and the means for mass education and communications offered a new opportunity in the history of the world. America had the practical knowledge to lead the earth into a golden age of peace, an age of freedom for the bodies, minds and spirits of the masses of the human race.

Then I began to think upon how I had seen this opportunity abused, how in America science had become the tool of shortsighted self interest, how the educational system and the mass news media became the means to delude and enslave the minds of the people. By the early 1970's, the fast spreading moral disintegration of a great nation, a nation that once held forth hope for the whole world, had begun to look irreversible.

I had come to the meditation garden to dwell upon thoughts of the Creator and the noble deeds of great men but control of the mind was not easy for me. Hardly realizing what I had done, I had allowed my mind to turn to thoughts about the political events and social conditions that were so very painful for me to see during the years just before my last experiment with suspended animation.

America was in a deplorable state. The spiritual ideals upon which the nation was founded were regarded impractical by leading educators, political figures and even the clergy. Truthfulness was considered irrelevant to the conduct of international diplomacy. The flagrant immorality on every level of the military was a byword. Our State Department appeared to be little more than a tool serving special interests and the information released to the public concerning its actions only a smoke screen. Our National Security Council seemed to be concerned chiefly with the security of investments of private corporations, especially those which were exploiting the resources of small countries. America's reputation for stripping third world countries of their natural resources resulted from an unholy alliance between the State Department, the great conglomerate corporations, and our "Intelligence" Agency.

The nation's courts had become a mockery to justice. The practice of law made men wealthy. They spent their energies upon litigation that involved property, inheritances, insurance settlements, commercial transactions and corporate business. A selfless and dedicated lawyer serving the cause of justice was hardly to be found. There were men with high ideals who took up the practice of law but they soon found how difficult a challenge they had accepted.

It was not a matter of the legal system being either all black or white, since many honorable men were involved. However, the jury system of law was abused and perverted. The hypocrisy of suggesting that it was an effective tool serving in the cause of justice was transparent to any intelligent person. Strict rituals and specialized terms were used so that, regardless of how the jury was selected, the lawyers and the judge dominated the rulings. Often, the spirit of the law was flatly denied while the technicalities of its letter were twisted to suit the private interests being served. This attitude was incomprehensible to a jury of laymen. They were bullied into submission to the court experts. By using obscure legal terminology, it was easy to make them feel they were incompetent and ignorant of the law and helplessly dependent upon these "experts." The legal terms and court procedures combined with the array of legal devices designed to confuse the layman had made a farce of the jury system. The right to a speedy trial had been stretched to mean years and legal fees had become astronomical.

Like fish spawned in dirty water, with few exceptions, neither the legal brains of the country, nor the educators who grew up with these conditions seemed to notice the discrepancies. Law, politics and wealth had become interwoven. By inheritance they were family tradition. Cooperation among the "haves" preserved political power with the group. The prisons played a special role. Geared to the mistreatment of slum offspring, instead of being intelligently operated rehabilitation centers, they were hells that exposed prisoners to insensitive guards and to brutality from each other. Homosexual rape was the rule. The inmate who complained of mistreatment from his cellmates was tortured and sometimes murdered! The legal profession was able to take credit for the condition of the prisons because from their ranks came the overwhelming majority of the nation's judges and lawmakers.

In flagrant denial of every principal of Christianity, it was the educated and influential people of the land who owned the slum houses. These people knew children would live in the hovels they owned. The under-privileged were nursed up where filth, malnutrition, greed, vice and violence ruled. Just as the poor of Europe in earlier times had sold their babies to monster makers who would deform them into sideshow freaks, so the "respectable" people of America condemned the children born in slums they owned to be deformed mentally, morally and spiritually. Of course, their real estate agents handled all the details of the lucrative slum property investments.

The sleeping public was uninformed concerning its stake in the natural resources of the land. Oil, minerals, coal, timber and water power were sold to private interests at a small fraction of their value by uncaring or corrupt government agencies. Plans were being pushed to clearcut America's national forests to the ground and to reforest by planting single variety crops of fast growing trees. Then it would be necessary to kill the life within the soil and streams with tons of poisons to allow the single growth crops to flourish in defiance of natural law.

Occupied by such thoughts, I had sunk into a hunched position with my elbows on my knees and my head in my hands. My body was tense and my face drawn. About that time I heard foot steps approaching. In a moment Dr. Karoll appeared at the gate to the meditation enclosure.

"You don't appear to have had a very satisfying meditation, David," the Doctor's voice carried an undertone of concern. "Surely you are not longing to be back in your old circumstances."

"Oh, Dr. Karoll, I hadn't realized that you were back from the worship service. I hope that you enjoyed it."

"We surely did...Well, enjoy is not quite the right word. It was a joyously elevating time, a renewal of joyous spiritual fellowship with each other and with our Maker." The doctor paused a moment, then he asked how I like the meditation enclosure.

"This garden sanctuary for meditation is very beautiful, Dr. Karoll, but this morning I was not able to keep from thinking about the past. For a time I was back agonizing in the midst of the confusion again but not longing to be part of it. Being with your family and friends has shown me a contrast that made me more aware of the insanity of my time. It is depressing to think of the anguish that was experienced by so many people. Why had a nation like America, founded upon beautiful ideals, with a wealth of natural resources, so quickly become a land of incredible wastefulness, greed and selfishness, and of such monstrous cruelty to other peoples?"

"You were living in a great testing time for human beings, David, a testing for the individual character which had been built into each soul, you might say."

"Hmmm," I paused, "Well, there was certainly a special test coming from one particular direction and we were not looking so very good. I guess there was a sign of our condition in the phenomenal success of slick, expensive pornographic magazines which outsold by far all popular home magazines. They were on sale almost everywhere and even carried on the racks in some of the large chain grocery stores. To compete with them, the women's magazines were beginning to imitate them. Indulgence in every human weakness was encouraged by newspaper advertisements, radio and television commercials, and by motion pictures. Cigarette and soft drink advertisements used sex hand signs and phrases of the younger generation which made them actually pornographic for those who understood them. There was pressure from every side upon the youth of the nation to seek the immature values of short-sighted self-interest. They were taught to ridicule and to despise those who tried to oppose corrupt government, those who were willing to speak clearly to the issues and to make the kind of personal sacrifices that their ancestors had made in founding the nation. Their heroes were the notoriously immoral actors and actresses and their measure of success was money regardless of its source.

"David, you did live in desperate times. There are many parallels in earlier history to what you saw happening in America. The rise and fall of the Roman Empire is an example of the growth of a nation into greatness through industry and discipline followed by a rapid decline through immorality and self-indulgence. Rome was notable for justice in the days of its greatness. A fair trial was guaranteed every Roman citizen. Changes were coming quickly when Apostle Paul made appeal to Caesar for his right to a fair trial. He would have been freed by an honorable man like Julius Caesar but Nero had him beheaded with no more concern for the justice due him as a Roman citizen than if he had been a rebellious galley slave."

"I must say, Dr. Karoll, that does sound like a parallel."

"All of these things were necessary experiences, David." Dr. Karoll did not sound like he was able to appreciate the tragedy of what I was relating to him.

"You've made statements like that before, Dr. Karoll. I'm sure you've good reasons for making them, but will you take time to explain what you mean?"

"We'll get to such questions soon enough, David."

With that statement the Doctor turned and motioned to me with a nod to accompany him to the house. I knew Sunday dinner must be ready. Some friends had been invited over for tennis and to spend an evening of fellowship with the Karoll family.

.

CHAPTER 15

A Child's Attitude

"Shall we never cease to stamp human nature, even in childhood, like coins; to overlay it with foreign images and foreign superscriptions, instead of letting it develop itself and grow into form according to the law of life planted in it by God the Father, so that it may be able to bear the stamp of the divine, and become an image of God?"

—*Friederich Froebel*

The weather was just right for tennis. The air was cool with a hint of chill, but the sun was bright and a gentle fragrant breeze intermittently moved across the lawn court. The couple that had been invited by Dr. Karoll and his wife, Louise, were John and Amy Farland. The evening was planned in part to prepare me for eventual exposure to society, since it was hoped that I would some day become a normal member of the community. I would not guess the Farlands' ages for I knew that life spans had been increased. Something about this couple told me they were quite old...in my terms. Physically they appeared to be vigorous and athletic middle age, perhaps between forty-five and fifty.

We played a few sets of doubles. Alice and myself were paired together. My game had improved. Dr. Karoll had encouraged me to work out on a practice backboard to improve my physical condition and stamina. Alice played beautifully, but the two of us were no match for these old people. They had stamina and their control was delightful to see. Dr. Karoll's wife, Louise, was especially adroit at placing her shots and this made the game fascinating for me, in spite of the uneven scores.

While Alice and myself were watching a set being played between her parents and their guests, I commented that it would be quite interesting to me to know how competitive sports were carried on in a society that was so different than that I had known.

"Oh," said Alice, "you will appreciate the change. Sports are much more a part of the activities of individuals and families than you can imagine. We have not been participating as we usually would because of your presence. Normally we spend a full day of every week at our community center. We have seasonal sports activities and year around sports. All of us take part in tournament games and matches which are going on constantly. Teams for every level of skill and matches that offer competitive sports to every member of our society are an essential part of our way of life."

"Well," I said, "will wonders never cease. You seem to have decided that heaven was supposed to be here on earth and have set out to make it that way. A dream like this is just too much! I remember how I enjoyed team sports and how empty a place there was left in my life after I got out of high school. I couldn't continue any team sports on a satisfying basis. Participating regularly in active sports was impractical unless you became a professional ball player, but then it would have ceased to be pleasure. Professional baseball players were bought and sold like a commodity. Even if a person could enjoy that kind of ball playing, the field was limited. Only a small percentage of people who had excelled in a high school sport could possibly be accommodated. Then it would be emotionally unsatisfactory. A full time occupation with professional athletics would hardly allow the development of normal family life or other aspects of a man's nature."

Alice was sympathetic toward me. She seemed to understand how frustrating such a situation would be to an athletic person and knew that my feelings stemmed from personal experience. "Your times were like the darkness before the dawn, David. Yet, many things about the days that you lived in were a great improvement over earlier times. No other country on earth equalled America for giving youth an opportunity to become educated. Anyone with a suitable attitude could obtain a background in the world's finest literature, a knowledge of the religious thinking and philosophy of the great minds of all times, education for his livelihood, and the knowledge of how to properly care for his own body and mind. From the standpoint of having the opportunity available, no one was limited in America. Courage, perseverance, hope and love for mankind were rewarded amply. A superior person could rise to the surface from any condition of birth. I imagine that you'll protest that this wasn't so, because many persons were born into conditions that seemed to prohibit them from such opportunities for self development. As we look back, it appears that it was there for anyone in America. Many examples exist to prove that, without regard to race, creed or color, a man could rise from abject poverty to world renown. Still we couldn't say that the situation was ideal or allow conditions like those of your time to exist today."

It made me impatient to hear Alice justify the inequality of opportunity from birth that prevailed in America. I thought to myself that she could not visualize what it was like to be born in the slums of a major city, especially if one was a member of a minority group. Surely, she couldn't mean that slum children had a fair chance to become leading citizens. I was about to burst out with a protest but stopped myself. In previous conversations I had made a fool of myself every time I assumed one of Dr. Karoll's family or friends was expressing a shallow or heartless point of view. Now I was more cautious, especially since it was Alice to whom I was speaking.

"Alice, I believe that the chances for the son of an upper class family to become a successful citizen in our society over those of an illegitimate child from the slums must have been ten thousand to one. People who talked about equality of opportunity were unwilling to examine the statistics on such questions. Occasionally a professional ball player, or a fortunately born black man could distinguish himself, but it would've been a mistake to say this proved there was equal opportunity for all." Although I had picked my words carefully, my voice betrayed that my feelings were high.

"You, perhaps, missed the key thought, David."

"What do you mean?" I asked a little shortly.

"Why, I said that a person could rise above any environment that they were born into in America, if they had a suitable attitude." Alice emphasized the last two words.

I was silent for a time. I thought back to my childhood and the financial difficulties that resulted from my father's alcohol problems, the shabby clothing I had worn and the ill fitting shoes, the neglected teeth, the humiliation of being given cast-off garments. What had made the difference for me? Why didn't I lose heart and join the crowd? There was no doubt about it, it was the attitude toward my circumstances that made the difference. The opportunity to get an education was plainly something to be prized. The reward for effort to acquire knowledge was unlimited...no door would be closed to me...no position too high for me to aspire to. I grew up in a home that created this attitude. My mother, the daughter of European immigrants, passed on to me her own feelings of deep gratitude for the privilege of going to school that they had instilled in her. Alice's words were true in the light of my personal experience.

"All right, Alice," I was feeling stubborn. "You can say that a suitable attitude was all that was required, but surely you will agree that the forming of a suitable attitude depends in a large measure upon the early development of the child."

"You could put it in more emphatic terms, David. You could say the child's attitude was a direct result of its early environment. The child's attitude is a composite of the thoughts, the words and the actions of the people around it from the time of its conception until it reaches the age of twelve."

"Then you agree that the minds of many people born in the slums were molded into an attitude which condemned them to a life of bitterness, frustration and confusion. A thinking person would not regard them as having an equal opportunity simply because, theoretically, they could rise out of their material want and ignorance." I was still feeling righteously indignant.

"Isn't that just common sense, David?" Alice said gently.

I was silent again. I had controlled my inclination to speak sharply in response to statements Alice had made which seemed to deny the injustice in our society. I had, nevertheless, thought to myself that she did not understand very well. Now I felt foolish. While my words had not been sharp, I knew that my self-righteous attitude had revealed itself in my voice.

Alice was not offended. She always seemed to look beyond my words to see the good intentions. The way that everyone assumed me to have good intentions and took no offense toward me for my 'holier than thou' attitude raised new questions in my mind about myself. How often, I wondered, had I misunderstood the good intentions and wisdom of my own contemporaries, if I was so often inclined to misjudge and downgrade these remarkable people?

"Do you see now," Alice said, "that our concern for children today will be much, much greater than it was in your day? Think back to what history taught you about the beginnings of the industrial revolution. Ask yourself what social condition was the most deplorable as a result of the manufacture of goods in factories around the year 1880."

As I thought about her question, I was shocked by the implications that came to my mind. During the early days of the industrial revolution the children were cruelly exploited for labor. No sooner than the child of a poor family could be compelled to do the simplest tasks by brutal treatment, it was pressed into service. Pitiful half starved children of seven or eight worked for twelve hours a day in the stench filled atmosphere of poorly ventilated factories. They knew nothing of hope for the future. Men, women and small children worked side by side. They all used the same filthy sanitation facilities. Brutal mistreatment of women and children was common. The depraved men, the product of such an environment, brutalized them in unlighted areas or behind packing cases in the factories. The conditions of the slums they lived in were incredible. The worst of the Negro slum areas in my time would have seemed a peaceful haven by comparison. Progress of the race seems related to the manner that a society trains up its children. I was beginning to re-examine the comparatively enlightened times of my youth. Compulsory free education had not solved our problems. I could imagine that there were many children in my day in circumstances appearing more inhuman to citizens of the year 2103 than the child labor conditions of the 1880's had appeared to us.

"Does this mean that it is a social responsibility now to mold the very attitude of the small child?" I asked in astonishment at the idea.

"Not only to mold the attitude of the child, but to determine that it has a suitable genetic heritage as well," said Alice.

"Incredible!"

"Just a natural evolutionary development. We are putting into practice the ideals upon which America was founded," said Alice matter of factly.

"But wouldn't this press everyone into the same mold? Wouldn't this be far worse than mistreating the body of a child...to mold its mind. How can this be?" The idea stunned me. This sounded like the worst of Communism and Fascism combined!

Alice couldn't help smiling at my consternation. "David, David," she said, "can you imagine how the nineteenth century farmers reacted to the idea that they must send their children to free public school? How do you think they felt about having their own children taken out from under their authority and taught things their parents didn't know?"

"But that was different," I said.

"Only in degree."

"But such a thing could be abused to create a society of mental slaves."

"That was a failing of your times. The youth were subjected to a barrage of false information and mental conformity was demanded. Your form of government had become so distorted that for anyone to call it a Republic or a Democracy was a sign of either abysmal ignorance or childish hypocrisy, yet such thoughts were drilled into the minds of children by your educational system. These children grew up and became the editors of your newspapers, your political leaders, your doctors, lawyers, clergymen, and the professors of your universities."

"Ouch!"

"Well!" Alice waited for me to pursue my objections further. I knew it was true that the power to mold the minds of children had been disastrously abused in my time. Our educational system had become a self-perpetrating evil. It was responsible for the inability of the people to govern themselves. The youth were indoctrinated to accept a corrupt political machine as a Democratic government. I knew that the original intention for public education was that it might free the illiterate and superstitious masses from bondage. No one dreamed that it was destined to mold them into docile acceptance of atrocious abuse of political powers by their "elected" leaders.

I fell silent and looked away to observe the tennis match. Dr. Karoll returned a smashing serve by John Farland. The two couples volleyed the ball with the kind of skill that I might have expected from seasoned professionals. It was set point in favor of John and Amy Farland. Alice and I both watched with keen interest as Louise Karoll scored the next two points to give advantage point to the Karolls. John Farland's next three serves were brilliant. By an ace on Dr. Karoll, Mr. Farland made the set point to give them an eight-six victory. It was easy to see that all the players enjoyed the game thoroughly. I saw no sign that personal feelings about who won affected the pleasure it had been for anyone.

CHAPTER 16

Noah's Flood

"There were giants in the earth in those days; and also after that, when the sons of God came in unto daughters of men, and they bare children to them, the same became mighty men which were of old, men of renown."

—*Genesis*

A ll of us had had enough of tennis and were ready to refresh ourselves before the evening meal. Dr. Karoll and I left the court last. As we walked toward the house, he turned to me and said, "David, you'll be interested to know that John Farland is well versed in the principles of anti-gravity. He is also familiar with the cosmic energy power transformer that now furnishes all the power needs of the earth in a super abundance. We have power for any purpose without the need for fossil fuels. Pollution of the air arising from fuel consumption is no longer a factor anywhere on earth, nor is radioactive waste. John will be glad to explain something of these two discoveries to you later this evening."

"I'll be looking forward to that," I said. "Those are two questions that I've been wondering about. It looked like our science was stymied on both of them. The idea that it was impossible to obtain energy without some equivalent of fuel consumption was drilled into the students of physics. A man could be picked up at the patent office, put into a mental institution and classified as insane by law if he tried to patent a device which produced energy of itself or through manipulation of the force of gravity. I once knew a practical and highly capable person who had this happen to him."

"There was nothing new about that, David. You remember how Galileo was required to retract his findings by the Church on pain of death. Science was a jealously guarded possession of the Church, and thus, any new science was heresy."

"Well," I said, "there was plenty of resistance to new ideas, especially where religious prejudice or profits would be affected. But the times of the alchemists and Galileo can't be compared with the great scientific age that I was living in. Why, no time in history could equal it. We made far reaching advances in technology and medicine. In a space of fifty years, we advanced from man's first flight in a heavier-than-air craft to supersonic jets, and then in just a little more time, we had sent a man to the moon."

I was beginning to swell with pride as I thought to myself what a record in scientific advancement was made by my generation, even if commercial interests had misused it.

Our conversation was terminated prematurely. We were about to enter the house to shower after our tennis playing when Louise turned toward us and mentioned that in about forty-five minutes we would have dinner.

After dinner, all of us gathered in the family room as we had done previously with the professors from Utah Isle. While the conversation lingered upon the day's activities and the weather, I was intently observing John Farland and his wife, Amy. There seemed a difference between them and the other people I had met. While they were in the same physical condition as the others, their bearing and proportions did not seem to equal them. John Farland and his wife looked more ordinary, more like my own contemporaries. Both looked Scotch-Irish, were light of complexion and a little freckled. They had sandy reddish hair with grey in places and were somewhat angular in figure...slim and a little wiry. My seeking to understand the social structure was reason enough, I felt, for me to ask personal questions.

"Mr. Farland," I said, " would you mind telling me your age?"

"Why, not at all, David," he said. "I am one hundred and thirteen and Amy is two years younger."

"Sir, this seems unbelievable. I've seen pictures of people who lived to be over a hundred but they didn't look like you. They couldn't have played tennis and were hardly able to participate in community life, much less be normal, active members of it, as you and Amy appear to be. Why, your age means that you were alive before the shift in the poles of 1998 and that you survived it."

"Yes, David. I was eight years old when the earth changes came. There were not many of us who survived the catastrophe, but of those that did, a good percentage were children."

"That's surprising," I said. "Why would it not be quite the opposite? Hardly any children would've been able to withstand the upheaval and the terrible struggle for existence that must have followed."

"Perhaps, you don't have the picture," said John Farland, "or you would easily understand."

"Please tell my why," I asked.

I had read some of the prophecies of Edgar Cayce but many events predicted by him which had taken place during my long sleep had not happened quite like I envisioned. References to them kept my imagination working overtime. Chance bits of information, casually mentioned in the discussion of some other subject, often caused me to lead the speaker away from his point to answer my questions.

"The answer's very simple," said John. "The children were able to trustfully accept the offer to come aboard the celestial ships for safety in the last thirty or forty hours before the shift of the poles. Older people were too suspicious. They felt it might be a trick and couldn't believe the warning."

"Come aboard celestial ships!" I exploded. "You mean that's how you survived?"

"Apparently you didn't know about this. Dr. Karoll mentioned that you had discussed the earth changes. I assumed you knew about the rescue operation."

"No...no, I didn't. This is fascinating," I said. "Please go on!"

"It seems to me, David, that many people knew about the celestial ships in the early nineteen seventies. Wasn't that so?"

"Yes, of course," I answered. "Many people saw through the government's effort to confuse the picture. Whatever the reason, it still may have resulted in good, perhaps even saving a panic. Perhaps they thought the people would fear a merciless invasion of the planet by a superior race. Our own nation crushed the American Indian with little or no conscience. Judging by our own conduct, what could we expect from a superior race from outer space? But there were some sincere investigators who were convinced of the celestial visitations and who vigorously opposed government perpetrated deception of the public."

John Farland paused as though he were trying to decide how to tell me in the best way what had taken place. "It is difficult to us now to understand the extent that distrust and fear ruled the earth, David. It's not that people are innately different today but the difference in their feelings is the result of the different circumstances surrounding their birth and childhood."

"There were some frightening stories about the UFO," I said.

"With few exceptions, the celestial ships," John Farland continued, "or UFO's, or whatever you called them, were on a mission to earth to preserve it from destruction by man and to save some life forms from extinction when the changes came. While many life forms required no help, still, many of the warm blooded creatures might have been lost if steps were not taken to save a few pairs of them."

"You are making this sound like a Noah and the Ark proposition." I laughed at the idea.

"You're so very right, David," answered John Farland seriously. "There's more of a parallel here than you would dream."

"Really!" I was surprised at his seriousness.

"To put things in the right perspective, we ought to go back to Adam and Eve, but right now we'll try to limit ourselves to Noah in order to stay closer to the subject," sad Mr. Farland. "You'll get a better idea of it all if we touch on the Noah and the Ark experience."

"Every subject that I ask about seems to open another door. These ideas are so different from what I grew up with," I said. "I hope you'll have patience with me. You have to keep giving me additional background just to get me to understand the answer to each of my questions."

"It's a pleasure, David, and I'm glad to share what little I know."

"First," John Farland went on, "let me show you why there is a connection between the rescue of myself and others in 1998 and Noah's great operation. To begin with, Noah was the name of a nation, not of an individual. There was an individual man referred to as Noah who was the head of that nation. He was among those called the sons of men that were incarnated in bodies which did not have a tail at the end of its spine and horns on its forehead, as did many in that time. Because of his superior appearance and abilities, he was elevated in time and became the leader and judge of his country."

"Oh, no!" I said. "You've really lost me now. I thought that man arrived on earth with a body that had evolved on another planet and was in a state superior to what it is today."

"Noah's body was superior to bodies today."

"Just a minute, David, you don't want to get off into that question now." It was Dr. Karoll interrupting. "You remember that we didn't have a chance to discuss your theory when the professors were here but told you our concept of how man got in a flesh body on earth was different from yours. We will take this subject up later."

"Thank you, Dr. Karoll," I said. "There are so many different ideas for me to absorb that I can hardly stay on any particular one of them when our conversation brings up another vacant spot in my understanding.

"Please go on with Noah, Mr. Farland," I asked. "I'll try to listen and hold my questions about details until later."

"All right, David," spoke John. "You know that the Bible is partly a legendary description of ancient events. In many a legendary story, as that of Noah, there is a faintly preserved record of an actual event of vast importance to the people of earth. The possible truth behind such stories is more plausible now, because we have data to work with not available in your time. When scientific thinking was directed upon the findings of archaeologists and integrated with information obtained intuitively by men of your times, like Rudolph Steiner, Harold W. Percival and Edgar Cayce, the Biblical records soon took on a different light."

"It is fascinating to imagine there really was a Noah," I said.

"The man we call Noah was the leader of the nation but the people were not under an authoritarian government. It was a great nation of souls, many with the type of ape-like bodies we just mentioned. Also, there were many other strange combinations of half-man, half-animal bodies on earth. In those times, conceptions took place which produced grotesque and sometimes startlingly beautiful combinations of man and animal bodies."

"Are you speaking of the centaurs and satyrs and sphinx of mythology?" I asked.

"Yes, those were a few of the mixtures, David. These had their beginnings millions of years before Adam. Many existed that there is little or no record of now. The period of years that souls have been in the earth covers, we think, some ten million years and this is difficult for mortal mind to conceive. However, because of the error that reached such proportions during Noah's time, a sudden violent change in the earth was about to occur. This was only about thirty thousand years ago. You might think that it was a natural change which had to occur when our globe cooled down to a certain point. However, the real cause for the changes was the failure of souls on earth to use their creative energy in harmony with universal laws. The inconceivably lovely earth was no longer able to be sustained when misuse of creative force was so rampant."

"I don't know what you mean by that, but please go on."

"The Flood came with the breaking up of the ice shell that enveloped the atmosphere at that time. The ice shell had the effect of making the whole earth into a giant hot house. These were the conditions for millions of years before the coming of man when life forms were developing and the vegetation was so lush. The sunlight was diffused by the ice and the air was saturated with moisture. Daily everything was drenched with dew when evening fell. Conditions were so changed at the time of Noah's flood that new species of vegetation and animal life could not enter into physical manifestations so freely as they once had."

"I guess evolution slowed down after that," I said.

"A gradual diminishing of the diversity of life forms then set in but changes continued in the animal kingdom through natural evolution."

"I don't think I understand about the ice crust."

"In the earlier hot stages of the forming of the planet, the water vapor was kept at stratosphere level by the high temperature of the globe. It condensed into tiny crystals at its outermost extreme and as the globe cooled, the ice cloud thickened. It was gradually compacted into a sphere of ice containing much of earth's water. When earth cooled sufficiently, the whole planet became an incubator for developing life."

"What a beautiful concept!"

"This was the condition when Adam, the Adamic race, first acquired flesh bodies. The flood came when the thin outer crust of ice began to break as the diminishing inner pressure of the hot liquids and vaporous matter no longer supported the inner earth crust. This created unequal forces on the fragile ice shell above. There were other conditions which you would find difficult to envision. For example, matter itself was of a different density and there was a different density ratio between air and water; heavier atmosphere and less dense water. The crust of ice had existed outside earth's atmosphere for many million years. This, of course was the period when plant and animal life had its beginnings and flourished in great beauty and abundance."

"You have painted a beautiful picture, one I would like to believe, whether it is true or not," I paused. "Now, was all this prepared for Adam?"

"It was not intended that there should even be an Adamic race living on earth when it was first created."

"Then for whom?" I asked in surprise.

"It was Divine Mind expressing Itself for Itself."

"Hmmm," I said thoughtfully, "I guess that brings us back to Noah and the Ark. But before that, could you discuss a little further about the way good and evil got mixed?"

"Well, first David," said John, "we'll have to give you a definition of the sons of Belial, the sons of God, and the sons of men. The earth was evolving beautifully until the rebellious souls, the sons of Belial began to interfere with the pattern of events taking place on the earth. The sons of God were supervising the introduction of life forms and guiding the evolutionary processes. They were not souls in flesh bodies, but spiritual beings who were in at-one-ment with God. When Adam fell, they bred from the animal kingdom a special body for him in which to have his three dimensional consciousness. This hybrid body was called hu-man. The sons of men were of the Adamic race and, though fallen, yet they were dedicated to doing God's will on earth. The sons of Belial were those souls who first brought distortions in the plant, animal and the mineral kingdoms. They had immersed their consciousness in matter for sensual experiences for ages and no longer had any recall of their beginnings. They were dedicated to self satisfaction alone."

"The Bible doesn't tell it that way," I said. "At least, not as I remember it."

"The sons of God and their celestial ships were mentioned in passages of the Bible. It does tell how these sons of God also became sidetracked, some of them seeking sensual experiences with the Adamic race. We have a mention of this in Genesis; 'The sons of God looked upon the daughters of men and saw that they were fair; and they took them wives of all which they chose.'"

"You mean that, like in the stories of Greek gods, souls that had never been born in earth bodies temporarily materialized them and mixed blood somehow with earth peoples?" I asked, recalling Greek mythology.

"Yes, that's the idea. And these mixtures produced amazing men, just as the book of Genesis and Greek myths tell. They had marvelous psychic abilities and could direct nature forces by mind power. They introduced to earth life devastating power for good and evil. In fact, the scripture says, after that God was sorry he made man. Sons of God, those who did not err, brothers of the fallen souls of earth, inspired and directed the building of the Ark through the individual called Noah, who had at his disposal the man power and resources of the nation of Noah. It was their responsibility to make sure that the hu-man body and other life forms would not be lost in the Flood. If the human body were lost, it could not have been redeveloped in the changed conditions after the Flood."

"What did the change mean to man?" I asked.

"It meant that the creative power of souls could not be misused so freely to create disharmonious mixtures of life forms, the harmful insects, the carnivorous animals, the plants that strangle others. It meant that man would be allowed to continue to use the hu-man body, the temple, the meeting place of himself and his Maker but his powers would be more restricted. The Ark saved evolutionary developments of ages and, of course, the human body. At the same time, the Flood cleansed away the bulk of undesirable mixtures. However, there was still an hereditary strain of these man-animal mixtures which persisted until only about twelve thousand years ago."

"Hmmm, a strange story but it rings true," I said. "I hope nobody stays lost."

"Each soul will eventually overcome its desire to experience life in a three dimensional earth body. Each will stop devouring lower life forms to sustain a flesh body, no matter how long it takes, no matter how many incarnations," Dr. Karoll volunteered.

"This story will give me a lot to think about," I commented. "If there was such an Ark, it certainly must have been a forty year project to build it. One thing is sure, it isn't reasonable for it to have been manned by only eight people, and half of them women."

"You are right about that, David," affirmed Mr. Farland. "There were more than eight people, else we would not have the five races on earth today. The eight were all that held a pure dedication to the purpose. They supervised the operation. It did take a well constructed craft to withstand the elements when the earth crust gave way at the poles after the ice shell crumbled, melting as it fell to earth and causing the Flood. Noah's Ark was maneuvered on the Flood waters to one of the poles and, as it collapsed, the Ark rode the Flood waters inward."

"What a story," I said. "What happened next?"

"Just after the poles collapsed, a portion of the earth crust about the equatorial zone broke up and moved outward due to centrifugal force and formed a ring about the earth on the orbit that is now the moon's. Gradually it was driven into a globe by cosmic rays, you would call it gravity, finally becoming the moon. The remaining earth crust moved inward and stabilized about the inner core. When the waters subsided, the dry land area was greatly reduced by vast oceans."

"That is certainly a fascinating description," I said. "Naturally, I can see that after the Flood, the sun shone as a ball of fire in the sky and the phenomenon of the rainbow was visible to inhabitants of the earth. The incubator conditions were over and the weather became harsh by comparison. Life forms hardened where they were, more or less, and vegetation did not thrive as it had before. I guess you might say that the heyday was over."

"That's the idea exactly, David."

"Well, I can see the parallel with the mushrooming of science in the twentieth century and how devastating it was becoming. But, please, Mr. Farland," I said. "Don't go any further. You have me almost dazed with your description of prehistoric times. I want to go over it in my mind and think about all this for a while."

"We didn't get to your question about our power source, David," said Dr. Karoll. "It's probably best that we take up that discussion another evening."

CHAPTER 17

Crystal Palaces

"I died for Beauty, but was scarce
adjusted in the tomb,
When one who died for Truth was lain
In an adjoining room.
He questioned softly why I failed?
'For Beauty,' I replied.
'And I for Truth...the two are One;
We brethren are,' he said."

—Emily Dickinson

A week had gone by since the evening with John Farland and his wife. It had been a time of adventure for me. Alice had taken me upon several extended flights in the air car. We had visited briefly at the university on Utah Isle and the architecture I saw there was beyond my most elaborate dreams of what could be done with structural principles. Instead of imitations of ancient architecture, or tiresome rectangular vertical projections of steel and concrete, or meaningless structures with facings and facades, there was an honest exposure of functional structural parts combined with graceful curves and decorative patterns from nature. Like the arches of ancient cathedrals, the structural parts were designed and proportioned to do what it appeared they did. Natural laws of physics with their mathematically constructed curves were given three dimensional form in these buildings. This gave structural members the grace of living things, like flowers, stems of plants, or ribs in the wings of a butterfly. The effect of this architecture was calming to one's spirit, perhaps like taking a walk in a forest of virgin timber. In their interiors an abundance of clear pools, fountains, tropical plants and rock gardens with little streams and water falls brought living natural beauty inside these buildings on every floor, purifying the air and perfuming it with the scent of flowers. To stand quietly in contemplation of such architecture was as satisfying as listening to a symphony. Alice said that to live with it was to daily grow more conscious of its beauty and more grateful for human cooperation and fellowship.

We had observed several structures that reached into the clouds when we journeyed over the continent. Some were reminiscent of the Eiffel Tower but breathtaking variations of it, rising to great heights.

Even many of the smaller structures were so tall and light in construction that it appeared to me that they would be blown over by the wind unless they were anchored to massive foundations. Alice was pleased to see my keen interest and arranged to have a professor of structural design accompany us and answer my questions while we were at the university.

The professor, an unusual appearing man with almost transparent skin, hairline, wrinkles on his face and a large high forehead, was introduced to me as Dr. Dubrock. He was one of the 'long heads,' the physically elongated people that had moved into the earth from a planet of another solar system. A delightfully pleasant person, he was able to make engineering principles seem like common sense. I questioned Dr. Dubrock about the tall structures I had seen with special reference to the foundations.

"Dr. Dubrock," I began, "in my time, one of the chief considerations in constructing a very tall building was the foundation design. New York City became a show place of tall structures because of its underlying strata of solid rock. Manhattan Island especially offered the necessary support for tall buildings. The structures were heavy and designed to resist overturning by any storm or quake. What new technique makes your light weight structures possible?"

"We merely studied the handiwork of Mother Nature," said the doctor, "and decided to learn how she designed her tall structures."

"You mean these buildings have roots!" I laughed.

"Yes, they do."

"How are they constructed?"

"Holes for root-like anchors are drilled in circular patterns. Depending on conditions, they may curve and fork and may have a bulb at the end for special anchorage. Sometimes we bore holes deep into subterranean rock. Generally, this design calls for a central high strength steel cable surrounded with concrete. This gives the effect of both a concrete piling and a root. You can see how this approach makes our tall structures practical."

"No, I can't," I said. "A tree may bend with the wind or quiver with an earth tremor but tall buildings are relatively inflexible. Our structural steel, while not brittle, had little elasticity and acted like putty whenever excessive stresses were imposed on it. The kind of tall buildings that we passed in the air car on our way from North

93

Carolina could not have been constructed with either reinforced concrete or with structural steel, in spite of the roots they may have."

"Ah, yes, you are quite right, David," said Dr. Dubrock. "It was necessary to imitate Nature's flexibility as well as Her anchorage. Even before the shift of the poles, the materials and know how were available to design far more imaginative structures than were being built in those times. Design initiative was stymied by your political system which gave highest authority to the money lenders and enslaved the construction industry to serve shortsighted self interests."

"How could we have erected these tall flexible buildings?" I asked persistently.

"You have very high strength steel tension cables for prestressing concrete. These cables with a useful tensile strength of one hundred tons per square inch could have been employed to serve as the elastic tendons of a tall structure. You already had high strength concrete mixes which produced a crushing resistance of five tons per square inch. Using this concrete in properly designed prefabricated compression members, in combination with high strength steel cables for tension, an efficient and exceedingly practical design for a tall flexible structure could easily have been made."

"How would you load the concrete evenly enough to make use of more than a fraction of its great crushing strength?" I questioned.

"In order to load the entire cross section of a brittle material evenly, it must bear upon a plastic material that is confined," said Dr. Dubrock.

I thought about this idea for several minutes before I answered. "I think that I see what you mean. If one used individual struts of concrete, properly contoured and with suitable joints, assembled the segments with tendons of steel cable threaded through them and suitably anchored, we could design a flexible structural skeleton for a tall building. The elasticity of the high strength steel would cushion the shock of earth quakes or high winds and the concrete would be carrying only compression loads."

"Yes, David, it is a design principle from Mother Nature. We shall never equal Her efficiency, but we may imitate Her," said Dr. Dubrock.

"It is apparent that concrete is not used above ground for building construction any longer," I said, as I looked toward a large laboratory building nearby.

"Well," said Dr. Dubrock, "with our unlimited energy supply from cosmic rays, aluminum and glass have become the most plentiful building materials on earth.   Aluminum is earth's third most abundant element, after oxygen and silicon. The power required for the electrolysis of the aluminum ore was the limiting factor and chief expense to producing it.   Now glass from sand and aluminum from clay furnish our commonest building materials. In addition to the supply of aluminum, we have magnesium from sea water which contains a half million tons of it per cubic mile. Such raw materials are unlimited and a minimum of human exertion is required once the machinery is set up to produce them. Scientists of your time were in the process of developing glass far tougher than had been considered possible a few years earlier. Now glass has qualities of elasticity unequalled by the finest steel."

"Marvelous, marvelous!" I was delighted. "Limitations that once throttled the imagination of engineers are simply non-existent. Glass certainly provides the most beautiful and enduring building material I can imagine. It used to be structurally worthless because of incompatible expansion rates and brittleness. By using a confined plastic material like pure aluminum in joints between glass structural sections designed for compression, and braided glass filament cables for tendons to hold the structure together, an engineer could design a crystal palace or a suspension bridge or an Eiffel Tower."

Alice was delighted with the way Professor Dubrock enlightened me concerning engineering techniques. My limited knowledge of engineering seemed like a child knowing his abc's compared to an educated citizen's, like Alice. She could have given me the same discourse as the professor, I learned later, but wished to spare me from becoming more conscious of my inferior education. The university professors' task was primarily to develop the students' abilities to imaginatively apply knowledge. They had been relieved of teaching students the fundamentals, I was informed by Alice. Knowledge of engineering principles was introduced into the mind quickly and easily, she said, by hypnotic techniques. When I raised my eyebrows at this, she said we would discuss it one evening with her father. The casual mention of engineering education by hypnosis opened a new area of thought to intrigue me. I remembered experiments teaching languages that were remarkably successful.

With the arrival of the weekend, I wondered what new experience awaited me. Arrangements had been made to bring John and Amy Farland back for an evening but changes in plans interfered. I was disappointed. The discussion of gravity and cosmic power was planned for the evening and I had resolved not to lead the conversation into other subjects again.

CHAPTER 18

The Darkness Before the Dawn

"My task which I am trying to achieve is, by the power of the written word, to make you hear, to make you feel...it is, before all else to make you see. That and no more, and it is everything. If I succeed, you shall find there according to your deserts encouragement, consolation, fear, charm...all you demand, and perhaps also that glimpse of truth for which you have forgotten to ask."
—Joseph Conrad

S ince plans had altered for the Saturday evening, Dr. Karoll suggested that possibly Alice and myself would like to see a currently popular stage play. Entertainment, I thought to myself, might hold as much an element of surprise as many other things about this enlightened society. I freely admit this thought was secondary to my anticipation of the thrill of escorting Alice to the theater.

Apparently Dr. Karoll had expected there would be such occasions, for I found that he had already ordered appropriate clothing tailored for me. So many things like this were being done for me that I was again diverted into questioning my state of consciousness. I had just finished dressing and, after observing the reflection of myself in the superbly becoming outfit, I found myself struggling to hang onto my sense of reality. Just then I heard Alice knock on my door. One glimpse of her made me forget all questioning of reality and decide that if I was dreaming, or that if I had died and was in heaven, then I had best enjoy it to the fullest.

Alice's gown enhanced her natural loveliness and added to her air of noble and pure womanhood. Whether it was the delicate color of her dress or its folds and pleats that did this, I could not say, but there was something about her which made me think of the strong and beautiful women of ancient Greece. The fabric was a shade of lavender trimmed with gold edging and decorated with small symbols brocaded in gold. While modest and feminine, still the dress revealed the beauty of her form and posture. As she stood there smiling, my ideal of all that was loveliest and most virtuous in woman seemed crystallized before me.

She sensed the effect that she had upon me in that moment and was both delighted and, very surprisingly...to me, a little abashed.

She turned away from me and for an instant she was not altogether in command of her emotions. Seeing this reaction had the impact upon me of an electrical shock. I experienced a thrill which had the sharpness of physical pain. It could hardly be imagined by anyone who has not had a similar experience. For an instant, it was as though the earth and all the stars in the heavens stood still. Then it was over. Alice regained her poise and I wondered if it had really taken place.

She smiled her approval as she looked at me, and I was delighted that she liked what she saw! My evening apparel was a semi-gloss forest green except for a narrow soft white collar, cuffs at the sleeves and trousers, and a deep "V" patch of white from the throat to the waist. The cuffs, collar and the "V" patch showing were an integral part of a removable light inner coverall-like garment. This liner was attached by bands of pressure sensitive fastening material. Like a fresh white shirt, it served to provide a fresh change but in a more complete way. This new style tuxedo was cut to give a good fit through the waist but allowed complete freedom of movement through the arms, shoulders and hips. It allowed the body to breathe, made a fine fit and was both very practical and good looking. It honestly accented masculine characteristics. The focus of attention was upon the head, neck, shoulders, hands and the carriage of the wearer.

Fifteen minutes after we reached altitude, Alice began letting the air car down to earth again. She circled the building so that I could have a good view of it in the little remaining day light. The architecture of the theater was like music in three dimensions. The mathematically developed contours followed the requirements of acoustical formula and its structural elements were exposed on the exterior surface. The entire theater was suspended a few feet above the ground by a network of fine cables laced to surrounding frames. The cables were strung taut to produce a stressed skin action on the exterior shell of the theater and supported it like spokes to the hub of a wheel. Its design was imaginative, artistic and highly functional but its seating capacity was for not more than three hundred people.

A road with a walking and biking path beside it led to the theater and what I took to be several bus-like vehicles were moving on it. Most of the people were walking or riding bicycles. The parking area was not visible from the air. Entrance places led to an underground parking area and, for craft like the air car, three small landing platforms offered a special convenience.

Alice set the craft on one of the underground parking entry platforms as I watched with admiration for both her and the performance of the craft. She activated a mechanism to lower the air car into the subterranean chamber. The arrangement was such that we debarked below ground, walked a short distance through a passage way, through a spacious lobby and then up a ramp into the theater itself. When the audience was all seated, the ramp folded in to improve the acoustics, Alice explained.

As we entered the theater, Alice began to tell me how important a place in society the theater had and how broad were its uses in developing individuality and encouraging the free exchange of ideas. The sum of what she said was this: Thousands of community theaters just like the one we were in dotted the countryside. They offered all an opportunity to develop and express theatrical talents. The function of the theater was to educate and ennoble people everywhere, as well as to provide opportunities for self-expression and individual development. Unusual incidents, scientific discoveries, archaeological finds, personal achievements and similar events were dramatized, accenting the human element. The theater lifted up before the race the heroism, the drama, and the adventure of mankind's struggle for greater harmony and understanding of itself and of the forces of nature.

The competition which existed among the community theater groups was keen and exciting, just as it was in their athletic games. Recognition for excellence was the inspiration for great effort and any group had the potential of moving into the fore to receive acclaim throughout the earth. Development of the arts was on par with the sciences. Artistic talent was equated with spiritual development. The day to day struggle for physical necessities no longer drained away the time needed for individuals to achieve a high level of proficiency in performing arts. Works of art were regarded as windows providing openings into the race mind to reveal the beauties and intricacies of man's higher nature.

Man's natural instinct and need for competition was sublimated to provide incentive for the refinement of human nature through using it to motivate youth toward the elevation of the values for which men strove. Social standing could no longer be bought but was attained only through distinguished service to the race in some form and especially through all of the arts. I thanked Alice for her discourse but had to apologize that I was hardly able to absorb such philosophical thoughts, especially not just then when I was experiencing so much beauty and wonder.

When I looked about the interior of the theater, I could see that it was designed to eliminate the need for voice amplification. It was small and the acoustics so excellent that close personal rapport could be established between actors and audience. The interior was not gaudy but subdued. It was decorated with relief figures. Alice explained that theater decorators tried to create a mood of receptivity and dignity that would harmonize with whatever the production depicted.

"Isn't this theater quite a distance from your home, Alice?" I asked. "From the time it took to get here in the air car, it could be three hundred miles. Your community theater would have to be closer or no one could walk or ride bicycles as we saw them doing when we landed."

"You are right, David. This is not our own center. The particular drama to be given here tonight is the reason we came. A great variety of plays are always being produced. However, when a particular play is timely or thought provoking, it may gain nationwide attention and be produced by a number of community theater groups. It is, perhaps, like a popular song or a successful musical show of your day. The ideals which stimulate their production are broader and more satisfying, perhaps, and the competition for the national limelight keener; but, otherwise, it seems much in the same spirit.

"Stage plays are a superior way to inspire and teach and there are few more effective ways of implanting reverence and respect for the human potential in the hearts of people. The experience of live performances of inspiring plays can hardly be equalled by other media. Our great thinkers are quick to work with skilled playwrights to introduce their ideas, whether they are for improving the administration of world government, for dealing with developing minds of children, or for furthering our understanding of the destiny of man."

"It is difficult for me to see how you avoid the pitfalls that such use of this means of communication must include," I said. "Why, you could mold the thinking of the people to any point of view. Government supervised propaganda, which uses the theater to channel the thinking of the people, sounds like a hopelessly undemocratic approach to communication."

We were interrupted from pursuing the discussion further as a sudden hush in conversation signalled that the performance was about to begin. The atmosphere became charged with the same electrifying thrill of anticipation and excitement that I remembered from times at stage plays in New York. The man who was to play the lead role stepped from behind the curtain. He was a man about my own size and build and, much to my surprise, dressed in a smartly fitting business suit of the early nineteen eighties. Alongside him stood the playwright, a woman whose poise and bearing reflected self confidence and intellect. This particular woman had an extraordinary quality about her that is difficult to describe. Perhaps one would say that she was radiating intellectual beauty.

"Dear Friends," she started. Her voice had the richness of quality which is the mark of a highly developed personality. "We have a play tonight that has a degree of uniqueness which we feel will fix in your memory some of the historical events it portrays. We hope that it will give you a new insight into a crucial period of our history. We must never forget that times of testing in the earth are for the refining and purifying of our character and improvement of our race. The disintegration of America in the 1980's was precipitated by our disobedience of moral laws, laws that have always been written in men's hearts."

She paused for a long moment as though to give dramatic impact to her next words.

"I have just been informed that the actual person out of the past whose life story provided the inspiration for tonight's play is here with us in the theater. We will not reveal his identity but hope that his presence will add power and meaning to our play." Then after a slight pause, she said, "...and now we present to you *The Darkness Before the Dawn*."

At first, the meaning of this introduction did not register upon my mind. When Alice turned toward me with a knowing smile, I suddenly realized that it was myself to whom reference had just been made. My surprise could not have been more complete. I was dumbfounded. The curtain was rising and an intense silence hung over the audience. I gripped the arm rests of my seat and determined to give no indication of my feelings for fear of drawing attention to myself.

There would have been no way to prepare me for the experience of seeing a live play such as began to transpire before me. The use of scientific knowledge, technical skill and artistic talent to produce the scenery was a marvel to me. A method of projection on a screen that was actually a mist-like vapor or fine dust trapped between several layers of transparent material, each layer responding to a different kind of light, provided a three dimensional effect for background scenery. The acting was superb. The accuracy of the portrayal of America in the late 1970's and early '80's left me speechless. It was done as an historical play, but it required a narrator to bridge over the great difference in points of view from those times until the present year of 2103.

I was not prepared for the contrast drawn between the times. Our society of the 1960's, '70's, and '80's was made to appear more grotesque and to have more distorted values than any social order out of the past I was familiar with. Activities of politicians and industrialists which in my time were thought of as needing some regulation were now viewed as heinous crimes against mankind and our environment. For example, the furnishing of modern technology's weaponry to undeveloped nations in order for them to carry on warfare was portrayed as inconceivably immoral, not only upon the part of those directly responsible, but upon the part of every single person who knowingly contributed to the effort, whether by owning stock in the companies, working for manufacturers or munitions, or by being willing to pay the taxes that they knew would be used for such purposes. It was a matter of individual responsibility for every literate citizen to make a moral choice to support or oppose the decisions of his government, no matter what the personal cost.

To these people of the Twenty-Second Century, the most vicious of all crimes against humanity was not the warring of one nation with another, not even the use by America of atom bombs to destroy helpless civilian populations in the cities of Nagasaki and Hiroshima of an already defeated Japan. In retrospect, the human race now regarded the misuse of the channels of communication as the most inhuman and destructive error of the Twentieth Century. All other abuses paled beside this and were secondary to it. The abuse of our technology they regarded as a byproduct of this one principal error which enslaved the minds and distorted the thinking of the masses.

This was amazing to me. I had thought we might be most critical of ourselves for the destruction of our natural resources and the pollution of the land and water with poisonous chemicals. The play did point out how our city water treatment plants took drinking water out of polluted rivers and did little more than clarify the water with coagulants and filters and kill the water borne bacteria with chlorine. From my own background in chemistry, I knew that dissolved contaminants coming from chemical processing plants or crop run-off water containing insecticides remained in our water supply, unaltered by coagulants and filtering. Horrible though it was that we allowed global contamination of the land and air and water with long lasting poisons, it was the poisoning of minds, the minds of the common people, with fear and hatred, with immoral desires, with disbelief in the spiritual nature of man that ranked as the supreme error of the Twentieth Century.

As the play moved on, my mind was constantly being jolted by the great difference in the perspective of these people with regard to human values. The errors of my time appeared so glaring to them that it seemed no one could have been quite insensitive enough to live in them without vigorously objecting to what they saw. Theirs was no self righteous attitude as they looked back on the errors of their predecessors. Quite the contrary. They believed themselves to be the very people who had committed the errors. Now, having been born in later times, they recognized their past failure as a lack of faith in God! Lack of belief in their responsibility on an individual level had enabled them to tolerate America's atrociously immoral government. Indifference, fear of reprisal, and failure of the well educated segment of the public to express vigorous objections to the infringement upon the right of individuals finally allowed the government to fall into the hands of those who lacked basic moral values.

The play went on to show how understanding of the purpose of life in the earth began to break forth when privately sponsored scientific studies established factual data concerning the natural laws governing reincarnation. This information provided an intellectual basis for mankind to change its direction. Peace, order, beauty, true justice and equality before the law for all peoples on the earth resulted when an understanding of the exacting natural laws to which each is subject became common knowledge. Scientists were able to establish that cosmic laws governing the reappearance of each individual had always preserved perfect justice, regardless of any temporary illusion of injustice. This was the key idea and theme of the play and the reason for its title, *The Darkness Before the Dawn*.

The belief that physical death ends all experience was the greatest darkness of my time. This widespread loss of belief in some kind of eternal life, examined in retrospect, was seen as the beginning of moral decay of the nation. It justified the prostitution of science to indiscriminately furnish the public with contraceptives. Scientists ridiculed the Virgin Birth of Christ and discounted the virtue and power to generate constructive influences of religious figures who lived chaste lives. The times offered no intelligent reason to dedicate one's life to selfless service of the race either for eternal rewards, or for the good of posterity. Gifted youth were using powerful drugs that would render them physically and mentally unfit to be parents. They drifted aimlessly, wasting their talents. Educators had become little more than mere hirelings. Impotent religious leaders, blind leaders of the blind, could provide no rational basis to oppose the widely held and scientifically endorsed belief in absolute death for the individual human unit. Intellectual leaders ignored the data from near death experiences which a few pioneering researchers examined. Such a condition was portrayed as the darkness which covered America.

As the play moved on, the old Chinese proverb, "one picture is worth a thousand words," came to life for me more vividly than ever. Advanced techniques for the projection of scenery in three dimensions with movement, sound and occasional odors had been applied with powerful effect. Because of all this, watching the scene concerning the great money collapse in America was the most stirring part of the evening for me. The play went over it briefly, giving the picture of it that Dr. Karoll described but in a way that I could understand better. America had been unwilling to correct her unsound money policies. All of the major European powers were forced to take steps to protect themselves as America's run away inflation threatened to disrupt international exchange and literally steal the wealth of other nations. By the early nineteen eighties, something like fifty percent of America's wealth was owned by only one percent of the population. They were quite indifferent to the disaster they were creating for the common people.

America was forced to take the desperate measure of confiscating all the silver in the possession of the American people. This became necessary so that it could be used for bullion to provide credit with an International Monetary Fund Bank in Europe in order to support the value of our currency in foreign exchange. The play showed how our system could have been saved by some honest reforms. It also showed how our government had become so corrupt as to be impotent in its response to meet a danger to the public. A final plea for us to take corrective measures along with a warning from the European Common Market nations and Japan gave America six months of grace to make changes before they would refuse to accept American money. The warning by the European bankers was kept a closely guarded secret from the public. Because there was such a vast amount of American currency abroad to be converted into the IMF currency, the credit furnished by the silver became exhausted. On the set day, all Europe refused any further dealings with American currency. The money panic that followed caused a complete breakdown of the mechanisms by which cities maintain their life. In one week, transportation, utilities, forces of law and order, and communications had ceased functioning from coast to coast. The major cities became great death traps which were devoid even of potable drinking water. People on foot struggled to reach the outskirts of the cities. Every artery was jammed with wrecked or stalled vehicles.

Adding to the horror of it, the public's human quality of sensitivity had been dulled to such an extent by the poisons in their bloodstream from spoilage retardants and insecticides in food and by the never ending stream of violence and cruelty they had witnessed on the television screens that they had lost compassion for each other. Our nation's inhuman use of technology upon the defenseless peoples of Indochina, poisoning their soil, dropping of defoliants, fire bombs and high explosives had hardened our own hearts, so that we were equally merciless toward each other in the emergency. The scene depicted staggered my mind. During the financial collapse, people became like beasts. Cannibalism became a way of survival!

While this episode was being portrayed, tears flowed freely down my cheeks. In a moment this was over and the play moved on to show the peaceful communities that survived the collapse. Foresight and intelligent cooperation had enabled many small groups to prepare for the trouble. About one third of America's population survived. The most important of the surviving communities were those groups of dedicated people who were determined that a beautiful America should rise again from the chaos.

The groups that survived had made intelligent plans. They recognized the irreversible nature of the political corruption. The most successful of them had selected isolated valleys in regions where terrain and vegetation prevented easy access and planned their self sustaining communities two or three years prior to the actual collapse. Such groups had chosen themselves a rendezvous and made plans to assemble the needed materials and equipment to fully prepare their area after the anticipated collapse brought all commerce to a halt. All equipment and materials needed were available after the money failure, for such items had no value to the leaderless hungry masses. These communities eventually developed means to communicate with each other by radio while travel was still unsafe and impractical. Later they selected representatives to gather together to re-establish their nation's government, honestly basing it upon the ideals and concepts of the original Constitution of the United States of America.

The play showed how this simple community life and closeness to nature was a time of re-thinking concerning the ideals of America. The early American practices of sharing of spiritual experiences and having community prayer and meditation began transforming those who survived the collapse. America's youth were deeply interested in the new information about the psychic nature of man and scientific evidence to support the belief in reincarnation. During this time of living off the land, the study of Edgar Cayce's life and the teachings given through him helped many to become convinced that they would be reborn themselves into the better world they planned to help create. This provided the incentive for heroic efforts to establish a just government.

The Night of Ignorance ended and a new Dawn broke over the earth. Much effort and many failures were ahead but the direction was clear. Peace on earth was inevitable. Virtue had finally become recognized as intelligent self-interest. The ideal of unselfish service to others, the expression of the Christ Spirit, filled the nation and created an atmosphere of fellowship and cooperation which soon spread throughout the earth. America resumed its position among nations as the birthplace of freedom, a land where there truly existed freedom from mental and spiritual enslavement, as well as the freedom from injustice and physical wants.

The curtain fell and the audience sat in reverent silence. It was not an occasion for clapping but I knew that everyone present would have the opportunity to show his appreciation in person to the playwright and cast members later.

The evening's experience at the theater with a beautiful companion, the sense of well being generated by my surroundings, my improved health and befitting apparel, all added to my self-confidence, so that I felt equal to meeting the cast and playwright. The theater was small but the large lobby below gave the audience, playwright, cast and all who participated in the presentation an opportunity to intermingle and share refreshments together. The play had stimulated a kaleidoscope of powerful emotions in me. The cast and playwright were entranced to have me recount from firsthand experiences my own recollection of some of the events of their play.

CHAPTER 19

A Modern Residence

"They shall beat their swords into plowshares and their spears into pruning hooks; nation shall not lift up a sword against nation, neither shall they learn war anymore. But they shall every man sit under his vine and under his fig tree; and none shall make them afraid."

—Micah
Old Testament

I t was Friday morning. The professors from Utah Isle were on a special visit and were planning to spend the entire day at Dr. Karoll's house. The four professors went into a conference with Dr. Karoll to decide how best to use the opportunities of the day. After ten or fifteen minutes they came to an agreement. They planned to spend several hours discussing their views and the data that each of them had gathered concerning me. The conversation would be recorded and transcribed later. They wanted to cooperatively assemble their information into a scientific paper. Dr. Karoll asked Alice to be responsible for me during this time. Assuming that, in addition to their work, the professors would perhaps spend some time on the tennis court, I suggested that the two of us have the time to visit some far off places in Dr. Karoll's air car.

"Where would you like to go today, David?" said Alice cheerfully.

"Well, Alice, you know how interested I am in the practical application of your science to concerns of every day living. I know that your father's house is an exception, having survived from my time and been updated. But tell me, do you have plants that prefabricate homes from different raw materials than we used?"

"Yes, we do," said Alice. "Would you like to visit such a plant?"

"I certainly would."

Alice conferred with her father a moment and came back smiling. She informed me that Dr. Karoll was glad to have us go. The air car was floated out and we had ascended into the clouds before another ten minutes had elapsed. As we headed for the home building plant, Alice explained that there was no longer a population explosion problem on earth. The entry of souls into the earth plane of consciousness

108

was strictly controlled. Regulation of the number of the souls to be born and supervision of which types, that is, which classes, whether souls in need of being guided in evolutionary growth, or to function in certain aspects of society, or to be master souls, was a normal activity of the many sided world government, she said.

I commented that such a "big brother" government was surely a far cry from Jefferson's ideal that the best government governed the least.

"We are now obliged to allow a great influx of souls from certain other systems whose planets are aging so they are no longer able to support all their inhabitants. There is one group which must return here because they owe a great debt. They had their beginnings on earth and developed far in advance of many civilizations which came after them. In their failure to learn to live in peace with another earth nation, they caused much havoc and made an exodus to another solar system. All of these souls who once lived on this earth must return and complete the development of perfect physical bodies on the planet where they first had their beginnings."

"You mean that our globe is involved in some kind of interplanetary housing project?" Such a broad conception of man's position in the universe took me aback.

"Why, yes, David, only it is inter-solar system rather than interplanetary. Neither our physical bodies nor theirs could live on any other planet in this, our own solar system, you see."

"They we are making place for these souls to enter earth and so now we have a population explosion by interspacial immigration?"

"Well, David, your term 'population explosion' suggests something out of control. This is not the case. We are creating living conditions that more than fulfill the noblest dreams of city planners of your times. Inter-solar system government will never allow more people to enter earth than can be welcomed joyously into our midst."

"Then the factory that we are visiting is making dwelling units to accommodate the space intruders."

"David, how can you possibly allow yourself to use such a term or even think in such terms?" Alice was not irritated yet her voice tone compelled me to recognize the ill will that I was expressing.

"Don't you realize that man on earth would not even have survived through the Twentieth Century had not millions of his elder brothers from outer space given assistance when it was needed? Why, more gratitude than we can express is due our space brothers. Unbeknown to us, for ages they have worked tirelessly to stimulate our evolutionary development. At any time they could have taken our planet from us easily as taking candy from a baby, had they chosen. In fact, a host of them have been guarding the earth for millenniums to protect us from aggressively evil races that would have conquered the planet long since and enslaved the adamic race. Truly, you have no idea of how wrong you are to think of such souls as intruders!"

It was humiliating to me to think that all through the ages we have been like helpless babes, needing protection from invasion. This idea stung my pride and I didn't like it.

"I must admit that it irritates me to think about it...this is a difficult idea to get used to. It's exasperating and frustrating to me to think about. Why, the people of earth won't even look the same before long. They'll all be getting longer heads. I don't like it a bit."

"David!" There was a new note in Alice's voice now. "Our family has learned to love you and we want to help you to become one of the members of our society who is qualified to vote and who is allowed the privilege of marriage."

"Well?" I said, not too politely because I was irritated.

"A person is examined in every facet of his nature before he is given such privileges. We are able to determine the emotional traits, such as honesty or dishonesty, courage or cowardice, gratitude or resentment and ingratitude, as easily today as one could test a person's skill in algebra or geometry in your times. We have many exacting methods to do this, for in addition to the analysis of astrological indications, the configurations of the hand, handwriting and voice analysis, the indications of body proportions and science of iridology, we even have a basis to evaluate personality by examining the blood microscopically. In addition to this, an instrument related to the lie detectors of your time is used during extensive written testing procedures to learn much of one's evolutionary position with regard to his life philosophy. We have also developed optical instruments which make the human aura visible to allow the further evaluation of one's level of development. A team of persons trained in these various phases of testing is able to make comprehensive analysis of data thus obtained and so determine the degree of maturity of any person. If you are not able to become manly in your thinking, David...if you don't overcome the immature feelings of pride and...well!"

Alice was very moved as she spoke these words to me and for a moment my mind was like a blank for I could not imagine why her emotions were so involved.

"Alice!" my heart was racing now.

Seeing her blush, was, I think, the sweetest and most humbling experience I had ever known.

We didn't speak again until the air car touched the ground forty-five minutes later at the assembly plant.

Tender thoughts toward Alice completely dominated my mind, until I was startled out of my reverie when she broke the silence.

"We're here! Won't you come along and let's go inside?" Alice opened the door and as she stepped out, I noticed how her lithe form moved with both the gracefulness of a princess and the deft coordination of a natural athlete. If she was preoccupied with any thoughts other than our visit to the dwelling unit plant, she gave no sign of it. As before when we left for the theater, I found myself wondering if I had not let my imagination play tricks on me.

The plant manager himself came out to greet us. Apparently Dr. Karoll had called ahead. The doctor's position as a widely recognized person and my own unique status in the society evidently called for the "red carpet." The manager introduced himself as John Faire and said that a luncheon was planned for us with the plant's key personnel. Mr. Faire chose to personally conduct us through the plant prior to the luncheon. I was not quite ready to come down to earth from my emotional pink cloud, but my engineer's nature forced me to respond to the opportunity being presented.

"I'm interested in seeing how you handle the utilities," I said in answer to John Faire's question as to what portion of the plant I should like to visit first.

"We'll begin our tour at the point along our assembly line where the utilities are being installed. Much of the preceding assembly work uses methods that are not new to you," said Mr. Faire, "and the technical knowledge is elementary. I'll be glad to answer questions you may have."

In a few moments, a small wingless vehicle with an operator approached us flying about ten feet above the ground. It dropped to earth next to us. Mr. Faire motioned us to step aboard. After we ascended about two hundred feet, we were carried to a large enclosure of an irregular shape located about three miles distant from the place where we had set the air car down. The perimeter of this building had a shape which might remind one of a natural lake as seen from the air. It must have been in the neighborhood of a mile long and up to half a mile wide in places. The roof was a series of irregularly spaced peaks and valleys like a vast tent enclosure. Its color blended in with the surrounding countryside. A remarkable job of camouflage from the air, if this were a defense measure, I thought. When I asked about it, I was told that this was part of an overall effort to blend and harmonize with the environment.

We dropped down and entered an opening in the roof which appeared as we approached. Once inside, I saw that this enclosure had a minimum ceiling height of about sixty feet. The interior was free of any columns but had taut vertical hold down cables at each low point. These single cables were spaced from one hundred up to two hundred feet apart. Radiating out from the high points and also in concentric circles around them were cables in the plane of the roof supporting it with a design borrowed from Nature's master engineer, the spider. A cylindrical unit about eight feet across and eight feet deep, like a liquid storage tank, hung by its top from the intersecting cables at the low points, and a hold down cable stretched vertically to the floor from its bottom. To me it was a new design concept and my first question was, "What holds it up?"

"It's like the roof was held up by sky hooks," I said in a puzzled wonder. "I've never seen anything like it."

John Faire and Alice both smiled at my consternation.

Alice pointed to eight foot diameter balls at the underside of each high peak and the taut cables that radiated to the low points where the vertical hold down cables attached to the bottom of the cylindrical units. "You might say that this roof is being held down rather than up," she said with a smile. "The balls are levitation units which can support the weight of the roof and twenty-five pounds of snow on every square foot of it."

"What a fine engineering tool! You really do have sky hooks." Then the thought occurred to me that the cone-like valleys would collect water during a heavy rain or melting snow. "Where are the roof drains?" I asked in astonishment.

Alice smiled again and pointed to the cylinder shaped units at each low point on the roof. "Those atomizers can handle the water at a rate of twice the heaviest rainfall ever recorded to fall in this area, and they eliminate the need for down spouts or provision for run off water."

"Atomizers!" I said. "You mean that you send the water back into the air as mist just as fast as it comes down? It seems impossible."

"We have an unlimited source of cosmic energy available, waiting to be tapped. We don't hesitate to use it in harmony with nature whenever it is convenient," said John Faire. "This volume of heated mist rising from these units soon creates an up-draft that even diverts much of the rain from falling on our roof."

The operator of our intra-plant air car guided it over to the area designated by Mr. Faire. In a moment we were standing in the midst of the workmen installing the plumbing, heating and lighting in the partially completed living enclosure units. It became apparent to me as I watched them that there were no exterior connections to furnish power or water to the units, nor any provision for waste water outlets from the plumbing units which were installed. This seemed puzzling to me and I began to make a careful inspection of the systems to see where the lines went which fed the water to the faucets and drained the water from the wash basins and other plumbing. Mr. Fair noticed my interest and said, "Well, I see that you've discovered that our living enclosures are completely independent units. They have no need to be hooked up to an outside water or power supply. One of these units can be lifted up and carried to a far away mountain top. After it is anchored down properly, it is ready for occupancy. The functioning of this unit is one hundred percent non-polluting. The power required is tuned in like radio waves so that, once settled, a family living in one of these units needs only to grow the food they require for their bodies in the ground surrounding their home. They then will have all they require to live independently. All the mechanisms of this unit are designed to function indefinitely."

"What about the plumbing?" I asked. "Why don't they need water and sewage connections, even if they can receive the power you broadcast for heating and cooling?"

"Why, you had the technology in your own times to handle the water and sewage the way we are doing," said Mr. Faire. "It's quite simple. As you have noticed already, we have separate plumbing systems.

The drinking water is condensed out of the air and there is a supplementary rain water storage tank. Water from these can be added into other systems as it is needed. The wash water system for bathing and household washing purposes is independent and has it own filtering and purifying unit. While it is always kept pure enough to be used for drinking, when the water is purified and reused it is undesirable for humans to take into their bodies. It lacks certain subtle vibrations which are gained from nature, from air and sunshine, and includes some undesirable ones. This detracts from its value for the body."

"What about the commode system? How is this handled?" I was interested in this because of the plaguing question of pollution in my times. Commode units were being installed as I watched. They were very compact, having neither inlet nor outlet for water supply. No tank like for a flush toilet appeared to be connected with its operation. Constructed as they were, the user would find the posture benefits of oriental commode installations. I remembered how these so surprised and inconvenienced westerners. The unit did have a small tube, perhaps one half inch in diameter, that went down through the floor, and ran to the edge of the enclosure. Being entirely independent of other systems, the commode needed only attachment to the floor and provision for the discharge tube.

"You could have built something like that commode unit in your time except for the kind of power supply it has," answered Mr. Faire to my questioning look. "It uses a non-volatile fluid and, with relatively simple mechanical action and heat, it removes the water and processes the solids into pellets. These are returned to the soil as fertilizer but not to grow food."

"What is wrong with using them to fertilize vegetable gardens?"

"Human waste is not used because it brings an emotional influence into the food itself when it is so used. Effects like this were not able to be measured in your time but are now easily detected. When used on food plants as fertilizer, the subtle vibrations still persisting in the human waste have adverse effects upon our astral body. The emotions of people affect the matter which has been taken into their own bodies and stimulates emotions in others if it has not been purified of them by a more extended contact with nature. It is man's duty to return all organic matter to the soil in a suitable form that Nature may re-absorb it into the cycle of life. The way wastes were handled in your time was unfortunate. The earth's capacity to support life was rapidly being destroyed."

"I think that we all intuitively knew that," I said, "but we seemed helpless to cope with the conditions. Wealth and power had accumulated into the hands of private interests. Enslavement of the people was far progressed. Those in authority pursued policies which were in ruthless disregard of posterity."

Alice touched my arm and said, "David, if you get into a philosophical discussion with Mr. Faire, you probably will not see much of this plant operation. Besides, why dwell on the past? All of these mistakes were part of the pattern of evolutionary growth for man. Those days are gone."

"They may be gone but they seem so close me that sometimes I awake in the night feeling that I am still in the midst of them. Then I imagine that the things I am now observing are only an unattainable dream," I said with feeling.

Mr. Faire suggested that we should move on if I was ready because there was not much time before the luncheon. We stepped into the intra-plant air car at his suggestion and moved a hundred fifty yards down the assembly line to where the lighting panels were being installed. Mr. Faire demonstrated to me how these panels could light up with any color of the rainbow and with an intensity varying from a barely perceptible glow to a brilliance that was almost painful. The light was without heat but into the lighting panels were also incorporated the heating and cooling surfaces. They functioned in these capacities either independently or simultaneously. Mr. Faire explained the panel construction. In between two layers of a glass-like material was sandwiched a layer of active light giving material with a fine metallic screen embedded in it. The active material, a mixture of various minerals, responded to a source of high frequency emanations, varying in wave length and intensity to produce the changing colors. The metallic screen responded to another source of emanations which caused it to produce either heat or cold. Each room had such a panel about six feet in diameter embedded in the ceiling. A separate humidity control unit insured that suitable moisture conditions were maintained.

"What is the need for the variations of colors and the brilliance that these lighting panels are able to produce?" I asked. "Why wouldn't a rheostat controlled white light have been sufficient?"

"Don't you recall how effective a means for healing the colored lights were for you, David?" said Alice. "These lighting panels are used to stimulate the mind forces and to bring a balance in the activity of ductless glands in the body. They are one of the tools to aid in preserving the youthful vigor of our people so that they may function to an advanced age. We also have a control unit to cause the lighting panels to go through a series of color changes. This symphony in color is similar to music in its soothing and healing effect. Color can be used to aid meditation and may have a balancing effect upon the emotions."

"It appears that you have simplified many things that we had begun to work with in the Twentieth Century. Your improvements are like the difference between our early radio tubes with a heated filament, control grid and plate, and the solid state transistor units we discovered years later," I said.

Our time was running out. John Faire suggested that we move down the line to where the completed living units were being tested. The in-plant air car was only a moment en route. At the far end of the plant the completed units were picked up through an opening in the roof to be transported by air to the homesite locations. They were several sizes, generally regular polygons of five to eight sides. Their bases allowed full rotation to follow the sun once they were put on a foundation. Their entire exterior, including a one piece roof, was of glass. Mr. Faire explained that glass had come into its own after the discovery that it could be made tough and flexible. Since the raw material for glass was unlimited in supply, this development made it the most suitable material known for building dwelling units. A family could move into one of these fully furnished units with no more than the clothing they required. The mechanisms, the exterior design and the construction materials used were such that they were hardly affected by time. This struck me somewhat negatively, despite the convenience of it all.

"It looks like you would deprive people of their individuality and the freedom to express themselves by furnishing families with complete homes. For many people I knew, building a home, decorating it and keeping it up was almost the chief occupation they had. Doesn't this inhibit an imaginative person?" I asked.

"Our values have changed, David," said Alice. "In your time, one's house had become too much a status symbol and a means to express individuality. A home should be as near to heaven as it can be made to be but in the darkness of your times, the appearance, the condition, the money value of a person's house was one of society's ways to measure individual worth. This especially created inequality in the circumstances for children. During the Twentieth Century, the degree to which one developed his physical coordination and strength and preserved the perfect functioning of his physical body or progress achieved in development of his character was hardly considered a measure of successful human experience. At the same time, obvious signs of an undisciplined nature, such as a distorted physical body from over indulgence and physical inactivity, a face lined from thoughts of avarice, or lust, or fear, were hardly imagined a disgrace if one had acquired wealth. Your way of life paralyzed much of the natural expression of individuality. People tried to express themselves through their homes because they had so little outlet for their creativity."

"What do you mean? I think it is important to keep a lovely home."

"It is, but personal achievements in science or in the arts or music or composition should be the means to express individuality and to distinguish oneself. To purchase artistic works rather than to produce them is self-deception if one thinks of this as self expression, and is a poor substitute to satisfy this basic human need. Self-conquest is the sine qua non for the expression of true individuality. A man has actually nothing to offer the world but his own truly unique individual character. To be a living example of creativity and individuality helps every other soul to enhance its belief in its own God-like nature. This is the sacred gift each one may present humanity, and each one of us does this by his own progress toward the creation of a Christ-like character, toward physical perfection, and the development of artistic talents."

As Alice made this statement, it reached right inside me and burst like a flash of light over my mind. Complicated philosophies and religious dogmas were summed up by her in just a sentence or two. It was so simple to understand her that I felt that if she could have just lived in my time, her words would have had a powerful effect on a nation. When I said this to her she sweetly smiled. Before she answered, John Faire explained that the point of view Alice had just given was as universally accepted by their society as the opinion that slavery was wrong had become in my time.

"We had such a high opinion of ourselves," I said, "that few would have believed the ideals of one hundred years later would make us appear to be barbarians."

Alice suggested again that I might lose some of the value of my visit in the plant by being so preoccupied with philosophy.

John Faire understood my feelings and said, "I think its appropriate for David to be more interested in philosophy than in our manufacturing plant. Our progress as a race hinges more upon creating personal goals which enable the solving of our social problems intelligently. Following this, provision for material aspects of life is easily accomplished."

We departed the plant for the gathering in the dining area. John Faire introduced Alice and myself to the group and, after an inspirational reading by one of them, we partook of simple fare similar to that I had learned to appreciate in Dr. Karoll's home. The same reverence for the act of eating that I saw in the doctor's home was prevalent. Meal times were used for meditation upon the Source of Life and were a time to be grateful to Mother Nature. Music that was piped in added to this atmosphere. The dining room was decorated in simple good taste. The walls were lined with portraits of great men and by some special quality of the paint or lighting these had the effect of three dimensional living persons present with us.

We thanked John Faire and his associates for their kindness and departed for the mountains of the Old North State.

CHAPTER 20

World Government

Alice and I arrived back from our visit to the government operated residential unit assembly plant in time for a leisurely swim before we had supper with the family and the professors. After the meal, we all settled ourselves before the open fire for an evening of discussion. While the others were still engaged in individual conversations, I sat before the fire and let my thoughts wander into the ancient past. The flickering blaze, with its enchanting power to stimulate the imagination, carried me into a fantasy of a lifetime in Egypt with lovely Alice as a companion. Mrs. Karoll had decorated her gracious family room for the evening with a large arrangement of wild flowers placed in an old Egyptian urn. This, I assumed, had sent my thoughts to the land of the Nile. The aroma of the burning wood added to the charm of the atmosphere and a spirit of fellowship, like sunshine, pervaded the room.

The familiar glow tube of the vision-phone interrupted before our conversation had taken a direction. As I compared their communications with those I had known, I thought to myself how every detail was improved. All was wireless and the entire system supervised and operated by the civil service. The glow tubes in each room silently indicated incoming calls and, in addition, a high pitched musical signal operated when it was switched into service. Dr. Karoll's position qualified him to have direct person to person service with any location on the globe. Depending upon individual responsibility, a family's service might be restricted to the local community except on occasions when specially authorized otherwise.

The call was for Dr. Karoll advising him of a meeting of the governing body for the community, the Centuria, of which he was a member.

After the call, Dr. Karoll took a few minutes to explain some of its details to me. The nation was divided into communities, each comprised of one thousand families, and their allotted proportion of single adults. Each family unit held one vote and the community elected one hundred of their members to form its Centuria. This highly sensitive group met weekly and the meetings were always fully televised to the local community. A new election could be called for by petition at any time if the people were dissatisfied with even one member of the Centuria.

This group in turn selected one of its members to represent it in a higher governing body. In elections of centuria members, everyone knew the candidates personally and no campaign expenses, sponsorship by private interests or the like were involved. As the matter of government was explained, private interests in the sense of financially powerful groups had been eliminated as an influence. Exploitation of natural resources or even ownership of land was a thing of the past, as far as private interests were concerned. Dr. Karoll had the honor and distinction of representing the local Centuria. An important congress of Centuria representative, the Decamillennia, a body of one hundred men in the same position as Dr. Karoll, was impending. The local meeting was to discuss the issues upon which Dr. Karoll, as spokesman, would represent the local Centuria before the Decamillennia. This higher governing body of one hundred men represented one hundred thousand families, or ten thousand Centuria members. One representative from each Decamillennia made up a still higher echelon called the Decamillennia Council, also composed of one hundred individuals.

The Decamillennia Council selected one of its members to be representative to the World Government Council, whose number was thereby related to the voting members of the world's population. It was presently made of up eighty-three members and total world population stood at around four billion souls.

The details of local government were organized and the means developed and carried out on the Centuria level but phases of human activity which required cooperation on a wide scale were planned at the Decamillennia level. The concerns which related to the overall welfare of the race and posterity, such as insuring an equal opportunity for self development for every soul, the preservation and enhancement of natural environs, and proper use of natural resources, were pondered and evaluated by the World Government Council and augmented by the Decamillennia Council.

Members of the Decamillennia were men of integrity and character. This was assured by scientific means to accurately analyze character. Even in the process of his selection to be a representative in the local Centuria, Dr. Karoll explained, each candidate's auric colors and other physically measurable evidences of his character were fully visible to the people. His auric colors, for example, revealing his emotions, are projected upon a screen while he addresses the people.

When the Centuria elected its representative, a more elaborate use of available practical means was employed to determine that the candidate was motivated by the highest of ideals and endowed with a high degree of capability to carry them out. All qualified voters were required to be learned in the sciences dealing with evaluation of human personality. But standing before the Centuria with his auric colors showing, no man could deceive this especially sensitive group. To aid the Centuria in making it selection, all needed services in connection with making an individual's character known were a routine provision of civil service agencies. The full print of the Decamillennia candidate's hand, voice prints, and similar evidences of his nature were available. His overall personality, the measure of his emotional control and discipline, his sincerity and his evolutionary development is thus openly set before the Centuria. The prospect of such a revealing exposure of a man's character, according to Dr. Karoll, causes one to search his own soul before offering himself as a candidate. An insincere person would be disqualified from the honor of public service as effectively and simply as a foot race excludes any but the fastest runner from the winner's circle. Science had made narrow self interest incompatible with political authority from the very lowest level on up to the World Government Council.

"Character development is the very purpose of life in the earth. Positions of responsibility and authority test and develop character and so they are considered a great honor. The world has focused its best scientific minds on the question of how a Christ-like nature may be individually developed. The competition among men now is to be the better servant of the race. The progress of each soul may be evaluated and individuals are grateful to learn about themselves and how they can make progress. In the truest sense of the word, we are seeking to create a society which encourages the most cooperative and self sacri-ficing expression of life of which man is capable of as an individual, to become a perfect expression of the Christ-Consciousness," said Dr. Karoll in closing his discourse on government.

"Surely you still have problems with human ego," I said. "What happens when the Centuria realizes that, in spite of everything, they have sent the wrong man to the congress of the Decamillennia?"

Dr. Karoll explained that when the Centuria did assign its voice to an elected representative, it was retained by him only as long as no one raised objection to his decisions. The call for a vote of confidence in their representative by the Centuria could be initiated by one mem-ber at any time, even when the Decamillennia was in session. This was accomplished by portable vision-phones kept always at hand by Centuria members when the congress was in session. These provid-ed intercommunication among the Centuria while they observe the televised activities of the Decamillennia. There were no secret meet-ings or agreements at any level among the governing bodies. Such a refined system of communication used in this manner, according to Dr. Karoll, made a practical reality of the American Dream: Government 'of the people, by the people, and for the people.' It functioned down to the individual level. No man, said he, could hold a representative's place, even in the Centuria, for twenty-four hours, if his actions did not express the will of the body that elected him. The support of private interests as a factor in attaining a political office had become completely irrelevant. Any qualified voter had a fully equal opportunity to be a candidate for the Centuria and thus, potentially, could rise to a position on the World Council.

After this short discourse about government, my thoughts could not be diverted to any other subject. I began with questions arising from my skepticism that Utopian dreams could ever become a work-ing reality. A representative government, I thought, would always be plagued by corruption.

"Why is your system not subject to the misuse of the channels of communication like ours was, and why can't politicians appeal to the childish and irresponsible nature of the masses to gain power to enslave them?" I asked.

"Well, David, in the first place, the masses of emotionally and morally immature people all have a fully equal opportunity to develop to whatever degree they wish. But they don't have the initiative to qualify themselves to have a voice in government," said Dr. Karoll.

"They don't!" I fairly shouted. "Who decides who qualified and who doesn't?"

Everyone in the room burst out in good humored laughter. For a moment, I must have glowed purple for I did not see how there could possibly be any humor in my question. The room fell silent as they quietly allowed me to fume. When Dr. Karoll thought I might be rational again he began, "David, did you have a license to fly a plane?"

I sat there glowering in silence, wondering if I was amidst a group of people representing the top rung of some kind of caste system enslaving thousands of voiceless peons farther down the line. The group could hardly contain its humor at the ridiculous figure that I made with my indignant self-righteous pose. Alice took the lead hoping, I think, to bring me down off my high horse without bruising me more than could be helped.

"David, do you imagine that your environment developed in you a sense of fairness and justice superior to that of my father and his associates?" she said, with a gentle, uncritical tone and some not altogether concealed humor.

To save me from the embarrassment that engulfed me, Mrs. Karoll stood up and suggested we all have some herb tea. She commented that the tea she had made for us had special properties to make one alert and to improve the operation of all the mental faculties. As I raised my eyebrows at that statement, some broad smiles went around the room. We all knew Mrs. Karoll so well that I couldn't help smiling myself because she had unintentionally made a joke at my expense.

In a short while we had again settled about the glowing fire with a fragrant steaming drink. I thought to myself that, according to the theories of reincarnation, we might all have gathered this way in the distant past. Perhaps we had enjoyed the same kind of fellowship as primitive tribal fathers imbibing in some fermented beverage as they talked of the lore of their people, sharing stories and songs about their beginnings.

The group sat in silence awaiting my response to the last question that had been directed toward me by Alice. Perhaps it was the property of the drink, or perhaps the opportunity for more thought on my part; at any rate, my mind seemed clearer and I answered Alice slowly and painfully. "As a matter fact, Alice, before you spoke, I was thinking that I was mistaken about the nation's advancements since my time. I figured all of you must be a part of a ruling class exploiting the lives of countless masses. When you thought my outburst was funny, it shocked me to think how cold blooded you must be. After you spoke, I realized my self-righteousness and pride had made a fool of me again. Still, I just don't see how you can deprive the common people of a voice in the government without having despotism. Besides, the question Dr. Karoll asked about a pilot's license seemed irrelevant, and it irritated me."

"David," said Dr. Karoll, "I didn't mean to insult your intelligence with my question. I hoped you would see the point I was making. We simply require people to prove their right to vote by demonstrating that they are responsible emotionally, mentally disciplined, knowledgeable, and have the ability to think rationally. All are allowed to vote who prove their qualifications by passing examinations. You didn't think it was unfair to require a man to actually prove his ability to fly a plane and demonstrate his knowledge of navigation and weather before allowing him to take responsibility for the safety of his own life and that of others?"

"Of course not," I said.

"This is just a parallel to the course of action which mankind decided it was imperative to pursue in order to successfully govern itself. It seemed evident that only those citizens who identify their own best interests with what is best for the race, who have this understanding and have exercised the self discipline to become informed, could be allowed to participate in governing a nation. Otherwise, we could not hope for an honest administration, one dedicated to and capable of solving man's dilemmas in trying to control greed and shortsighted self interest without restricting freedom," said Dr. Karoll.

"This seems utterly contrary to the ideal of democratic government," I objected.

"It is easy to have good hindsight, David," said Dr. Karoll. "When we look back at your times, the approach then being made to self government appears quite immature. The idea of equality had been planted well but was not growing in soil that was free of weeds. Your politicians made a great issue of free enterprise so that there would be incentive for the individual to excel in matters of business. However, where a voice in government was concerned, regardless of his efforts, every man was flattened to the same level. The poorly educated, the indolent, the irresponsible, the self-deluded masses who eagerly and naively believed when politicians promised to take from the rich to give to the poor; all were lumped together with your most responsible and learned men at voting time.

"Don't you remember how vigorously economic equality, as proposed by socialists, was opposed? Wasn't it considered democratic that people who worked harder than others should have the right to give their children advantages which other children's parents couldn't afford? Wasn't such thinking contrary to the basic concept of being 'born equal?' How obvious it is that any governing body will reflect the average quality of the individual voter's thinking."

"But allowing every one to vote, regardless of his education or economic status, was the very basis for democratic government, I thought," I said in surprise.

"Americans of your times were imbued from childhood with the fatal error that one vote for each person of a predetermined voting age means democracy. There is hardly a better way to insure failure of popular government than by subscribing to this faulty reasoning. The common people parroted phrases taught to them in grammar school about their freedom and right to vote. Their opinions upon politics were manipulated through the mass media. While they talked about being free, their minds were in chains, and so the masses were little more than well fed slaves.

"All channels of communication were owned by private interests. This alone would have predetermined that the nation's governing body should degenerate into an instrument to deliver the wealth of the land to private interests. Your newspapers had many fine champions of true democracy but the power of money was stronger. The so-called political parties became instruments of private interests, vying with each other for the political power to exploit the public. The winning team divided the spoils and set about their work of taking care of the vested interests which had installed them in office and to whom they had committed themselves to serve faithfully."

"But, Dr. Karoll," I interrupted, "we, also, had many great leaders elected as government officials down through the years."

"You surely did, David, and many of them are with us today in positions of governmental authority. Integrity was the first prerequisite for a candidate for office in the early days of America. At that time, only a very small percentage of the population could read or write. There was no radio or television and only the wealthy class was able to be informed or politically active. Those who founded the nation did not anticipate the effects of mass education. They would have made carefully worded provisions in the Constitution if they had foreseen what effect mass media communications could have upon the republic they hoped would someday unite the world in brotherhood. Perhaps Thomas Jefferson set the stage for the decay of democracy with his belief that America would do best to have as little government regulation over trade and commerce as possible. He felt that the government which should do the least to regulate the money system, transportation, food production or similar activities was the best for a nation. Keeping law and order and dealing with other nations, he felt, were the principal functions of government. In the early days of America, because of this thinking, there was no deterrent if the strong chose to exploit the weak in areas of trade and commerce. Evidently, many political leaders felt such affairs were a private matter. From the very founding of America, forces were aligned to enable the wealthy to accumulate more political power and, by inheritance, to preserve and enlarge the monumental inequities in the land."

"Tell me," I demanded, "how could America have become the great nation in the earth that she was, if we had all those weaknesses in our government right from the start? How could such unquestionably humanitarian leaders like Abraham Lincoln and Woodrow Wilson or Herbert Hoover ever have been elected as Presidents?"

"You needn't be on the defensive, David," said Dr. Karoll. "There have been many great humanitarians on America's political scene. The nation was founded upon beautiful ideals, the same ideals we are simply trying to realize in a very practical and real way in government today. We are Americans like yourself. America's failure in your time was our failing, too. Many who lived with you in the Twentieth Century are again living in America and they realize how they erred. Pride was the chief failing of America. Had the common people not elevated themselves in pride over the people of other lands, America would not have lost her way. Corrections in the laws would have been made to uphold the ideals set in the Declaration of Independence and make them a reality in the land. Then, America would have led mankind into an era of peaceful co-existence and human progress. She would have wrought a transformation in government of the entire earth. Even the shifting of the poles could have been avoided had America not departed from her ideals of trust in God, of the brotherhood of men, of purity and equality."

CHAPTER 21

The Virgin Birth

"If there comes a time when the power of the vicious so preponderates as to make any recovery hopeless, then an Intelligence lets a fire god or a water god give to the race what its thoughts have called for. Then follows the destruction of the race by water or volcanic action: the crust of the earth shakes and opens, flames pour forth, and the earth crust sinks while the waters sweep over the land and submerge it. New land rises out of the ocean and awaits the coming of a new race."
—Thinking and Destiny
H.W. Percival

"**D**r. Karoll, just when you have me listening carefully to your reasoning, you make a statement that sounds irrational and my confidence in you is shaken." I felt frustrated at hearing Dr. Karoll speak in riddles. "What possible connection could there be between the morals of America and a way to avoid a cataclysm of nature like the shift of the poles? Aren't you falling back upon an ancient superstition to imagine Divine retribution for immorality by catastrophe of geological origin?"

"As far fetched as it may sound, David," said Dr. Karoll, "it is now a scientifically established fact. Misuse of sexual energies by the people on earth does unleash destructive forces causing volcanic eruptions, earthquakes and the breaking up and submerging of land masses. Mythology suggests how this occurs. The story of Sodom and Gomorrah is just one account on record. The Guardians in the celestial ships burned these cities and made the sites uninhabitable because these cities hindered the progress of the souls born in them. At other times, the Guardian Intelligences allow the release of those natural forces which cause earth quakes or volcanic action. This was the case when Pompeii was destroyed. The similarity in the stories of Pompeii and Sodom and Gomorrah is not just a matter of coincidence. Sexual forces should be used in harmony with man's purposes for being in a physical body. Use of contraceptives by the general public had encouraged a great increase in sexual activity for self indulgence."

"Far fetched is putting it mildly, Dr. Karoll," I said. "You would have been called just plain crazy by the most astute jury of religious leaders, psychologists, anthropologists, geologists or any other group of educated men of my time. I'm afraid that I would have agreed with them, too," I said a little apologetically.

"Perhaps we're off the subject in a way which isn't helpful right now," said Dr. Karoll. "Suppose we ask our professor of political science to bring us back to the discussion of how our government operates." With that Dr. Karoll nodded toward Arthur Hilliard that he might take the initiative.

Here is a man who is three-quarters space intruder and one-quarter Hindu, I thought to myself; apparently, we had to get outside help to get over our impasse with corrupt government. I turned to Dr. Hilliard without waiting for him to speak. I was feeling a little cynical on the sex question and did not want him to start a philosophical discourse that would draw us away from what Dr. Karoll had just been saying. "Dr. Hilliard, I assume from what Dr. Karoll has just said, no birth control is allowed because it is not in the best interest of the people! Surely you have a problem with over-population. Alice has told me that this is not so, but how is it that the children of the irresponsible and politically voiceless masses do not overrun the earth?"

"If there were such a problem, it would indeed be an irresponsible government that was at fault, David," said Dr. Hilliard.

"Oh, no! This is too much," I said. "You mean that the common people are not allowed to cohabit or have man-woman associations except as the government allows?"

"We talked about this before, David," said Alice. "Didn't you understand what this actually meant to human society?"

"Well, who decides which person can marry and which cannot? Does this mean that some...well...a good percentage of the masses have no sexual expression...that it is not allowed?" This whole area of thought was puzzling and antagonized me.

"You've asked several good questions," said Dr. Hilliard. "First of all, David, you must understand that each individual decides for himself whether or not he wishes to marry. The opportunity is offered equally to all. All who exert the self discipline required to qualify for marriage are extended this privilege."

"But even so," I said, "isn't there a great deal of resentment?"

"There is no basis for resentment. Because of their understanding of reincarnation, many do not wish to marry for spiritual reasons. In the early days of the Christian church there was a profound understanding of this subject. The creative spiritual force which results

129

when sexual energy is sublimated through continence and prayer has always been the great cohesive force behind Catholicism. The monks and nuns of not only Christianity but of all the great religions understood that miracle working power was based upon the sublimation of sexual energy and its transmutation into a higher form of creativity."

"Well," I said, "that's a pretty extreme point of view. That couldn't be a basis for very many people to give up such a normal expression of their nature. How is it managed that so much control is able to be accomplished?"

"You are quite correct in your assumption that the masses have very little of the bodily sexual expression. This is because correct attitudes toward sex are learned from infancy. Even those who do marry hold the ideal that such is a sacred experience and only for procreation. You see, a true marriage is based upon relating the procreative act to spiritual laws. The purpose of marriage is very sacred. It allows two people to express sacrificial love in cooperation with Divine Love so as to be channels for the entry of souls into the earth."

"I'm not ready for ideas like this," I said. "Is there any history to back up what you are saying?"

"Pythagoras outlined the conditions to be fulfilled by those who would prepare themselves to have superior children. The most superior man in history was born into a community of Essenes who followed the instructions of Pythagoras. They studied how to prepare the mother, taking her into training at the age of three. They understood the astrological signs and other conditions governing the return of earth's spiritual leaders through reincarnation."

"I never thought of Pythagoras as anything but a mathematician. And I certainly never heard his name mentioned in connection with experiments in genetics," I said.

"The virgin birth is an advanced concept in the practical application of the teachings of Pythagoras. Conception was by materialization of the seed from another level of matter or consciousness by a soul who had attained mastery of natural laws governing such. The virgin birth itself is not so exceptional in religious lore but the double virgin birth of Jesus Christ is unique in the records. The records read by psychics say Mary was also immaculately conceived and born to the Essene maiden Anna."

"Why this term—immaculate?"

"It refers to freedom of the conception from any taint of desire for a sensual experience through their flesh bodies on the part of the mother or father. Conception may be achieved through aportation of the sperm of a man living in a physical body by spiritual forces. In the case of the Master of Masters, the first to achieve this mastery, Jesus, the projection of the seed was by Him from another level of consciousness. Through the virgin Essene Anna, He projected the female aspect of Himself as Mary and then His male aspect through Mary as Jesus. This was unique in the history of the human race. It has great significance for mankind."

"Then the father, Joseph, must have been prepared by training to accept both the idea that Mary was not illegitimate and that her impregnation was of the same order," I said.

"He was."

"Then Jesus was truly the son of Virgin Mary by immaculate conception, you say?"

"Yes, David, this is true. And the first Christians, the founders of the Catholic church, the gnostic Christians, understood these concepts well. They have actually been common knowledge among the scholars of the ancient Mystery Schools from their beginnings."

"You have gone too far for me," I said. "These ideas are beyond my comprehension. I never would have believed that you could make a Virgin Birth sound like a scientific fact." I paused thoughtfully before speaking again to ask, "Suppose a couple should disobey your laws and have a child, then what?"

"They forfeit their lives, but the child is allowed to live."

"That sounds harsh," I choked. "No! It sounds inhuman!"

"It sounds so to you because you have a different understanding of death," said Dr. Hilliard. "Our science has transformed the old concept of death. In fact, death, as you thought of it, has been abolished from the earth."

"Forfeiting one's life and being put to death sound like the same thing to me," I said, with a note of sarcasm.

"Departing a flesh body is making transition to another state of consciousness. Death does indeed occur to the physical body and the false I, the personality. The unconscious mind of the entity has continuity but the personality is a temporary vehicle like the body. The physical body is only a gathering of dust around a form generated by the unconscious mind. And the personality is only a reflection of the set of influences one is working with in a particular life span on earth."

"Dr. Hilliard, you say things with a definiteness that stuns my power to think. I'm not able to absorb them. My powers of reasoning are short circuited. You speak as if it were rather inconsequential for a person to lose his body, or voluntarily give it up to experience being parent to a child. I never visualized a government with such all pervading powers. Your thinking is so foreign to my times I haven't the capacity to understand it. Government by the people in combination with the idea of rebirth, Divine Justice, no sexual privileges for the masses, chaste marriage, select group of voters...all this is too much for me!"

"David," it was Alice speaking now, "if the greatness of ancient Greece resulted from application of teachings introduced by Pythagoras with regard to eugenics, wouldn't it be a crime against our race to ignore them? If the birth of Christ resulted from this knowledge, is it any wonder that dedicated men and women are applying it in order that souls may enter into the earth under circumstances more in harmony with their spiritual nature? We believe that a civilization equal to the most spiritual times of Lemuria and Atlantis will again rise in the earth because of the re-discovery of this knowledge. The promised Millennium hinges upon its applications."

"Please bring me back down to earth and relate these things you are telling me to government of the people, by the people, and for the people," I said, feeling stubborn and intellectually lost.

"We are trying to do that," said Dr. Hilliard, "but must work with the mental handicaps you have acquired from your times."

"When you talk like that I have no way to answer you," I said.

"Well," answered Dr. Hilliard, "ignorance of the purpose for earth life was the reason for the Twentieth Century preoccupation with material goals and your frantic activity to acquire them. Manufacturing skills brought into being by efforts of inventors were intended to serve the ideal of freeing man of material want, so that he could develop higher aspects of his nature. Mankind failed to grasp this opportunity. To the contrary, indulgence of the sensual side of human nature on a gigantic scale followed the industrial revolution. Advertizing techniques capable of rendering the mind helpless to resist had enslaved the masses to pursue material goals and sensual satisfactions. The marvelously elevating potential of radio and television was used instead to cloud the minds of the people, dulling their intuitive sense of right and wrong."

"That's a pretty sharp criticism of advertising," I said. "How would people know what to buy without advertisements? Don't you have any kind of advertising?"

"Advertising as a commercial activity has no function in connection with distribution of the nation's produce. We guard our people from all that would program their minds to express selfish desire or that would destroy their moral fiber. Surely you understood that the techniques of advertising of your time hypnotized your youth to make mindless responses to inane slogans and enslaved them mentally by the time they were adults. We do use some of the techniques your advertising industry discovered but only to ennoble the thinking of our race."

"It sure sounds like a 'Big Brother' government to me. Even a man's soul isn't his own," I said. I could not help being shocked at the idea of the non-existence of a free press or of complete control of all channels of communications by the government.

"David, you'd do well to stop and think a bit before answering. Possibly you're allowing prejudice to interfere," warned Alice. "Shouldn't you let your powers of reasoning have a chance to operate? You might be able to see that our government has truly become government of the people, by the people and for the people. It gives more genuine freedom to the individual than was ever dreamed of in your time. No group or class infringes upon the rights of others, nor upon the rights of posterity."

"Well, I certainly must say that with all our freedom to exploit natural resources, we were stealing the rights of posterity. 'Let posterity solve their own problems,' was the common point of view," I commented.

"Yes, David," said Dr. Karoll. "But promoting an understanding of reincarnation can provide incentive for men to give their very lives to improve the lot of posterity. The freedom of a citizen should be unlimited, as long as he is not destructive and contributes his share of time to serve the common good. In the interest of the general welfare, a government can allow unlimited freedom to express individuality in service to others but selfishness must be sharply limited."

"Who votes," I said. Too many new ideas were confusing me and

I was trying to get the conversation into an area that I would feel more able to talk about.

"Anyone who is currently eligible," said Dr. Hilliard, "just as Alex outlined earlier. Anyone who can prove his capacity for self-government has a voice in the world government through its elected representatives."

"Isn't there private enterprise anymore?" I asked.

"Not of the kind that allowed private ownership of a nation's vital industries like communications, food production, clothing, building construction, banking, and transportation, to fall under control of small groups of people," said Dr. Hilliard.

"As a matter of fact, David," said Dr. Karoll, "the feverish activity to produce consumer items has discontinued. The activity today centers upon acquiring self knowledge and developing the soul faculties. Furnishing material needs does not require the priority it once did."

"But what about all of the people's needs for clothes and shelter and food and entertainment?" I asked.

"And transportation, you might add," said Dr. Daren, who had been quietly listening to the discussion.

"Yes, that's right; the automobile and truck building industry was one of the country's chief manufacturing activities," I said, "and the gasoline and oil to keep them running required another giant industry."

"You had quite an industry built upon the ill health of the people, which included great hospitals, insane asylums, drug producing organizations and an army of doctors and nurses," spoke Dr. Daren, the medical scientist.

"None of these are under control of private interests?" I asked.

"No, they aren't David." It was Riley Knudsen, the powerfully built professor of anthropology speaking. "Mankind has gone through a transition. The industrial age changed the struggle for barest necessities to keep body and soul together into capacity to over produce everything needed. Industrialists of the late Nineteenth Century and the Twentieth Century fought with each other to gain strangle holds upon vital industries. Like Robber Barons of old, they amassed fortunes through their control of transportation facilities, manufacturing the key products, utilities and natural resources. The strong willed and brilliant men devoted themselves to the struggle for wealth and power. To perpetuate the conditions created, they maintained an economy of scarcity and high rate of goods consumption. Wars were their most effective means. As if hypnotized, people spent their lives frantically serving the false values of the times. Instead of building fine communities, recreation parks, and homes that would endure down through time, your new productive capability was diverted to very perishable consumer goods, war material, and housing projects that became slum areas almost before the last pour of concrete hardened."

"Many people knew all this," I interjected. "We just didn't know how to combat it. We knew things were wrong but hoped that they would change for the better as education improved. The tragic conditions in the world sometimes seemed hopeless and purposeless to many of us, I suppose."

"All this was not purposeless as it may have appeared, David," Professor Knudsen responded. "There is a parallel between the evolution of man as an individual and as a race. The race is progressing through the creation, growth, disintegration, and regeneration of nations, just as individual man is making progress through experiences of birth, life, death, and rebirth. The law and order in the universe, the intricacy of his own physical vehicle, and the wonders of the visible world of nature are ever before man to lead him to seek his Maker in humbleness. Our God is Time, Space, Patience, Love and Immutable Law."

When Riley Knudsen stopped speaking the room was quiet. An atmosphere of awe and reverence settled upon us. We could not remain unaffected, for it seemed that he had spoken a prayer from the heart, baring his deepest religious convictions. Several minutes went by while we sat before the fire watching the red-orange glow of the dying embers. Finally, Dr. Karoll spoke to thank Riley Knudsen for providing such fine thoughts to sum up the evening's discussion. Since the professors planned to leave for Utah Isle before breakfast in the morning, we all exchanged a word or two before saying goodnight to each other.

CHAPTER 22

Adolf Hitler

"Therefore judge nothing before the time, until the Lord come, who both will bring to light the hidden things of darkness, and will make manifest the counsels of the hearts; and then shall every man have praise of God."
—First Epistle to the Corinthians New Testament

"Good morning, David." Dr. Karoll's greeting had a special note. "Good morning, sir," I said. "You seem especially cheerful this morning."

"We learned some thrilling news yesterday, David. One of the earth's great leaders was born a few weeks ago. The configuration of his hand print at birth indicated a highly evolved and gifted soul had entered into the earth. Through research into our records, a study of the astrological indications and with the confirmation of our psychics, we have established his identity. His life in the earth should bring blessings to mankind."

"Who might this be?" I said with keen interest.

"In ancient times, he was the great spiritual leader and king, Nebuchadnezzar of Babylon. He has often earned honor and risen to authority in historical times but he became a pariah in your time," Dr. Karoll paused, "for he was Adolf Hitler."

"Adolf Hitler!" I fairly shouted in astonishment.

"Yes, David," said Dr. Karoll. "Does it surprise you that we feel he will bless earth during this life before him?"

"Surely, you are not serious with me, sir?" I said unbelievingly.

"Very."

"But I don't understand at all how this can be," I said. "Wasn't he one of the arch-criminals of all time...the very symbol of man's inhumanity to man?"

"Many people thought of him thus, David, but no one is able to judge another without having access to the full details," sad Dr. Karoll.

"You can hardly hope to convince me that there was any good in Adolf Hitler," I said. "Perhaps I don't have the facts about him, but

136

please remember that he was in power while I was growing up. People thought he started the Second World War."

"Well," said Dr. Karoll, "what did you think of Voltaire? Was he a great and good man, would you say?"

"Why...why, yes," I said. "He was one of the most brilliant minds in history, deeply religious and humanitarian in the truest sense. He envisioned and longed for the time when man would treat his fellow-man as brother throughout the entire earth. He opposed the church of his day only because he believed it perpetrated injustice, and for this he was maligned as an atheist."

"Yes, David," said Dr. Karoll, "but there were times when Voltaire, like Hitler, thought about some not so humanitarian short-cuts to realize his dream of a well ordered society. Impatient with their short-sightedness, he questioned the worth of the common man. Also, he set aside his better judgement and did his health serious harm by the use of drugs."

"Well, this may be," I said, "but his dedication to the ideal of establishing a peaceful, just, well ordered world government marks him as a great humanitarian."

"You need not defend Voltaire to me, David," said Dr. Karoll with a slight smile. "You see, he has been reborn later in the person of another fine leader who is in a position of responsibility today."

"This kind of statement is not acceptable to me, Dr. Karoll," I said after a long pause. "You must introduce me to this idea in a way that draws cooperation from my reasoning powers. I don't see how Voltaire, whom I greatly admire and respect, and the brutally aggressive Adolf Hitler could possibly have anything in common." I could hardly restrain myself from speaking out much more critically of Dr. Karoll's statement.

"Please, don't spoil David's breakfast, Alex. This is too lovely a morning and too early to discuss a subject so touchy with him." Mrs. Karoll interrupted us with a smile.

I started to defend myself for I didn't like being referred to as touchy, but just at that moment Alice came in. "Well!" she exclaimed with a twinkle in her eyes, "am I just in time to observe the reaction of a twentieth century mind to a twenty-second century news item? Have you just told David about the rebirth of Adolf Hitler?"

For a moment I felt like I was being made the brunt of a joke. I could feel the color rising along my neck. I caught myself and tried to manage a smile. I must have revealed all my emotions in my face. The humor of the situation struck all three of them at once and they could not refrain themselves from laughing aloud. In an instant the humor of it struck me as well and I found myself sincerely laughing with them. After this, we spoke no more of Adolf Hitler during our breakfast, but enjoyed it quietly. When it was over, I asked Dr. Karoll if he and his family could take time to clear up some questions that they had started spinning through my mind.

"Surely, David," answered Dr. Karoll. "You know that your presence with us is the reason that my regularly assigned duties to our community and government have been partially suspended."

"This still seems a dream to me, sir," I said. "I'm still inclined to wonder when I'm going to be awakened."

"As a matter of fact, David," said Dr. Karoll, taking my thoughts for a cue, "life in the earth is a kind of dream. Much that we think is real has no permanence. Life in physical bodies may best be thought of as the means created by Superconscious Mind to enable us to become aware of, and eventually to overcome, our separateness from the Maker. We are allowed, in this very real seeming dream, to exercise our free will destructively, if we choose, without actually harming anyone but ourselves. And even this is not as harmful as it appears, for we are learning better by experiencing the problems we have created for ourselves."

"Yes, David," said Alice, seeing that I was about to express my objections, "Adolf Hitler did not and could not harm anyone but himself. He never overcame Divine Justice for an instant. The individual God-Self of each person has all the power of God-Almighty to protect and preserve perfect justice for that individual. The God-Self allows the flesh body or mind of its human expression to be injured only when it needs such treatment in order to meet and learn of the error of its own thinking. It is to the soul's benefit, not harm, to painfully lose a physical body in order to gain a needed lesson. As one of your mystical poets said, 'Through pain comes the breaking of the shell that encloses the understanding.'"

"Now I suppose that you are going to tell me that the untold numbers of people who suffered and died in prison camps and concentration camps in Germany deserved to go that way," I said, in disbelief, "and

Adolf Hitler did their souls, if not their bodies a spiritual favor?"

"Exactly," said Dr. Karoll matter of factly. "Of course, as you use the word 'deserve,' it would not express the true picture. The right way to say it would be, 'their souls made the choice to go that way.'"

"What is the basis for such a pat answer as that?" I demanded. "How can you know this?" I thought about it a moment and then commented. "Say now, it would have been wonderful if the Jewish people could have believed that! Why, the bitterness they nurtured towards Germans, toward all non-Jewish people for that matter, was based on their belief that they were a virtuous people who, through no fault of their own, were blamed for all the world's troubles. They claimed the Christians were still persecuting them for the crucifixion of a false Messiah."

"I think I hear some twentieth century anti-Jewish sentiment in your voice, David," said Dr. Karoll with a note of surprise.

"I imagine that you do, Dr. Karoll," I said. "It would be difficult not to react to the ill feelings that Jewish people expressed toward the non-Jewish portion of the human race. Having no stake in the welfare of any nation, they readily preyed upon their less clever non-Jewish brother to create hardship and poverty. The clever, non-productive ways they obtained their wealth generated the hatred, which they called 'prejudice,' and the vicious cycle continued through centuries. Living dispersed throughout many countries gave them insidious financial advantages in international commerce. The predisposition to take advantage of all non-Jewish people was bred into them in early childhood. Thus, they preserved their status as a despised minority. As a new nation without old prejudices, America was an easy mark for them to gain a foothold. With their naturally superior abilities they were soon in a position to dominate the businesses they selected. The broad fields of entertainment, retail clothing, jewelry, and advertising were their natural choices, for they were highly lucrative and pandered to the weaknesses of the public. They had no scruples about undermining the nation's moral values and so the promotion of the incredibly profitable field of pornography was their special territory."

"David, let me explain why you shouldn't go on with this train of thought," said Alice.

"You'll be giving me the answer to a puzzle that is as old as recorded history if you can provide intelligent reasons for the blessedness and cursedness of the Jewish race," I said skeptically.

"Did you notice that you mentioned only the failings of the Jews?" asked Alice quietly.

"Well, David," said Dr. Karoll, "as strange as it may sound to you, our examination of the akashic records revealed that you had even made a name for yourself as a Hebrew in several different lives during Old Testament times and as a Jewish Christian in the New Testament period. You would have been lionized if the Jewish people could have believed that you actually were the reincarnation of some of your identities as an Old Testament figure."

"I know that you're sincere in telling me such things," I said, "but I have absolutely no recall of them as you may know, and can hardly make myself believe that what you are saying is true."

"All right, David," said Dr. Karoll. "There are better reasons why you should not have felt as you did toward Jews. First, recognize that, had you been nurtured up in their way of life from birth, your own thinking would have been conditioned to accept their way of life and religious philosophy. Next, take into account the working of the law of thought, for it brings to each person what he has created. Whatever a man thinks and speaks critically about in others indicates rather those very tendencies in his own make-up which he has not overcome, and unconsciously despises in himself. Now, consider what your criticism of Jewish people actually means. If an individual has pursued a train of thought which generated prejudice and mistreatment of a minority, then his own thinking may best be brought into balance through a life experience as a member of an ill-treated minority. Each one of us must be given an opportunity to meet the creation of his own thinking. This is the real meaning of the Grace of God: The provision of unlimited opportunities for each soul to meet that which it has created for itself by thinking, until it chooses to generate harmony and perfect love only. The perfection of our character will result as we apply the teachings of Christ, returning good for evil, seeking to serve rather than to be served. This is exercising the Law of Grace and this process will eventually make incarnation in a physical body unnecessary."

"Then all of us who greatly admire their virtues or despise their faults may be born Jewish from time to time?" I said.

"The Jewish race occupies a unique place in serving the needs of mankind. Don't their contributions to progress stand like beacon lights down through the ages? Haven't they produced great musicians and philosophers? Doesn't the Jewish Heretic, the Essene called Jesus of Nazareth, illustrate the place of the Jewish race on earth in the most constructive sense. You see, the extremes of good and evil are brought into sharper focus and the inner struggle is intense for souls incarnating as Jews. Some souls are inclined to spend a number of consecutive lives in a particular race. Because each nationality has certain prevalent thought patterns, these persons may gradually reflect some of these in their faces and bodies. Some may dwell in their thoughts upon the lovely and self-sacrificing aspects of their culture and become especially beautiful. This is all simply the action of impartial natural law, the law of thought. Mind is the builder of our physical bodies, as well as the creator of the mental and psychic destiny that each soul must meet. The noblest leaders in all the earth have always been true Israelites. These souls migrate to whatever nationality is closest to expressing mankind's highest ideals. You will see this in their faces, no matter what their blood lineage."

Dr. Karoll paused to give me a chance to absorb what he had just said and comment. All four of us sat in silence perhaps three or four minutes. Finally, I said, thoughtfully, "Shall I assume that several million souls chose to be born into the Jewish race in Germany just so that they could be put to death in concentration camps? Shall I try to believe that all the intricate details of coordinating the lives of millions of people and, also, a myriad of events too complex to imagine, were all worked out to give Adolf Hitler a needed experience at being dictator? This seems impossible."

"It is impossible for man with his finite mind to conceive of Infinite Love and Mercy and Power and Intelligence," said Dr. Karoll slowly. "Religions, generally, teach that God is able to mete out perfect justice to every individual, while, simultaneously, giving him freedom of choice within a given set of circumstances. Those who reject this great teaching of Judaism can hardly identify themselves as Israelites. An individual's actions and words, not his nationality, identify him."

"Please tell me how that could possibly be?" I asked, with a new appreciation of how involved a proposition people were admonished to accept by faith in one religion or another.

"Through deep meditation one can see how it is possible," Alice answered softly.

"Can anyone really achieve that?" I asked.

"Not every one has the inclination. Only a small percentage of people in your times had the desire to exercise such self discipline in combination with the intense desire that is required to see truly the God of Abraham and Isaac and Jacob," said Dr. Karoll. "A great leader in thought who was your contemporary, Erich Fromm, saw clearly the universal character of the God of Abraham and the Brotherhood of man."

"You have given me an outline of the development of the race of man as a long process of sowing and reaping in order to learn right from wrong the hard way," I said, avoiding an impasse with meditation again. "You make it sound as though the understanding of every aspect of society revolves around knowledge of reincarnation. You have repeated again that each person is reborn in order to meet and balance his own creations. How can you speak of someone who must owe a tremendous score, a man like Adolf Hitler, call him a great hero, and tell me that he is being welcomed back among us? An inconsistency appears to be present here. There must be a serious gap in my understanding of your point of view."

"We are inclined to expect too much of you, David," said Mrs. Karoll gently. "It is partly because we learned of your exceptional powers of reasoning from the psychic examination of your past, as well as from your hand prints and other means."

"Well," I said, feeling good natured at this answer, "whenever I am not able to follow your reasoning, I shall have to assume that you are paying me a kind of compliment."

They all smiled with me at this, and Mrs. Karoll suggested that we pause from our discussion for some of her herb tea. Dr. Karoll assured me they were glad for me to continue with questions concerning Adolf Hitler. They wanted me to be satisfied intellectually with their attitude toward his return and to understand why his part in the great world war did not trouble them.

"Be patient, David, please," said Alice in answer to my thoughts. "To be able to feel no condemnation in your heart toward anyone, you must have acquired either much scientific knowledge, or have an uncommon degree of religious faith, or else have a spiritual illumination in deep meditation. To achieve any of these is difficult for one who lived in a time of widespread skepticism and vicious criticism."

We drank our herb tea, savoring it, in silence. Telepathic communications in Dr. Karoll's family rendered conversation at times superfluous to their enjoyment of each other's company. It must have been a full fifteen minutes during which no audible exchange took place before I hesitatingly asked them to please go on with the discussion of Adolf Hitler. Dr. Karoll, I felt, knew what troubled me without my asking.

"How can a man responsible for stupendous crimes against mankind be welcomed back to society?" I asked. "And besides this, how can such a person ever balance the score he owes the rest of mankind...or live with himself, for that matter, if he learns of his past?"

"Oh, he will learn of his identity, but not unless we know he is able to confront this knowledge with equanimity," said Dr. Karoll.

"Is that possible?" I asked, with surprise.

"Well, yes it is," said Dr. Karoll. "It's a basic tenet of New Testament teaching that anyone who chooses to accept Christ into his heart is freed from the burden of his past mistakes, isn't it? A person who has truly had the inner experience of inviting Christ into his heart knows that such a release from the past would be possible and equally available to the soul that manifested itself as Adolf Hitler as to anyone else."

"Are we going to let him take advantage of the Blood of Christ washing away all sin?" I asked, trying not to sound facetious. I was unable to restrain smiling at the idea of Adolf Hitler being vindicated of his crimes by the blood of a crucified Jew. "Surely we couldn't let him off that easily?"

"You have got only half of the message there," smiled Dr. Karoll. "Jesus said that each one must take up his own cross. The advanced soul-entity identified with Adolf Hitler will already have done much work upon himself. In fact, he had an exceedingly painful and difficult life experience in America, beginning some time in the 1950's, in which he was introduced to some of his problems from the past, including the use of drugs."

"I get lost in the allegory of these mystical passages from the Bible, Dr. Karoll," I said, chuckling inwardly, "but I can see that the idea of reincarnation opens up a new field for humor. What a beautiful joke it is on those people who in their minds were administering justice to Hitler. I think they would object to Adolf Hitler being literally reborn and 'getting away with murder' by becoming a 'born again' Christian. This could be terribly frustrating to the Christians who think he should suffer throughout all eternity in the Lake of Fire. It might be a joke on some Jews, too, if they relished the possibility that he was getting the good old Christian treatment."

They all smiled at this and Dr. Karoll added, "Voltaire, whom the Christian world anathemized as atheist, would have the last laugh. He believed in an all-merciful God and rejected the vindictive figure created by the Church."

"Seriously, Dr. Karoll," I said, "do explain to me why Adolf Hitler is to be welcomed and even given preferential treatment."

"Men like Adolf Hitler are mankind's greatest heritage, David. Once towering genius was thought to be a product of chance combinations of genes. Now we recognize a genius as one who has achieved development surpassing his fellows through persevering effort, dedication and self discipline over a period of many lives. While the greatest of minds can become terribly distorted during infancy, yet ordinary minds, no matter how marvelously improved by good treatment, cannot be rendered genius. As a towering humanitarian genius, Adolf Hitler set out to serve not just Germany but the entire world. His goal was to develop a super race in Germany. It was to be superior in the way that Jesus taught: 'He that would be greatest among you, let him be the servant of all.' Hitler recognized the energetic German people, with their capacity for hard work and their productive genius, as capable of alleviating poverty and injustice in the earth. He was unaware that he and many of his compatriots had been Hebrews in the past but remember that actions are the only indication of true Israelites. He saw how the productive classes within German society were being preyed upon and the nation's morals undermined by a closely knit minority of highly capable people. Adolf Hitler intended to change such conditions, first in Germany, and then throughout the world, conditions which allowed a few to enslave many. The prejudice and misinformation spread about him gave a confused picture of this soul. The reality is rather that, as an instrument dedicated to serve the German people, he expressed the composite mind of the nation, both its good and its evil. It is no wonder that he was despised by the world, for he became a scape goat blamed as an individual for the error of the whole nation of German people. His great gift as a human being was to be the highly receptive individual who would truly express the mind of the people, thus providing very effective leadership."

"Well," I said, "will wonders never cease. You astound me with this idea that Adolf Hitler set out to be a servant to humanity and to transform the earth through the application of the teachings of Jesus."

"This is the way he looks to us today, David," said Dr. Karoll. "An examination of the akashic records for this soul shows that he has been a champion of humanitarian causes down through the centuries. Even in Germany, his first achievements were highly constructive and beneficial for the common people. Through fine and noble actions he gained power. He has been a beneficent ruler since ancient times. The law of thought rules the actions of all leaders of nations. This means that the composite of the thinking of the people is represented by whatever leader is set in authority over them, regardless of his actions or how the individual arrived at a position of power. The political leadership of any nation is the medium through which natural law enables the people to meet their own collectively created destiny. They are enabled to see the out-picturing of their own thinking in the actions of their leaders."

"Then Adolf Hitler was not a villain but merely an instrument of Divine Law as the channel through which the thinking of the German people expressed itself." I said, feeling like a school boy who was giving a right response without understanding what he was saying.

"That is precisely the idea that we are dealing with...precisely," said Dr. Karoll. "You will be interested to know that twentieth century seer Edgar Cayce said something to that effect. He said concerning Adolf Hitler at the outset of his rise to power: 'If imperialism does not creep into the hearts of the German people, the advent of this leader will usher in a Golden Age in the earth.'"

"With this kind of reasoning, Hitler could do no wrong, except to create unfavorable personal destiny. Right thinking upon the part of the German people would have made the difference. It was still justice to the millions who suffered during his rule, even including the Jews, but had the goodness in the hearts of the German people prevailed, that justice would have come to each one through some other channel, and possibly in some other century?" I questioned thoughtfully.

"Yes," answered Dr. Karoll quietly.

"Then it doesn't matter how a leader comes to power, perfect justice always reigns. The atrocities of a Spanish Inquisition, or a Roman amphitheater, or an Aztec human sacrifice ceremony, or a German concentration camp represent individual and collective reaping of that which has been sown or balancing of the Law of Thought?"

"Correct."

"It would be wonderful to be able to believe that," I said with a sigh.

"Judaism once taught this, and so, for that matter, has every major religion when rightly understood."

"But," I said, "it was plainly evident that Christians didn't believe it, much less the Jewish people."

"The faithful of all religions have always believed this. For a man to turn the other cheek or to bless those who abused him proved his faith in Divine Justice. Those who sought the Holy Spirit through prayer and meditation accepted these teachings by Faith, David," said Alice gently. "Now the testing time for faith is over in the earth. We have scientific evidence that perfect justice is simply the result of the immutable operation of natural laws. The laws of physics and chemistry that have been established by scientific investigation are less complex but no more exact in operation than the Law of Thought."

"Then," I exclaimed, "people would really have no basis to blame another, even a person such as Adolf Hitler, for the problems and hardships they suffer...but only themselves! When the thinking of the masses is unselfish, compassionate, honest, just, merciful and loving, they positively shall have leaders who will act that way!"

"You have the picture, David," said Dr. Karoll. "Potentially, the Kingdom of Heaven is right here on earth and always has been. Any person or any nation practicing the teachings of the Sermon on the Mount will create this Kingdom of Heaven, first within, and eventually, without."

"I wish you could persuade me to believe these things," I said slowly and perhaps a little too strongly.

"We won't have to," said Mrs. Karoll. "You will convince yourself because of your powers of reasoning. Alice will take you to the Records Center where you can examine the data files. You can see pictures of persons now living and compare them with those of their previous physical bodies. You will meet some persons and compare them with personalities who were exposed to the public in your time. The evidence will be irresistible to your scientific mind. It requires no more faith to believe in perfect justice than it took faith in your time to believe that water was a compound of hydrogen and oxygen."

146

"Identifying a person with his past lives doesn't prove that there's perfect justice in the world, does it?" I asked.

"The data gathered over the years since we began keeping such records points in this direction unerringly. Many psychics have independently reached into the ancient past to help establish this concept. Perfect justice is nothing more or less than the unerring operation of natural law in the lives of individuals."

"Then what was the case with the Jewish people who were in Germany at the time of Adolf Hitler's rise to power?" I asked.

"Why, in this case you had the psychic readings of Edgar Cayce to refer to," said Dr. Karoll. "He was asked this very question and answered simply that the group of people who had been incarnated as Jews in Germany at that time had been together as a nation some six or seven thousand years previously. As he described it, it was what you might call 'poetic justice.' They had, as a nation in Persia, conquered another nation and had proceeded to annihilate the people by the millions in a manner which generated for them the collective destiny that they met as Jews in Germany."

"In that case," I said, tongue in cheek, "they had no reason to complain. They should have accepted this treatment as from the Lord and blessed those who despitefully used them, just like Jesus tried to tell them, but they wouldn't listen."

"Whether you believe what you are saying or not, David, you have understood intellectually," said Dr. Karoll.

"This is too good to be true," I sighed. "We could have had a Utopia well started a hundred years ago with this philosophy."

"Don't think that it is all that easy, David, for a vast amount of effort is required on every level to keep human society in a constructive growth pattern. In acquiring this knowledge, we have overcome a hurdle along the way which eases some problems, but brings unforeseen challenges. For a comparison from your times, consider the industrial revolution introduced by the steam engine. The productive capacity for supplying man's needs was then no longer limited by the energy available from the bodies of men and animals, windmills and water wheels. However, the new productive capacity inevitably became the very source of those forces which became so destructive as to create a Frankenstein that threatened all life forms of earth. The future inhabitability of the planet earth was threatened. Were it not for intervention from those disciplined intelligences from the outer spheres, there would be nothing but desolation throughout the globe now."

"Surely this new knowledge concerning perfect justice to the individual could not hold a ghastly prospect such as that? I don't see how it could do anything but good. Wouldn't knowing about rebirth and that they reap what they sow force people to be good?" I asked wonderingly.

"This knowledge potentially will enable a small group of people to enslave the masses through their ability to control the circumstances of their own rebirth and retain their identity and position as overlords for centuries," answered Dr. Karoll.

"But the law of cause and effect would not allow this, would it?" I asked, startled at such a prospect.

"Oh, yes it would!" said Dr. Karoll. "Any misuse of his brother that a man can conceive, he is allowed to perpetrate. Man learns through exercising his free will and then meeting what he has created. There are always countless souls who still have negative destiny to meet. These would be drawn into experiences of enslavement and mistreatment."

"But if an individual knew the laws of reincarnation, he would be a fool to enslave others," I said, dismayed at the prospect of human error upon such a vast scale as to enslave the inhabitants of a planet for ages.

"We are getting into deep water, David," said Dr. Karoll. "You hardly understand or accept the elementary possibilities inherent in the human soul. So far we have been discussing souls who, like children, must be sent off to school or they will not go. This is the level of the masses. With the break through to higher levels of consciousness, and communication with beings from outer space, undreamed of possibilities have opened up for the leaders of the people. There are scientific ways to cause the rebirth of a soul into a given set of circumstances, to identify it with its previous personality and, thus, make possible the creation of a self perpetrating dynasty, enslaving the masses unmercifully. Eventually, it would destroy itself but it could last centuries."

"But why would anyone think they could defeat laws of nature?"

"By establishing several classes and relegating the masses to ignorance and servitude and by controlling the circumstances of their own return, or else by using known techniques to extend their life span indefinitely, you can see the way a group of superior people might attempt to overcome the law of cause and effect."

"How can you conceive of such a terrible thing even taking place?" I asked, horrified. "If superior persons understood that one reaps what he sows, they would be the last to make such mistakes, and the first to protect the earth from any who might have such leanings. Beside this, you have said that the leaders out-picture the thinking of the people. It looks like we have a 'which comes first...the chicken or the egg' question. Why do you think such things can happen?"

"The reason we can anticipate terrible error following a time of enlightenment, and release from the belief in injustice is because the akashic records show that similar things occurred in the past," said Dr. Karoll quietly.

"When?"

"Most recently in Atlantis about ten thousand years before Christ."

"The highly evolved individuals enslaved the masses?" I asked.

"Enslaved them and used their advanced technology to make them into automatons. They bred slaves like cattle and used advanced electronic devices inserted in their brains to cause unbearably intense pain by remote control, and thus utterly eliminate rebellion," said Dr. Karoll.

"Could they prolong their own lives, too?" I asked, shocked at such prospects.

"Indefinitely."

"What happened?"

"Higher beings, guardians of the planet, intervened. By influencing the minds of key technicians to make mistakes in the use of their cosmic energy converters, excessive force was released to cause subterranean explosions and the submerging of the continent resulted."

"Were these higher beings from other planets?"

"From the outer spheres was the terminology the Edgar Cayce psychic readings used in identifying them. Yes, to be sure, they were visitors from other planetary systems who had come to assist the race of men on earth at a critical time."

"I think that David has quite enough to think about for several days," said Mrs. Karoll. "Perhaps it is time to plan to take him to one of our record centers so that he may satisfy his mind on the more elementary questions of the continuity of the life of the soul."

"You are surely right about my having much to think about," I said with feeling. "I believe I would like a few days alone in some mountain cabin, if you feel it would be good for me."

"Wonderful!" said Alice. "We will give you sound recordings on the subject of meditation, reading material, and spiritually stimulating music to help you."

In the space of four hours all arrangements were made for me to go to a mountain retreat and the four of us were aboard Dr. Karoll's air car for the trip. I was to spend fourteen days alone before they would return for me.

CHAPTER 23

Words as Thought Forms

"Unless we take care to clear the first principles of knowledge from the embarrassment and delusion of words, we may make infinite reasonings upon them to no purpose: we may draw consequences from consequences, and be never the wiser. The farther we go, we shall only lose ourselves the more irrecoverably, and be the deeper entangled in difficulties and mistakes. Whoever therefore designs to read the following sheets, I entreat him to make my words the occasion of his own thinking and endeavor to attain the same train of thoughts in reading that I had in writing them."
—*From the preface:* Treatise Concerning the Principles of Human Knowledge
George Berkeley

"How long will it take us to get there," I asked as I watched the earth dropping out from under the fast rising air car .

"About twelve hours," said Alice.

"I'm surprised," I said, "I thought that we could reach Europe in three hours, much less be able to reach any mountain retreat in America in that length of time."

"We are going to let you be surprised, David," said the Doctor's wife, Louise. "Alice asked if we might not try to obtain the most appropriate meditation retreat possible and a distinguished master of the art to guide you."

"With twelve hours to make the journey in this craft, you could be taking me to be taught by a Tibetan Lama at some mystical Shangri La, high in the Himalayas," I said, laughingly.

They all smiled but no one commented on this remark.

"How high will we fly on the way," I said.

"We will stay at around eighty thousand feet, David," said Dr. Karoll.

"No matter what altitude, it must be necessary for there to be some kind of traffic control to avoid air collisions in such fast moving craft," I said.

"There are not many craft of this type operated in earth, David," said Dr. Karoll. "This allows us to use an individual air traffic control method which is very simple. Attached to the controls is a radar like scanning system which locates all objects within miles of this craft. It automatically alters our course slightly to avoid any object, even a bird."

"Why are there not millions of these craft, just as we had millions of automobiles in America?" I asked.

"Ours is a society of harmonious cooperation, David, not one of many factions vigorously pursuing competitive and separate personal interests. We have a transportation service which is operated in the public interest by the public. Almost all travel between population centers is by public conveyance. Within the local population centers there is provided fast convenient travel and, for any necessary individual travel in the cities, we have vehicle pools. There is little need for the individual conveyances of your day. Our people enjoy excellent provisions for walking and bicycling the short distances from public transit stations. Supplying public transportation, electric power, residential needs and public accommodations are naturally functions of our government."

"It was beginning to look like our whole system of transportation needed a drastic overhaul in America, not just because of pollution but for many reasons," I commented. "As for the source of power, it was beginning to be extremely apparent that our private enterprise system must continue to devour the natural resources of the land in a mad scramble for profits that would not stop until we rendered the beauty of a great continent into a hell of abused land, polluted air, and water. Real poverty, not the false poverty of a mismanaged social system in a land of plenty, but a real poverty arising from depleted soil and natural resources was fast closing in."

"David," spoke Dr. Karoll, "yours were times when, as far as your government was concerned, instead of providing the basis for cooperation that would have used men's best capacities to serve their common needs, it guarded the position of those who exploited natural resources and manpower, both at home and abroad," said Dr. Karoll.

"Well," I said, "we were not ready, I don't believe, for the kind of government you're suggesting. It would have produced chaos. America's aggressive men, who grasped control of various industries, of oil and railroad, minerals, lumber, banking, farm lands, or real estate, were highly honored as fine citizens. The fortunes and power they fought for gave them the incentive to organize industry and utilize science, as well as to learn how to motivate the laboring man. If our government had taken over private industry, everything would have ground to a screeching halt. Political intrigue, greed, inefficiency and infighting for power would have created an impossible situation. I think corruption among competing private interests, vying for power over our government, was more functional than if the whole machinery was operated by one corrupt faction which had gained control over all."

"Well," said Dr. Karoll, "you just asked why we don't have millions of air cars. With our system we could easily produce them, but as you see, we have no reason to do so. All our people have adequate transportation and are occupied with far more satisfying activities than being cogs in the machinery for producing millions of new model air cars every year."

We all lapsed into silence. As I looked out on the scene visible from our position above the earth, my mind went back to the first occasion I rode with Alice in the air car. Alice must have been receptive to my thoughts for she turned toward me and smiled. "A listening ear for your thoughts, David."

"I wonder sometimes if I need to express them with words around you and your mother and Dr. Karoll," I said, with a smile.

"Communication can be richer and deeper without words," said Louise Karoll. "Spoken words may clip the wings of thought. They may narrow down to a single band of color the rainbow of feelings we are trying to convey. A word ineptly spoken can shatter a glorious inner communication between spirits, just as one might burst a soap bubble and shatter the swirling tremulous sphere of scintillating color."

"As you speak words, Mrs. Karoll, they have the opposite effect, stimulating the imagination to construct an elaborate mind picture to fill out the meaning of your words," I said.

"Ah!" said Dr. Karoll, "now there you have the mystery and magic of words. The spoken word creates a form with depth and color in the thought world which actually expresses all that its speaker was thinking, both what he desired to communicate and what he may have wished to conceal. The same spoken word, depending upon the quality of the thinking of its speaker may create an elaborately beautiful form, complex as the exterior of a medieval cathedral, or one as simple as a river polished stone."

"Well," I mused, "You certainly generated a picture in my mind with those words, whether there are such things as thought forms or not."

"Even more mysterious than this, David, the spoken word of a

Master-Mind, imperfectly transcribed by a disciple, may still convey his full meaning, although centuries of time and the confusing idioms of an ancient tongue stand between."

"A statement like that would seem to be impossible to validate," I objected.

"From your present point of view, it may be. Such concepts may only be encountered successfully by the intellect after it has been disciplined to respond to the delicate and easily submerged intuitive faculties. When the mind is properly disciplined so that one consciously moves into the thought world, then he may see and know why this is possible," said Dr. Karoll. "However, this mystical power embodied in words spoken originally by a Master-Mind has been demonstrated again and again. Jesus said, 'I am the bread of life: he that cometh to me shall never hunger; and he that believeth on me shall never thirst.' How can a phrase like that, which is certainly unintelligible in our language, have the impact to transform a personality?"

"I have seen such a thing happen," I said, "and it is a mystery."

"What we have here," said Dr. Karoll, "is not easy to explain, for the unconscious mind of the individual, rather than the conscious mind, comprehended the meaning of such words and then stimulated the reaction at the conscious mind level. This, of course, is why persons having such experiences may have seemed to you unreasonable when questioned concerning their faith and unequipped to give a rational basis for what they believe."

"Ah!" I said, "You have touched upon familiar ground with me there. There was hardly a mind as hard to deal with rationally as a 'Saved by the Blood' fundamentalist."

"The reality behind their conversion experience was profound truth given to mankind by a Master-Soul, David," said Dr. Karoll.

"But how can seemingly senseless phrases contain truth?" I asked.

"Thought forms of beauty and truth created by a Master-Mind become living symbols, enduring down through the centuries. Living words of Master-Minds guide and ennoble the race of man. By their unique qualities, they separate themselves from all others. As the centuries roll by, they are burnished rather than eroded by the passing years."

"You speak riddles, Dr. Karoll," I said. "How can words be called living? Must we resort to those incomprehensible religious metaphors that frustrate the intellect?"

"The intellect, David, is inferior to the intuition and is lacking in mobility, just as an inanimate object can not be compared to a living creature. Anyone who is intellectually oriented is incapable of understanding a reference to living words, unless he is willing to control his intellect and cause it to cooperate with, and be receptive to, his intuition."

"That explains a whole lot," I said, "I did notice that among groups whose members had relatively undeveloped intellectual capacity, these intuitive religious convictions were quite common. Such people were inclined to belittle and feel contentious toward those who did exercise their rational faculties."

"Among such groups as you refer to, there was often a need for more intellectual development to provide the check and balance, and to prevent true intuitive whisperings from being confused with childish and superstitious distortions, hallucinations and other delusions generated by the imagination," said Dr. Karoll.

"Now you have helped me to understand much better, Dr. Karoll," I said. "I have known too many narrow minded, intellectually drab persons, who claimed religious conversion experiences, to imagine that theirs is a superior form of comprehension. How may I develop this receptivity to intuition without sacrificing my intellectual discernment?"

"Alex," said Mrs. Karoll, "wouldn't it be better to let David take up such questions as these in meditation? Through meditation, his own understanding will open up."

"To be sure, Louise," said Dr. Karoll.

"Is it possible that you are all conspiring to key up my interest in learning meditation?" I said, half seriously and half jokingly.

They just smiled at this. We again fell into silence as we viewed the cloud flecked scene below. Again my mind drifted back to that first trip aloft in the air car with Alice. Retracing my recent past, I found myself moving in thought from one event to the next, until I finally arrived back to my first waking experience in Dr. Karoll's home. At times like this, a subtle questioning from within nagged me. How much longer before I should awaken from this extended dream-fantasy to find myself being revived by friends in the year 1984?

CHAPTER 24

Psychedelic Drugs, Miracles and Magic

"I saw and heard and knew at last
The How and Why of all things, past,
And present, and forevermore.
The Universe; cleft to the core,
Lay open to my probing sense
That, sick'ning, I would fain pluck
Thence but could not, —Nay!"
—From the poem Renascence
Edna St. Vincent Millay

The word, hallucination, echoed in my mind from the conversation of just a moment before. If I woke up, how would I describe my hallucinations of the twenty second century to my friends?

This train of thought had gradually led me back to some experiences with psychedelic drugs which had interested me during the years just preceding my long sleep. Psychedelics like peyote cactus, psilocybin from the mushrooms, the ubiquitous cannabis sativa known popularly as marijuana, LSD or d-lysergic acid diethylamide which was first derived from a fungus that grows on wheat and rye, the wild herb henbane, the seeds of the morning glory, thornapple, and many of the others came into my thoughts.

The comments by Dr. Karoll about words having shapes and colors reminded me of my study of hallucinogens. I thought about an article written by a psychical researcher who had used peyote cactus juice to investigate its potential to awaken psychic faculties or possibly duplicate mystical religious visions. He described how, during his experience, an array of three dimensional curvilinear and many sided geometrical patterns rose before his vision when words were spoken, either by himself or by others. The shape and color of the three dimensional word figures conveyed far more of their meaning to him than the spoken sound of the words. The figures he saw seemed to be created by the sounds. Besides containing elaborate meanings, these figures also had certain peculiarities that identified them by some unique characteristic with each individual speaker's voice. In addition to all this, he saw other forms which seemed to be related thoughts arising from the mind of the speaker and, also, some opposing thoughts emanating from other minds, which attacked those issuing from the speaker. A very thought provoking article this had been, to say the least. Hallucinogen was a good word for the psychedelic drugs.

"Dr. Karoll," I said, breaking a silence of thirty minutes or so, "do you know about the hallucinogenic drugs and the way they swept across America like wild fire in the 1960's?"

"I have been expecting you to bring up this question, David," said Dr. Karoll. "There was nothing new about psychedelics for they are mentioned in ancient records. The Yoga Sutras of Patanjali, possibly the oldest written words known, contain a mention of their use to achieve astral powers. Patanjali warned disciples of Yoga that this was the dark path. William James and S. Weir Mitchell took cognizance of them and did penetrating research on their effects some seventy five years before the general public learned about them in the 1960's."

"Dr. Karoll," I said, "how can you possibly have this kind of historical data on an obscure subject so readily available?"

"You are not aware that psychedelic drugs in the hands of the masses are considered to have precipitated cataclysmic changes in society. This subject has been spotlighted because of its significance in world history. However, you already know that our learning techniques enable the unconscious mind to absorb volumes of subject matter in a few hours and recall specific data to the conscious mind at will."

"It is hard for me to realize how you can do this," I said. "I'm constantly being distracted from any subject I ask about by your phenomenal ability to answer me in such detail. Please go on and tell me how and why the psychedelic drugs influenced history?"

"They furnished evidence concerning other levels of consciousness and they compelled the recognition of psychic forces. This brought scientific minds into serious research upon the subject."

"How could the half-crazed, emotionally confused and shattered psychedelic drug users accomplish anything like that?" I wondered.

"Had you stayed conscious for another twenty years, you would know. After the first few years, during which so many persons using drugs damaged their nervous systems and minds, some discovered they were in possession of one of the tools used by magicians and sorcerers," answered Dr. Karoll.

"Are you saying that the medieval magicians used psychedelics...that their magic potions were the same as our psychedelic

157

drugs?" I asked thoughtfully.

"Precisely, David," said Dr. Karoll. "Not only the magicians of medieval Europe but also the Magi of Persia and India. These ancient wise men who were true Initiates of the Mystery School sometimes made use of them."

"That seems to ring a bell," I said. "I remember how often in fairy tales that feats of magic followed the drinking of a strange brew. But acid heads just entertained themselves with fantasy, or took the psychedelics for aphrodisiacs, since they had such an effect if the mind was turned in that direction. It's hard to imagine that they were capable of producing magical effects. How could they do that?"

"Psychedelics, David, trigger the endocrine system to release secretions which affect the electrical conductivity of the network of nerve channels in a way that makes more refined senses available to the conscious mind and gives it access to data ordinarily restricted to the unconscious. They have a unique quality about them which enables the conscious mind to continue to function while the vast powers of the unconscious mind are brought gradually into play. The conscious mind can retain control and direct its own unconscious mind like a hypnotist. In other words, temporary command of the ordinarily inaccessible soul faculties can be assumed by the conscious mind. As you are well aware, this can enable one to exercise phenomenal powers. Psychedelic drugs users of the earlier years had no idea this was possible. They were limited to the states of consciousness and capacities they believed possible by the very nature of the psychedelics. Mostly they experienced only a heightened awareness of sound, color, smell, and other sensations and fantasies because they were conditioned to expect only phenomena of sense experiences."

"Do you mean the acid heads could have accomplished healing miracles or committed mysterious crimes like black magicians had they known they were possible?" I asked with renewed interest.

"Yes," answered Dr. Karoll, "but there was more to it than just knowing the possibilities. The magicians and medicine men had developed the ability to focus their attention, visualizing their objective powerfully and distinctly for a period of time. They held the visualization clearly until they knew the required thought forms had been created. This ability required extensive self-discipline and training to develop. It was undeveloped in ordinary drug users. Lacking knowledge of these possibilities and lacking mind control, there was not the least chance that the ordinary user of psychedelic drugs could accomplish such things."

"Then what happened to make psychedelics have an effect on history?" I questioned.

"In the years that followed the 1960's knowledge of how psychedelics could enhance mind power began to be applied by materialistic but intelligent and disciplined groups. The supernatural powers available through these drugs soon made mankind aware of the reality of the black arts and introduced a form of crime which could not be dealt with by conventional methods."

"Please explain what you mean and how this was accomplished?"

"When such a group, or even just two persons, were able to agree upon a particular objective, the mind forces generated were able to move out into the atmosphere and take possession of persons who were susceptible, such as those who had damaged their own normal resistance to possession by a thought form or discarnate by excesses of alcohol or drugs. These people could be animated to commit bizarre crimes."

"That seems to fit a widely publicized murder of an actress and her friends, a mysterious crime of the 70's which I well remember," I said.

"There were other techniques which enabled them to steal by teleportation, to produce mental and moral aberrations in selected individuals, to cause accidents, to influence decisions of political figures, and to bring financial successes. Even some elements of the government's espionage bureau began to practice these black arts."

"What a terrifying situation!" I said, "How did society deal with such insidious forms of crime?"

"Constructive application of the same forces, when generated through prayer and fasting and selfless dedication to serve mankind, would have been successful. There were too few who understood and practiced these things. The people failed to do this and thus it came about that the forces of nature lashed out to bring things into balance. Those whose purposes were out of harmony with the establishment of spiritually oriented world government were carried away by the swirling waters during the shift of the poles. Some may not be back until thousands of years hence when circumstances are again suitable to allow them to meet the disharmony they chose to create."

"You make it sound like a natural disaster occurred which was selective about whom it affected. Surely, I am misunderstanding you," I said.

"Apparently you did not fully understand the role played by the celestial ships. Warnings of the coming shift of the poles were going out even in your time. Just a short while before the actual disaster took place, a great host of space ships descended to earth and offered to pick up all who wished their protection," said Dr. Karoll.

"But how did this sort the sheep from the goats?" I asked.

"Human nature took care of it, David," said Dr. Karoll. "Those who devise evil against others are suspicious. They were the ones who couldn't trust the celestial visitors. They assumed the dire warnings only a trick to persuade them to board the spacecraft."

"That was convenient," I said, solemnly, as I thought about the gigantic catastrophe.

Again, we lapsed into a thoughtful silence. During this silence of an hour or more, some unanswered questions about psychedelic drugs kept going through my mind. I found myself reviewing all the facts I knew that could lend credence to what Dr. Karoll had said. A personal friend, who had been the foster son of an Indian chief in Iowa, once gave me an interesting description of the way some of the American Indians used peyote to leave their physical bodies and visit far off relatives to learn how they were getting along. Fifteen or twenty of them sat in a circle inside a ceremonial tent, took the peyote buttons and then, as a drummer beat a monotonous rhythm they gradually went into a kind of stupor. After several hours, they regained consciousness believing they had been unseen visitors in the tepees of friends and relatives, perhaps hundreds of miles away. When news came by ordinary means later on, it usually confirmed the reality of their clairvoyant experiences.

I remembered another firsthand account of his about a different kind of phenomenon. His interest in the peyote cactus had taken him deep into Mexico where he saw a miraculous healing take place. The healing ceremony was simple but its success hinged upon the religious fervor which was stimulated by using peyote. Several peyote buttons each were eaten by a small group of friends, the sick person and the tribal medicine man. After several hours of prayer, healing from serious illness to normal health took place right before his eyes.

160

Also, he learned that peyote was used by the Indians when they needed extrasensory perception, such as for locating lost horses. The Indians who had made the use of peyote a part of their religious ceremonies were, he felt, the most mature individuals he had encountered in any society.

Dr. Karoll's comments introduced a particularly interesting new question on this subject. "What did you mean, Dr. Karoll, by making reference to the Initiates of the Mysteries in the same breath that you mentioned black magicians and psychedelic drugs?"

"In some of the Mystery Schools, the psychedelics were used to initiate disciples into the spiritual world. The mind expanding potion was used only once for each individual and the experience either made a Master of the student or broke his spirit. Novitiates were chosen with great care, and then only took the drugs after two years of spiritual, mental, and physical preparation. The relationship between the endocrine system, blood chemistry, the nervous system and the exercise of psychic powers was intuitively understood by mystics. Christian mystics and Hindu Masters gave practical instructions for developing spiritual faculties in their Holy Scriptures. They defined the kingdom of heaven as a state of mind. They taught that the Holy Temple is the threefold body of man and that when a human being is able to meet the necessary conditions of inner purity on physical, mental, and spiritual levels, he can control the endocrine glands and cause them to secrete mind expanding hormones. These ancient masters used psychedelic drugs as a helpful crutch. Of course, the psychic powers will develop naturally in anyone who actually lives the teachings of Jesus. This is why Jesus said, 'the things that I do shall ye do also.'"

"Dr. Karoll," I interrupted, feeling frustrated, "you have mentioned Biblical insights before. So much of the Bible is contradictory and so much of it offends my powers of reason that my mind is not receptive to it. Can you use a different approach?"

"It is difficult to find a better one," said Dr. Karoll. "The knowledge possessed by the Hebrew mystics embraced the whole range of the understanding of man's potential, both the possibilities for making his physical body subject to his mind, even invulnerable, and the capability to direct the very forces of nature. Jesus demonstrated these again and again, including the teleportation of his body and the precipitation of tons of food from other levels of matter."

"Well," I said, thinking how to lead the conversation away from the Bible, "since you relate conditions existing in the physical body to psychic powers, you might give me a specific example from some other source."

"Why, yes, of course," said Dr. Karoll. "There are many. In your times, Peter Hurkos illustrated, from the physical standpoint, how the practice of yoga may develop psychic powers."

"Dr. Karoll," I said, "Peter Hurkos was famous in America in the 50's and 60's and many articles and books were written about him. In all that I read about him, including his autobiography, I recall no mention whatsoever of a connection between his psychic ability and the practice of yoga."

"It was often mentioned, David," said Dr. Karoll, "but you didn't recognize it. Tell me, David, do you remember how Peter Hurkos first came by his psychic ability?"

"Why, of course," I said. "Everyone who took an interest in him knew that story. He was up on a ladder doing some painting, suffered a bad fall, and was unconscious for some time. When he regained consciousness in the hospital, he found that he could read the minds of the nurses and see details of their personal lives."

"In other words, David, a physical injury that jarred his spine and neck made him a psychic," said Dr. Karoll.

"You mean that yoga can alter the spinal column to cause one to become psychic?" I asked.

"That's right," said Dr. Karoll.

"I never thought of that," I mused. "I do remember hearing about people who were confined in mental institutions after a bad fall because they began to hear voices. If psychiatrists could not talk them out of this, they would be confined in mental hospitals. Does this mean osteopathic treatments should have been used to correct a spinal condition in order to stop the voices?"

"Don't you think that is a reasonable surmise, David?" said Dr. Karoll.

"Hmmm...then practice of yoga positions can develop psychic powers," I said slowly, "by altering conditions in the vertebrae."

"Yes," said Dr. Karoll.

"Then it isn't necessary to develop a saintly character to gain psychic powers but there are chemical and mechanical short cuts, psychedelic drugs and possible operations on the physical body?"

"Yes, David," said Dr. Karoll. "This information wasn't freely available to the public until the last part of the twentieth century. It was released to the masses of an impure society at a time when its disintegration was progressing rapidly. The reality of the psychic powers became commonly known. It was a necessary time for testing and purifying which sorted out from the masses a remnant of people who were to participate in developing a new and more spiritually enlightened society after the shift of the poles."

"That's a familiar train of thought from Christianity," I commented. "But what about the Catholic mystics? Did they use a short cut to gain access to these psychic powers and spiritual experiences?"

"The records of Catholicism include such a varied array of visions and psychic experiences that the answer must be 'yes and no,'" said Dr. Karoll. "The Catholic Church had a profound understanding of spiritual laws. The beauty of their saints has provided a guiding Light for the earth. But there were those who looked for ways which did not require so much self discipline."

"Did they know about using the sacred mushroom?" I asked.

"The Church had the information in their archives which came from their missionaries who worked among primitive tribes in Mexico and South America. It was carefully hidden and only a handful of scholarly monks were familiar with it but they did not relate it to true mystical experiences. The use of psychedelics by the monks and nuns would have wrecked havoc in the Church."

"Then how did the monks do it?" I asked.

"The method the monks used to have a mystical experience was different. They beat their bodies with whips made of many strands with tiny sharp objects tied to them. This treatment caused numerous small sores and the secretions and infection that occurred brought them to a feverish state, bordering upon death. During this time of weakness and fever, they sometimes experienced mystical visions like the psychedelic drug users."

"Now that rings a bell," I said. "I remember a friend who told me how he experienced a state of elevated consciousness during a high fever. He moved into another level of consciousness in which he was able to visit in spirit with others and have direct mind to mind communication. This one experience gave him a new understanding and changed his attitude toward his relatives and all the people he knew closely. It made him almost saintly in his tolerance toward everyone. I can see why this method practiced by the monks could transform character to make a saintly religious person."

"If it didn't kill him," said Dr. Karoll with a wry smile.

"Are there are any other ways to have psychic experiences without applying oneself to spiritual disciplines," I asked.

"A number of ways," said Dr. Karoll. "A unique way to achieve astral travel was practiced by Tibetan monks. They had special chambers prepared so that they could be isolated in utter darkness and silence for a year at a time. The entry was plastered over. An attendant furnished the monk his food, a small dish of cooked barley meal, which was placed through a small opening every other day and his empty dish removed. Other needed facilities were provided in the darkened chamber. When the monk asked to be placed in this chamber he knew that he would not hear a sound or see a glimmer of light for a full year. There was no way for him to shorten his stay except by dying, once he entered this chamber."

"Self imposed solitary confinement," I said in awe. "Wouldn't he go mad?"

"The monk had been conditioned to believe and accept his capacity for astral travel, although he had not been able to achieve it. During the ensuing time, a great inner struggle for the retention of sanity took place. Finally, the psychic nature would come to the fore to free him from the prison of his physical body and he would begin to consciously experience astral travel. Once this break through occurred, the monk found himself able to visit any place on earth at will. He returned to his body every other day just long enough to refresh himself and take the nourishment provided. This is an example of how psychic ability can be a forced development. It could be a selfish kind of diversion for the monk, merely a sensual experience on the astral level of consciousness. When acquired this way, it obviously did not hinge upon virtue or character development. It was so satisfying to the Tibetan monks that it was not unusual for them to spend several years this way, not consecutively, of course. The faculties developed by this means were intended to have been dedicated to serve humanity during his astral travels."

"It would seem that the human body and mind could not stand

that kind of an ordeal," I said with feeling.

"Few Westerners could, David," said Dr. Karoll. "These monks trained and prepared themselves physically and mentally in anticipation of the strain. Even then, it was not uncommon for one to die before his year was up."

"The way a subject broadens out when you discuss it to interrelate data from all over the world is a never ending wonder to me, Dr. Karoll," I said in admiration.

"There was yet another widely publicized event revealing how certain conditions may produce heightened awareness. You possibly remember the details," said Dr. Karoll.

"What was that?" I asked.

"Do you remember something in the reports from the first American and Russian astronauts which raised the question that they were temporarily hallucinating?" asked Dr. Karoll.

"Why, yes," I said. "I recall a ridiculous claim by the Russian astronauts that they were able to see the smiling faces of the peasants as they sailed over their homeland. In fact, I had an extended conversation on this question with a remarkable little old lady who was over eighty but still mentally alert and keen. Apparently, some of the details of the report from the American astronauts looked equally as ridiculous as the Russian accounts. The story she told me was this: She said the first news stories about the experiences of the astronaut Glenn gave her the impression he had actually had a psychic experience. This little lady, Miss Barr, had distinguished herself nationally as a fingerprint expert and had been interested in parapsychology for years. She was able to have access to the confidential report made by Captain Glenn because she was cleared to see secret government documents and, also, because she was a next door neighbor of the Kennedy family. Captain Glenn's written report said that he was able to see smoke coming from the chimneys of houses as he passed over the plains of America. He knew that he was at an altitude from which it was humanly impossible to even see houses but was conscientious about making this report. Miss Barr postulated that Captain Glenn unwittingly projected himself out of his body down to the altitude where he was able to see the things he claimed he did."

"This was a genuine insight, David," said Dr. Karoll. "The partial release of the inner body from the pressure of earth's ether allowed this experience to take place. The very existence of ether was then still being denied in scientific circles but this was the reason."

"Then the government withheld information on the subject?" I asked.

"Those responsible didn't want the public to become confused or raise questions which couldn't be answered," said Dr. Karoll.

Mrs. Karoll had quietly prepared a lunch for the family while the doctor and myself had been engrossed in conversation.

"Will you join us for refreshments?" she said lightly, "or has all that food for thought taken away your appetite for food for the body."

For the moment I had to admit that it had. Mrs. Karoll suggested that we all take a little red wine that Dr. Karoll had made from grapes grown on the sunny slope behind their mountain and relax for ten or fifteen minutes.

CHAPTER 25

Psychedelic Drugs and Initiation

"There is a principle of the soul, superior to all nature, and through which we are capable of surpassing the order and systems of the world, and participating in the immortal life and the energy of Sublime Celestial Beings. When the soul is elevated to natures above itself, then it deserts the order to which it was formerly compelled, and by a religious magnetism is attracted to another and a loftier, with which it blends and mingles."

—Iamblicus

We had all settled back into silence after Mrs. Karoll's graciously prepared dinner. My thoughts were occupied with the conversation with Dr. Karoll just prior to our interruption to enjoy some refreshment. Before long, I realized I had failed to pursue my thought upon a particularly intriguing aspect of psychedelic drugs.

"Dr. Karoll," I said, "you have not discussed in enough detail the way hallucinogens were used by Initiates."

"I'm glad your interest is sharp on this subject, David," said Dr. Karoll. "In your times, even persons who were open minded upon broader aspects of religious thought found themselves highly prejudiced about psychedelics, and only to be religious in the ordinary sense would close some doors. Many kind and generous people were religious in this sense. They naturally opposed ideas which infringed on their understanding of their religion because they had been conditioned not to use their minds in this area of thought. The Bible contained so many idioms from ancient cultures that could not be understood when taken literally that the 'don't question, just believe' approach was imposed by your spiritually blind leaders."

"Why do you bring up this point," I protested. "Initiates, you have said, can't be identified with a particular faith but are universal in their thinking."

"For a very good reason, David," answered Dr. Karoll. "You were exposed to a society which conditioned a broad segment of the public to reject the possibility that psychedelic drugs had the potential of greatly expanding mankind's understanding of the physical world with its life forms and the spiritual world. The idioms of the various religions and infinite divisions had caused the scientific world to stumble over spiritual realities. The blind faith approach to spiritual teachings required the powers of reason to be blunted. Neither of these groups, the scientific nor the religious, could be impartial in their examination of the psychedelic drugs because they produced phenomena which raised threatening questions concerning generally accepted 'facts.'

"Neither religious leaders," continued Dr. Karoll, "scholars, nor even the psychical researchers could very easily overcome the prejudice that hindered them from making constructive investigation of psychedelics. Many vested interests were threatened by psychedelics. But there was still another barrier even more difficult to surmount which severely hindered their evaluation by competent and well financed investigators."

"And what was that?" I asked, wondering when Dr. Karoll would get to the point.

"The necessity for two years of self discipline, including a nutritionally correct vegetarian diet, chaste living and thinking, and development of mind control through the practice of meditation. Such a thorough preparation is an absolute must in order to condition mind and body to experience the full potential of the spiritual illumination the psychedelics may enable one to have." Dr. Karoll answered earnestly. "Needless to say, persons who studied and used these drugs were quite sure that such disciplines were not necessary and would make no real difference."

"Well...," I paused to think about that for a moment, "I guess that lets me out for a while. Two years, you say," I paused again. "Why two years? Can you tell me something about the evaluation that could have been made, if a scientist had known and been willing to make the personal preparations?"

"Surely, David," said Dr. Karoll with a smile. "My point was to show it was not likely for anyone to stumble upon the information accidently. It took a truly dedicated scientific mind to investigate the psychedelics, for we have a field of investigation here which demands certain conditions to be met within the body and mind of the scientist himself. He must develop a clean strong body, purify his blood, have a clean mind, meticulously conserve his procreative powers, and have control of areas of the unconscious mind which were not being cultivated by the investigators of your times."

"Then who did meet these conditions," I wondered.

"Initiates of Egypt, India, China, Persia and Greece were such men, David. Mystery Schools for spiritual initiation have thrived at different times in history and in different places throughout the world. The neophyte accepted for initiation was a superb human specimen. Some of the Mystery Schools used psychedelics for the initiation rites. Two years of extremely disciplined training preceded a single experience with a psychedelic herb. This one psychedelic experience opened his spiritual organs, counterparts of the physical in a higher level of consciousness, and introduced him into the psychic world. A previously initiated Master accompanied him and, leaving their bodies, together they would go into other realms and communicate with lofty beings. The body was in a deep coma while they moved into higher levels of consciousness. After one such experience, the individual was transformed. He had a personal experience with the Universal Christ and became a 'new creature in Christ Jesus,' to use Christian terminology. Or else he was mentally and emotionally shattered, sometimes permanently. Great perils threatened a neophyte. For example, the soul, dazzled by the beauty and freedom of the psychic world, was in danger of wandering away and losing interest in coming back to its physical body. If this occurred, the physical body would die and the soul entity would have lost a great opportunity to make spiritual progress. To prevent this, masters stood by in prayer to draw the soul back to earth consciousness so that it could fulfill the humanitarian mission it had been trained to accomplish."

"Dr. Karoll," I said, "such a picture as you draw excites my imagination to a fever pitch, but my mind is strained to accept a word of what you say."

"Ah, David," said Dr. Karoll, "you could not help but be excited by this story for you have participated in such experiences yourself as a Gnostic Christian, although you have no conscious memories of this. Also, David, you have been initiated into the Mysteries in Egypt and Greece, India and China."

"Shall I assume from your reference to the Gnostic Christians that early Christians found in the Christ Jesus the same ideal, the same pattern for their spiritual life, which had been found earlier by Initiates of the Mystery Schools of Egypt and Greece, as well as Judaism?"

"Yes, yes, you have the idea, David," said Dr. Karoll.

"Then," I said, "would you say that the Christian teachings actually did contain the wisdom of the ancients and so this why those incomprehensible Christian idioms had a mysterious power to touch the soul?"

"This is true, David," said Dr. Karoll. "And while the reiteration of these Mystery School terms inoculated the conscious mind of many people to resist their real meaning, like a vaccination arms one against the pox, nevertheless, little children could respond to the Gospel stories with their heart. Older people, with innocent hearts like children, could be thrilled and comforted because they did not resist the inner meaning of the story of Jesus."

"Is there any real value in this kind of faith?" I asked.

Dr. Karoll was silent for a moment as he pondered how to best answer my question. "Initiates must consciously face the great personal responsibility of direct knowledge of the power of Christ within. Children and the gentle sweet old women and old men with simple faith and goodness like that of little children could wield the prayer power of an Initiate and, unknowingly, often did, and so contributed mighty forces to help mankind evolve toward the ideal of brotherly love throughout the earth."

"Dr. Karoll," I said, "I thought that I understood something of the psychology of religion but each conversation we have shakes my self confidence further. Now all appears hopelessly complicated and garbled. The picture you have given me suggests that pagan rites, mythology, blood sacrifices, reincarnation, miracles of healing, speaking in tongues, Mystery Schools, hypnotism, hallucinogenic drugs, trance mediums, chastity, vegetarianism, visitations from outer space, ghosts, Hawaiian Huna doctors, the lore of ancient Atlantis, and Mu, African black magic, cataclysmic earth changes, and Christianity are all intermingled and inextricably linked together. They appear all the more so as our discussions proceed. How are you going to bring me out from among the trees so that I may recognize the outline of the forest?"

"No one can do that for you, David," said Dr. Karoll.

"No one," I echoed, feeling puzzled and surprised at this answer. Dr. Karoll made no further comment. It was evident he was going to allow me to ponder his words for a while. I started to rephrase my question but then, instead, decided to quietly think upon our conversation. Knowing Dr. Karoll's way of stimulating my thoughts, I assumed he had already given me the answer. I tried to concentrate. It was not easy for me to do this, at best. Fifteen or twenty minutes went by in silence. Mrs. Karoll quietly brewed some of her stimulating herb tea and sweetened it with mountain honey from Dr. Karoll's apiaries. The tea made me alert, keyed up my mind, and relaxed my nerves. A few more minutes passed quietly.

"Meditation, of course," I finally said out loud.

They smiled at this and I felt I had achieved a victory.

"Meditation," I said it again more confidently. "You have done it to me again, I see."   No one made any comment as they quietly waited for me to offer whatever thoughts I had.

"You make me feel that I will not be a useful citizen in your society, or even of much value to myself, unless I learn meditation. I don't react very well to having pressure put on me to do something. I can't say you are doing this to me either, yet I feel under constraint. My attitude doesn't make sense to me. I'm well able to see that you believe meditation is the 'Open Sesame,' but something in me is objecting to the discipline of personal application."

Again no one spoke. Their sympathy for my inner conflict and the feeling I had of their warm personal affection for me was an influence that was reaching out a helping hand to draw me upward. I sensed that meditation was the way to transform my nature and that these changes would come at the expense of my ego. I was dealing with pride and knew it. I was faced with overcoming a frame of mind like the Pharisee who prayed, "God, I thank Thee that I am better than other men are." Still, I knew myself to be a fool for entertaining this thought, especially under the circumstances that I was in.

We flew on in silence. I knew the doctor and his wife and daughter did not need words to have communication with each other, but I was not sure of the extent they could read my mind! I guess I preferred not to know. Another hour slipped by and our twelve hour journey was more than half over. I could see that there was a great expanse of water far below. A giant thunderhead cloud below to our right told me that fifteen miles underneath us a good sized island was hidden from our view.

CHAPTER 26

The Meditation Tower

"I am the same toward all beings; to Me there is none hateful or dear. But to those who worship Me with devotion... they are in Me and I too am in them."

—Bhagavad Gita

The snow covered crags of the Himalayas were expanding in the vision panel as Dr. Karoll guided the air car earthward. Only in motion pictures taken from the air had I ever seen them before. The skyward jutting of upturned earth crust called forth an inner vision of prehistoric upheavals. The high flying experience I had just been through had heightened my awareness so that everything I looked upon took on more significance.

Our air car moved on down to the level of the higher mountain peaks and we slowed down to take in the majestic scene spread before us. When the idea had come to me of spending time in isolation amidst the natural beauty of a mountain setting, I was thinking a cabin would be available in the Blue Ridge near Dr. Karoll's home. In another moment, I was experiencing the spine tingling thrill of observing my retreat while poised in mid-air beside it in an air car over the Himalayas. Instead of a cabin, it was like an upside down egg sitting gracefully atop a tree trunk-like shaft, which clasped a jagged peak a hundred fifty feet below us. Like a tree with roots anchored in rocky terrain, the tower base had tentacles that gripped the irregular peak, following its contours and fastening to the solid grey rock. From its spreading base to the underside of the capsule, the tower varied in diameter from perhaps eight feet at the bottom to four feet at its smallest point. As we hovered next to the dome, our altimeter read twenty-seven thousand three hundred forty feet.

"You are going to leave me here?" I asked, knowing full well the plan. Questions raced through my mind and answers came with equal rapidity. Words seemed awkward and slow to express my thoughts. I was, indeed, to spend two weeks in this meditation capsule under the

172

tutoring of a Tibetan Master. The Tibetan was not going to stay with me but would come by astral projection for two hours each day. Our conversation would be by mental telepathy. His form would be made visible to me by his power of materialization when I lit several floating wick incense burners containing perfumed oils from various herbs and plants. My two weeks in this retreat far above the clouds were to be spent entirely alone. Dr. Karoll and his family were not even going to enter the compartment for a moment, nor give me instructions on how to manage during my allotted time in it.

As Dr. Karoll maneuvered our craft near to one side of the capsule, I could see that there was a provision for the air car to make a pressure tight mooring at its entrance. In a moment I stood in the doorway to my meditation school room. I had no more sensation of our altitude or position than if I was stepping from one room into the next in Dr. Karoll's home.

There was no need for parting words between us. Dr. Karoll and Mrs. Karoll embraced me warmly and Alice pressed my hand. I understood Dr. Karoll had given detailed instructions and that all needed provisions had been made for me. I stepped empty-handed into the air lock vestibule, closed and carefully checked the door behind me, then turned and watched through the vision glass with mixed feelings as the air car drew a few feet away from the tower and shot skyward. I was going to spend two weeks entirely alone, alone in the midst of rugged peaks in the highest mountain range on earth, to seek to become more aware of my own soul and my relationship with the Source of all life. Immediately with this thought came a surge of joyous anticipation.

I began to examine the interior of my meditation capsule in the sky. It was conducive to reverence and awe and wonder. Instinctively, I knew what my first actions should be. I gave my body a thorough cleansing in the sparkling clean, efficient shower and washroom provided, a vigorous rub down, and then applied a thin, lightly perfumed lotion. I donned the meditation attire provided me which was a vibrant deep lavender one piece suit . It was lined with a fine weave cotton throughout and the exterior was a loosely woven wool. This garment was cut to provide the freedom of a one piece coverall ski suit and had the quality of allowing the skin to breathe because of the fabrics used.

My clothing and all that I had entered with were placed in a storage closet. When everything about my person had been cleansed and put in order, I turned my attention to the furnishing of this unique structure. The egg shaped enclosure was around fifteen feet high. The entrance door opened into the lower level which part had the facilities mentioned and other provisions for the physical aspects of life. A ship ladder and trapdoor led up to the meditation chamber. When the trapdoor dropped and closed behind me, I stood in the center of a full dome of unbroken transparency which gave the sensation of standing on a cloud. Brilliant sunshine reflecting from snowy peaks revealed their jagged crests in clear outline.

I glanced toward the sun momentarily and found myself wondering why its rays and brilliance did not affect me adversely. When I looked directly at it, it seemed as though the glass dome was smokey at that area where its rays entered straightest. It looked to me like an illusion but later it became apparent that the dome was automatically made opaque where the sun's harmful rays would enter most directly during any particular time of day.

A planting strip made a full circle near the inside edge of the dome and a variety of exotic plants with exquisitely colored blossoms thrived. Under my feet was a soft standing pile rug, sky blue in color. Seven low tables, perhaps nine inches high and eighteen inches in diameter, were spaced around in a circle. On each was a large solid gold incense oil bowl. Each had its own design in deep relief on the side facing me. These pure gold bowls weighed possibly ten pounds each. The designs appeared to be religious symbols of different Mystery Schools. In the center sat a table just a few inches higher than the others that was large enough to sit upon in tailor fashion. The round center table had a heavy band of gold, possibly two inches square in section, running around its outer edge. Cushions of several different thicknesses and shapes were available. I felt pleasant radiant heat from all directions which, combined with refreshingly cool air, provided delightful physical comfort.

"David Alan Neuport," I was being addressed by a voice inside of my own mind and yet for a moment I was not sure if it could not be my imagination. "David," the voice spoke again, "don't be alarmed. This is Rama Sandlob, your meditation teacher. I am a Tibetan lama who was fifty years old when you were born back in the twentieth century. I am able to speak English but you are translating my thoughts into your own interpretation of them as you use the language. You may make conversation with me by simply directing your thoughts to me without speaking aloud but only forming them in your words."

"How wonderful!" I thought back. "It is an honor to me to be under your tutelage, sir. My school room exceeds anything that I could have imagined."

"The honor is mine, David. You are the subject of much interest among those in the earth who have developed psychic faculties. Your achievements of the past in bringing into the earth more knowledge of man's relationship to higher realms of consciousness are unknown to you at present. We know of them and give you the respect and honor which you are due.

"David, the influences that mold personality from the time of conception until the age of twelve make an incalculable difference in the achievements of an individual in a particular life. A soul entity capable of prodigious achievements when raised by enlightened parents may stagger amidst confusion, hardship and failure when it is subjected to unenlightened adults during its formative years. For your training it was needful for you to have a mother and father who were deficient in spiritual insights. Their confusion and frustration with their own circumstances were naturally passed on to you but this experience gave you the incentive to seek answers to the mysteries of life and to appreciate the internal struggle going on within others. While you have, in past ages, made a lasting contribution to the race, you are not nearly so developed or sensitive as many others who have distinguished themselves in history. Your intelligence is not so unusual nor is your sensitivity, but your powers of reason are exceptional. This combination made you more able to withstand the disintegrating forces of your times more successfully than many who are far more capable than yourself. This fortunate combination in you has enabled the God-Self within to use you to serve human society in difficult times. You have most to your credit the measure you have overcome selfish ambition. The wise of all ages have understood and taught that overcoming oneself, one's undisciplined emotions and appetites, is the very purpose of life. Service to humanity is the natural result of this self mastery."

Before going on with this strange conversation I had to pause and forcibly restrain my skepticism. When I had it sufficiently in hand I went on. "But, sir," I thought, "were there not many great composers and artists who were undisciplined in their personal lives, yet they gave much to mankind?"

"A discussion of this question is not appropriate just now, David. Meditation is the tool that will enable you to understand such apparent incongruities. We shall endeavor to keep your efforts in one channel. Tomorrow at ten a.m. you may light the incense burners for our first instruction period. In the meantime, you will want to become familiar with the entire meditation tower. Some of my assistants will influence your thoughts as you seek to be in readiness for tomorrow morning. God be with you until then."

"Thank you, sir, I shall be looking forward to seeing you."

I was alone with my own thoughts again. I spent another half hour looking at the panorama of jagged snow capped peaks that surrounded me. The sun was moving lower and the changing shadows altered the scene as I watched. After watching a breathtaking sunset, I decided to go down to the living quarters and explore its details. Just as I went down through the trapdoor, the impression came to me that my lavender meditation suit should be carefully hung in a place provided and a different outfit worn on the lower levels. The one piece meditation suit had feet and soles that felt like suede leather but the lower level garment, a soft gray in color, was in two pieces like an athletic practice warm-up suit and separate slippers were provided.

Information about what I should find and how I should conduct myself filtered into my mind. It was rather like I turned my imagination loose and thoughts were being created by it. My diet was to be entirely of liquids and I looked around to see where they were. Ah, the thoughts came, my liquids were to be prepared just before I used them from refrigerated vine and tree ripened fruits and vegetables that had been selected and stored for me. The device that would prepare the juice was already programmed to select the appropriate fruit or vegetable from its storage place and prepare it for me on a schedule. The diet had been determined specifically for the needs of my body and mind. First there would be a blood cleansing effect, then a nourishing period and, finally, stimulation of the endocrine system to raise my awareness and sharpen all of my faculties. This was to take place progressively over the fourteen day period. The highest mental and spiritual stimulation would be reached upon the twelfth day and be maintained for three days.

There was an exercise room at the base of the tower, if my impression was correct, and an elevator just large enough for one man would take me down. I began to look for the elevator which I had not noticed previously. Upon slipping into the cylindrical elevator and looking at the control panel, I learned that there were three levels at the base of the tower. The exercise room included familiar equipment with improvements. The most interesting to me was a versatile treadmill that could be set up or down to a steep angle, could be power operated at selected speeds and would keep mileage and time. A bicycle provided could be ridden upon it because the speed of the treadmill and its angle were remotely controlled from its handle grips. A ladder, similar in operation to the treadmill, had a gauge which gave readings in foot-pounds and in decimals of one horse power while it was climbed. Its speed was automatically controlled by the rate it was climbed. It was intended that I should spend several hours each day in the exercise room. Meditation, exercise, listening to music, reading, playing chess for recreation with a Tibetan monk by means of a glowing, remotely synchronized pair of chess boards, and being tutored by Rama Sandlob were all to be done alternately to a carefully worked out schedule. My willingness to undergo the training had been established and thus, these informative mental impressions told me, help would be given me by way of strong hypnotic-like mind force that would be applied as needed to overcome any weakness of will on my part. That thought made me shudder a little because I knew my schedule included a twice daily plunge into a tank of ice cold water freshly drawn from a deep well. I had been wondering just how they were going to get me to do that by mental instruction alone!

Above the exercise room there was a room for physical therapy with provision for steam baths, osteopathy, internal irrigation and the use of various rays. When a person required such treatments in preparation for advanced techniques of meditation, one skilled in these administrations would accompany the student for a few days. Above this was the music, reading, chess and relaxation room. The taped musical recordings were on units about the size and shape of a thimble with the fine magnetic wire winding between two spools inside of it. There was music with power to heal the body, the nervous system and to stimulate spiritual faculties.

The reading material included adventure stories and humor, as well as profoundly spiritual writings. I questioned in my mind why all of the literature was not of a devotional character, then I thought I became aware of someone laughing. "Evidently you have forgotten how the Bible read," was the thought that broke into my own train of thinking.

Without even raising my eyebrows at this invasion into my private thoughts, I responded, "What part are you referring to?"

"Surely one could not read the Old Testament account of Saul, King of Israel, and all the details of the story of David without finding high adventure, humor, pathos and every element of human emotion that is portrayed in the best works of Shakespeare. If one will allow his natural powers of intuition and imagination to reconstruct the scenes as he reads the Bible, he will experience a fascinating adventure."

Conversation in thought took only seconds. As rapidly as an idea formed itself in thought, it was possible to absorb it and respond. Rama Sandlob's assistant continued on with information about the meditation tower and my use of it. He told me how the designs on the golden bowls aided Rama Sandlob to make himself visible. By mind power he could organize the matter and energy which was made available while the incense oils were burning. It was an application of the principles that Moses embodied in the design and construction of the Tabernacle, the Ark of the covenant and the Mercy Seat and its accessories to enable Spiritual Beings of a high order to make themselves manifest to the high priests who were guiding Israel.

The same natural laws operating at lower voltage, so to speak, allowed the materialization of Rama Sandlob in the meditation dome.

All of this information pouring into my mind so rapidly began to make me feel agitated and nervous. I pointedly asked to be left alone with my own thoughts so I could relax. A mental impression of assent to this request came quickly, and then I had a distinct sensation of the departure of my mental telepathy visitor.

If my first few hours were as remarkable as this, I thought to myself, what will transpire in fourteen days?

CHAPTER 27

Rama Sandlob

"Tell all the truth but tell it slant,
Success in circuit lies,
Too bright for our infirm delight
The truth's superb surprise;

As lightning to the children eased
With explanation kind,
The truth must dazzle gradually
Or every man be blind."
—*Emily Dickinson*

Slowly a bluish haze began to gather before me. I watched it with growing unbelief from my position facing East while sitting tailor fashion in the center of the meditation dome. A form was taking shape from thin air. It became progressively more opaque and distinct until at last a man, ageless and ancient in appearance, sat opposite me. In the Hindu meditation posture of the full lotus, erect and motionless, he sat at the same level as myself about five feet in front of me. I say, 'he sat,' because I don't know quite how else to say it. Actually, he appeared suspended in air, as though supported on an invisible flat surface. His robe was the saffron color identified with the Tibetan lamasery. Simplicity in attire, shaved pate and a wisp of a beard from the bottom of his chin, marked him as the traditional figure of a Tibetan sage.

In the study I had made of psychic phenomena, the question of materialization had often come to my attention. Several of my acquaintances had witnessed these phenomena. There was extensive evidence including photographs and patiently gathered data from many sources to confirm that such was possible. I had examined documentation on this subject to be found in such volumes as *Human Personality and Its Survival of Bodily Death*, written by F.W.H. Myers. There was little basis for me to be skeptical of the possibility, and yet...yet, my mind rebelled at what my eyes were reporting.

"Honored friend, many of your brothers send greetings to you through me." The words sounded inside my head. There was no visible sign of movement from the figure before me. The expression in the eyes and face conveyed enough that more was unnecessary. My mind and my senses were at odds with each other and the conflict was

179

occupying too much mental energy for me to respond.

"You have many friends in the Unseen who are assisting you, David. This phantasm before you is to help you recognize we are here. It is needed to give your sense mind a focal point. This visible form you see is a projection of the astral body of Rama Sandlob. It will hold your attention and enhance your ability to make an attunement to the unconscious mind of Rama Sandlob. Address your thoughts to this astral form as you would speak words to a visitor who brought his physical body with him."

I was still unable to speak, yet I had no fear that my silence would seem discourteous toward my visitor. I knew all my emotions and thoughts were like an open book to this mind that was symbolized before me in an opaque haze. It must have been at least ten minutes before I was able to adjust myself to making conversation with a ghost, or phantasm, or hallucination, or perhaps, an astral projection of a Tibetan lama almost two hundred years old. I felt the need to be very respectful.

"Sir, it is a great honor to me to have you accept me as a pupil. Your reference to my 'brothers' who greet me through you is heart warming. May I ask the identity of those who call themselves 'my brothers?'" I sounded stilted.

"It is God's gift for me to be with you this morning, David. Through you the joy of fellowship with my Maker is offered to me as I seek His Face in yours and as He reveals another facet of His Own infinite beauty to me in you. My God walks the earth in every human being. Learning to know you, David, is learning to know another portion of Him and to serve you is to serve my Beloved Master."

I was quiet again for another ten minutes or so. These words seemed so pregnant with meaning that they ran through my mind again and again. I could feel my own powers of comprehension being stretched to absorb their implications. Somehow my usually limited attention span was not hindering me. Perhaps I was receiving the needed assistance to focus my mind from Rama Sandlob but I could not tell. I decided not to pursue the question referring to the identity of those Rama Sandlob spoke of as 'my brothers' who greeted me. Rather, I think I should say I was influenced to drop the question because it would be distracting and personal.

"Your appearance in so strange a manner is difficult for me to get used to. The thoughts you presented are profound and beautiful and it humbles me for you to address me as one whom you would serve. Something like a symphonic chord echoing after a clear single note sounded in my thought processes with each word you spoke. It was as though you taught me volumes of religious philosophy while you spoke only a few words. I feel like I comprehended broad concepts of religious philosophy and saw them woven into one great harmonious pattern. All this is now vibrating through my whole being like it was being imprinted upon each cell."

"You are not being taught anything, David, in the ordinary sense of the word. Long had erroneous thinking about the process of learning hindered man from understanding himself. No man can teach another. All shall one day be conscious of the infinite knowledge within. Each of us is in the process of being re-awakened to his former consciousness of God's wisdom and power within."

"That sounds like the teachings of Plato," I said.

"It is, David," said Sandlob. "The story of Snow White, of Cinderella, and Sleeping Beauty are examples of how spiritual truths are symbolized to aid the awakening of each soul to its real nature. Told fully and accurately, these ancient fairy tales ennobled and purified the thinking of the child. The child identifies itself, or a facet of its own nature, with each character of the fairy tale. The witch, for example, always trapped by its own evil devices and often burned alive, is identified by the child with the tendency to do evil which it finds in itself. The virtuous hero or heroine of the fairy tale, though tried to the uttermost, is always honored if they persevere in virtue to the end. Only in the half world of physical appearances do good or evil deceptively appear to go unrequited in kind. The classical fairy tales from ancient times were given by inspiration of God to serve man's spiritual needs just like the Bible. They have the power to awaken the soul to its true nature and destiny. Pioneers in the field of psychology like Carl Jung and William James saw fairy tales in this light."

"Why, it was popular to belittle fairy tales and change them in my times. Editors took out their characteristic elements like the inevitable reward for good and punishment of evil," I exclaimed. "Unrealistic, said the educational authorities."

"Yes, David, that error made them dull to children and contributed to the absence of sharply defined moral values among your leaders and the educated people of the land.

"There is hardly a person, David, who will not respond constructively to the right approach to his mind. Written on the subliminal consciousness of all is that inner knowledge which may bring forth a recognition of any truth. Man's innate desire is to see order and beauty and justice in the earth and his knowledge of how to bring it about is mirrored by his great religious teachers. The soul is Sleeping Beauty, and Prince Charming is Christ."

After making that statement, I noticed that Rama Sandlob was beginning to become transparent and fading away from before me. I quickly spoke in surprise. "Are you about to leave, sir?"

"Yes, David. You have much to think about and meditate upon. There will be unseen entities who will be working with you between now and tomorrow. Until then may you be guided and blessed by the Master within."

Rama Sandlob was gone and I sat silently in deep thought for some time before descending through the trapdoor to follow my scheduled routine.

CHAPTER 28

Cancerous Thinking

"I think lightly of what is called treason against a government. That may be your duty today, or mine. Certainly it was our fathers' duty not long ago; now it is our boast and their title to honor. But treason against the people, against mankind, against God is a great sin, not lightly to be spoken of."
—Theodore Parker

I was again sitting quietly in the meditation dome for it was approaching the time for the second visit from my Tibetan instructor. I made all the preparations for meditation with regard to physical cleanliness, and followed the ritual for mental-spiritual cleansing according to the outline given me. The ritual was concluded by listening to music composed upon a quarter tone scale. My mind was cleansed from mundane thinking by prayer. I sought to move into inner silence as I slowly chanted the sacred sound, Aaahhrriiieeeoooouuummm, sounding the chant smoothly, I formed each vowel by gradually changing the shape of the mouth cavity with my cheeks and tongue. A spine tingling awareness of beauty and power expanded inside me until it made me unconscious of ordinary physical sensations.

At first, his presence was like the sensation one feels when there is a static electric charge in the air. Then, as I watched, his visible form took shape before me. Rama Sandlob projected a pleasing sequence of syllables into my mind. I assumed them to be words of a language that was incomprehensible to me. The cheerful and light hearted sentiment they seemed to convey was, "the top o' the morning to you, David."

"And the same to you, sir," I answered involuntarily, smiling broadly.

Rama Sandlob smiled at that comment and said, "I wrapped my greetings around the thought of foreign sounds and you understood me perfectly, David."

"Now just a moment," I said, "on that basis we would need no languages at all. We could convey thoughts by imprinting them upon primitive sounds."

"When the intuitive faculties are functioning normally, this would be true," said Rama. "You have the record of the gradual loss of this ability faintly preserved by the story about the tower of Babel."

"Now, will you tell my why we need vocal sounds at all. Why not use thoughts alone?"

"Once we were able to do that. Now we need sounds for a crutch. You might visualize the reason from a parallel drawn with your method of broadcasting by radio," answered Rama, smiling. "Thoughts are vibrations of a different character than sound. Each spoken sound is like the radio carrier wave and includes the thought wave just as the radio wave includes the sound wave. From audible sound the intuitive faculties extract the inaudible thought vibrations that were impressed upon the sound waves. The mind amplifies them into intelligible thoughts to a greater or lessor degree, depending upon the hearer's intuitive faculties. By this power to imprint thought vibrations upon sounds, a thought picture given by a highly evolved person may tell more than a thousand words by themselves could ever do."

"I do not see why we need to use vocal sounds at all," I said, "if the human mind is both a transmitter and receiver?"

"They were not needed when men were truly honest in their communications with each other. Sounds to help us communicate came into use gradually as man departed farther and farther from his Maker. Over the centuries, they were crystallized into the limiting forms of language. Because of the deceptive use of simple words and sound, the intuitive faculties were dulled more and more. Words will not be eliminated again but the need for them in person to person communication will be diminished in time as man learns not to misuse either words or thoughts in an attempt to deceive his brother. Right-use-ness will bring the restoration of the normal faculties of the soul, or psychic powers."

"Then our built-in radio transmitter-receiver sets for thoughts will be in good repair again," I commented thoughtfully. I felt I understood this discussion better than when Dr. Karoll and his family talked about it.

"Your comprehension is excellent, David. It proves your own psychic receiving set is functioning," Rama Sandlob stopped addressing thoughts to me after these words and I felt he was offering me the opportunity to think about other questions.

For several minutes I thought back to the period just prior to the collapse, as I remembered it. I thought over what I knew, or thought I knew, about astral travel. Would Rama Sandlob have been using his powers of astral travels then to make himself aware of events occurring outside of Tibet? I wondered to myself. Astral travel is not necessarily enlightening, I had been informed. Since one's powers of comprehension may be as limited by the ego as they are in the ordinary physical consciousness, one does not necessarily gain understanding by astral travel.

"Sir," I asked hopefully, "can you tell me about the events of the year 1984? It is hard for me to imagine what made my friends abandon me in a cave while in a suspended animation coma."

"Possibly I can, David. You see, I participated consciously in the great battle that was being fought in the thought world of the earth. Those who were attuned to the Infinite Spirit found themselves involved in the struggle to preserve our school room, Earth, from desecration. Have you a particular question in mind?" asked Rama.

"How did it take place and why?" I asked. "Dr. Karoll told me something about it but I should like to know more."

"That's a pretty broad picture to cover, David. A large book could do little more than touch the surface. On the other hand, the question is elementary with regard to the principles involved. We can make a comparison of America in her dying days with a self indulgent human being, a person whose misused body has become loaded with the poisonous wastes from his excesses. As his self destruction progresses, he is less and less able to render a useful service in exchange for what he seeks to satisfy himself. His cravings enslave mind, as well as body, and so with craft and dishonesty he seeks to obtain what he wants. At last, in a state of physical, mental, and moral wreckage, he departs his body because an abused vital mechanism suddenly gives ways."

"A shocking comparison, sir," I said.

"More appropriate that you might imagine, David."

"But, sir, a nation is made up of individuals and its actions can hardly be compared to those of a single individual."

"To the contrary, David. The comparison is very real. There is the physical body with its individual cells and organs and there is the nation with its individual members, its organized government agencies and its various industries that each serve functions similar to those of organs in the human body."

"In a way, I can see what you mean, sir," I said.

"Then you can see a parallel to the human body in the effect upon physical aspects of land, air and water of a nation which does not maintain control of its unwholesome tendencies. What was called free enterprise became the tool for enslaving the common man. Just as surely as a self indulgent individual will experience physical limitations through sickness and, finally, death, so did the nation. When groups sought to have unlimited resources to indulge their whims, the masses had to be enslaved and crushed. Yet corrupt government can only exist when selfish thinking is rampant throughout the land on the individual level. It takes the selfish thinking of the masses to create a tyranny. Natural law brings upon the masses the outpicturing of their own thoughts. To force the people of any nation to accept pollution of land, air and water, corruption of the morals of youth with debasing entertainment, destruction of physical health with improper food, conscription of the nation's youth for aggression and disregard for the common people of backward nations, hinges upon the moral compromise of each person who contributes his thought power to support these activities. The fatal disease in the nation of America could well be equated with cancer in the physical body," said Rama.

"Cancer," I said, "hmmmm, what particular activity in the nation was like a cancer in the human body?"

"Many were, David," said Rama. "You might say that cancerous thinking was widespread and those who were especially successful in applying it in business were highly respected."

"You have confused me, sir," I said. "How can you compare any business to a cancer?"

"The nature of the cancer is that of a parasite. It multiplies its own cells by drawing what it needs away from the useful parts of the body. The cancer grafts itself into an organ, absorbs nutrients and grows ever larger and larger. It throws off waste like all growing things but has no constructive function to balance this. Its purposeless growth is like a human living a selfish life in society. It blights or kills the body of its host. Cancer is a disease expressive of short-sighted self interest," said Rama Sandlob, "in its most elementary form. Stockholders, like cancer cells that have invaded an organ in the human body, may become parasites. They may draw upon the productivity of others to sustain themselves and multiply their kind but contribute nothing."

"We had lots of shortsighted self interest in America but I never thought of it in those terms," I said. "A stockholder was a parasite? Those are hard words."

"Usually things are neither black nor white but some shade of gray, David. The cigarette industry of your times was, possibly, the most obvious example of shortsighted self interest. Seldom acknowledged was the fact that such an industry could not exist a day unless the common people were individually willing to compromise their personal ideals by serving it in one way or another. The existence of the vast cigarette industry revealed the extent of shortsighted self interest on the part of the masses throughout the nation. Each store keeper who sold any product he knew in his heart was harmful to his brother, each parent who did not object to their advertisement, each employee in advertising who did not refuse to aid in preparing copy for harmful products, each newspaper owner who allowed his paper to promote them; these individuals were guilty of cancerous thinking. The cigarette industry did not represent crime against humanity by a small faction of wealthy persons motivated by greed. Not at all! Every person who knowingly aided a harmful industry to function revealed his own willingness to prosper at his brother's expense and even to be a director in the activity. Every person who knowingly cooperated with his government when he believed it was perpetrating the harm of another nation or participated in the manufacture or distribution of a product he believed injurious to man or his environment, was, like a cancer cell in his flesh, committing treason against the human race."

"Then the kind of thinking that enabled the cigarette industry to flourish you would say caused the collapse of the nation?" I asked.

"That's right, David."

"Dr. Karoll connected the money system with the cause of the collapse," I said.

"This would be like saying a self-indulgent old man suddenly died because he happened to have apoplexy."

"Then Dr. Karoll meant that the money system was just the weakest link?" I asked.

"It's hardly possible to say it that way and be accurate, David," said Rama. "You see, cancerous thinking, that is the desire to get value without giving an equal value in exchange, had pervaded every level of your society. The danger of this error in thinking should be as obvious as the danger to health of a cancer in the flesh. Great corporations which originally prospered because they served the people gradually became perverted to serve first the interests of their stockholders. It was like observing a cancerous growth becoming engrafted into the flesh of a man's heart to see the politicians and those employed by the government putting their personal interests above those of the nation."

"Your analogy is shocking, but is clear enough," I said.

"This history of the rising and falling of civilizations," said Rama, "is the record of the see-sawing of life giving and disease producing thought. Noble thoughts produce health in nations just as in the human body. An elevated spirit demands obedience from mind and body. Disciplining all of his appetites, the noble man lives to serve others and uses his body as the instrument to make application of his ideals. A selfish human life is like a cancer cell and a minority that prospers by enslaving the common people is parallel to a malignant tumor. The enslavement of the cells of the body in an individual to serve his own sensual desires is like enslavement of the working classes of a nation. When a nation will allow mass production of contraceptives instead of teaching the virtue of continence to its people, we have cancerous thinking gone wild. To do this is akin to bringing down the curtain on the closing act. Many variations of cancerous thinking though there be, the most critical and destructive relates to the misuse of sexual powers on an individual level."

"Your analogies cover so broad an area, sir, almost all of the nation's troubles could be said to come from cancerous thinking."

"You might sum up all of man's travail, individually and collectively, by saying that it stems from selfishness, David."

"This point of view is difficult for me to accept without reservations. One individual we find born into circumstances which create problems with selfishness that are almost insurmountable. Another enters into the world with an opportunity presented that engenders his development into a superior person. Am I having a problems with words, even though you are conveying thoughts directly into my consciousness? Shouldn't the frame of mind we are calling selfishness be called ignorance? Is it not ignorance rather than selfishness when one creates painful destiny by disobedience to the laws of nature?"

"Oh, David, you are trying to oversimplify the question now. Stop and think a moment of the parallel that we have drawn between error in the individual and in the nation and then ask yourself these questions:

"Was there anyone who did not know in his heart that it was wrong to pollute the pure natural waters of a beautiful land?"

"Was there anyone who did not know it was wrong to allow any human child to be raised in the slums?"

"Was there anyone who did not know that it was wrong to furnish war weapons to other countries?"

"Was there anyone who did not know that it was wrong to permit advertising and entertainment which undermined the morals of youth?"

"Well," I commented, "it still looks like ignorance to me."

"No reasonably intelligent person could plead ignorance," Rama answered slowly. "It was not ignorance of the harm being done when those who owned factories dumped polluting wastes into streams. The right to pollute was a source of profit. They were in a position to use income gained through inexpensive disposal of waste in streams for lobbying or for legal assistance to obstruct efforts by the public to bring corrections. The plant workers as well as the owners were keenly aware of the foul injustice done posterity by the destruction of the natural environment."

"I'm not sure, sir, but I think you have just expressed your agreement with me," I said.

"Why do you say that, David?"

"Because of your belief that each individual meets himself in his personal circumstances, be they good or ill," I said, "and inherits the environment that, unbeknown to himself, he helped create."

"Words, words, words! How they do obstruct the understanding!"

We were both silent for a space of several minutes. During our silence Rama Sandlob projected ideas into my mind without using words until I responded, "All right, all right, sir, I follow you. I do not know how to use the graphic language you just used on me but I could not fail to understand it." I laughed out loud as I saw how ridiculous a position I had taken.

"Oh, you are using this language all the time, David. This is why no one takes offense with you. We understand what you are trying to say and we see how you have misunderstood our thoughts. Now, to get back to the question of equating ignorance and selfishness, suppose you re-state your view."

"Well, of course, I see that it is not so simple. The desire of individuals to take care of their families and to have the best that life offers for themselves is not evil or wrong or selfish in itself. It only becomes so when they set themselves apart in consciousness from any member of the race and are willing to satisfy their own needs by activities which place them out of harmony with the whole of society. In each individual we see the same conflict between desires and urges seeking expression within his own body that we see between factions within nations or throughout the earth. The man who does not control his appetites is well aware of the harm suffered by other members of his body, yet lacking incentive to do otherwise, may persist in an indulgence until it deforms and humiliates him. The desires and appetites of the physical body are good and serve needed functions. The key is to maintain balance among them. This can be done when the welfare of the entire organism is placed above its separate parts. Just as the individual human body is a functioning whole, so is the race a whole made up of many parts. In the long run, no one may prosper at the expense of another. All are equally dependent upon the whole. In his ignorance of the price he will pay a man willfully chooses to commit the only sin, the sin of self separation, or … selfishness."

"You have the picture, David," said Sandlob. "You could have stated that selfishness was not a matter of being ignorant of the results of wrong doing but a lack of faith in the Immutable Laws which govern the universe. This is just another way of saying error results from unbelief in Divine Justice. God is LAW as much as He is LOVE."

With that Rama Sandlob slowly faded away from my view and I experienced his "God be with you" as a three dimensional thought form of exquisite beauty.

190

CHAPTER 29

It Can Be Humiliating

"The Deity said: O dear friend! None who performs good deeds comes to an evil end. He who is fallen from devotion attains the worlds of those who perform meritorious acts, dwells there for many a year, and is afterwards born into a family of holy and illustrious men. There he comes into contact with the knowledge which belonged to him in his former body, and then again works for perfection."
—The Bhagavad Gita

Nights were an adventure in consciousness and as I awoke in the morning a sense of gratitude flooded over me. Sleeping was not the same to me for I was having new experiences and seeing differently; there were lovely colors and forms, music of surpassing beauty, and I saw thoughts as living things more real than physical matter.

When he materialized before me in the morning, Rama Sandlob affirmed meditation was the key to all I sought. "The soul must retrace its steps, but the way, though narrow and straight, should be joyous. Presenting oneself to God each morning with thanksgiving for the gift of consciousness and a prayer for direction is the way. Then, through meditation, will come the guidance, the incentive, the power and joy," were his words.

He instructed me to hold Christ before me, restrain my mind from entertaining thoughts, direct it to a point between my eyes and hold it there. To encourage me, he made reference to an incident in the Bhagavad Gita. It was when Krishna had just advised Arjuna to practice restraint of the mind: Arjuna thought over his instructions and answered that he believed it would be easier to restrain the wind from blowing than the mind from wandering. "Yes," said Lord Krishna, "this is so; nevertheless, if you persevere you will succeed."

Then Arjuna thought about the disciplines set before him and how all his earthly ambitions had to be abandoned. What, he asked, should be his fate if he spent his life in the effort at self discipline but failed to achieve the purity necessary for union with Krishna? Would he not have lost everything, he asked, having renounced earthly goals on one hand and failed to attain the prize of overcoming death? The

191

Hindu manifestation of I AM answered that his effort would not be lost. He would be born back into the earth to a family well advanced in spiritual knowledge, be awakened to the spiritual insights he had previously attained, and go on. Thus he would advance from one life to the next, laying up divine treasures, treasure in heaven, until at last he recovered all his God-like qualities and was restored to at-one-ment with his Maker.

Instructions for meditation were contained in the Gita and, although details were lacking, said Rama Sandlob, had I made application with perseverance, they would have shown me the way to rebuild my atrophied soul faculties while I yet lived in the twentieth century.

"David," said Rama Sandlob, "we are going to help you now to reawaken skills in meditation you learned in Egypt with Amenhotep IV, in Greece under Pythagoras, and in Palestine as the pupil of an Essene teacher for almost two years starting just a few months before Jesus began His ministry."

"How can you do that," I asked, "since in this life I have done so little? I read the Gita in my study of religion and found the teachings fascinating, but to practice them is quite another thing."

"From your interest in psychical research, David, you are familiar with accounts about persons who suddenly acquired abilities which ordinarily take years to develop. Speaking in foreign languages, sometimes in ancient or lost tongues, was not uncommon among certain religious sects. You also heard of persons who acquired overnight the ability to play a musical instrument or sing with outstanding virtuosity. These phenomena were recorded but not much understood in your times. Educators could hardly give recognition to these possibilities without altering established theories about the mind and its source."

"This is true, sir," I said. "These phenomena attracted my attention because of my interest in improving education of children as well as improving my own mind. I satisfied myself that some cases of 'speaking in tongues' were not meaningless babble. I found genuine cases of individuals speaking a language to which they had never been exposed. However, to my knowledge, they were never able to tell what they had said. How could there be value for one to experience this babbling even if it was genuinely a strange language?"

"To awaken formerly acquired abilities in you, David, it is necessary that you believe in such possibilities. What you have said about persons unconsciously speaking languages which they learned in earlier incarnations is true. There may be a value to the soul, even when no one can tell what they said, because the experience serves as a release on an unconscious level. The point is that such memories exist which, potentially, may become conscious memories. Languages often filter through from the soul's record because, as with musical aptitude, it is the soul that has been conditioned to give the automatic responses."

"Well," I said, "I see why language is most likely to show up but why is there no recollection of the meaning of the words?"

"There is recollection, David, but it is below the level of the conscious mind. If there were no inner recollection of the meaning of the words spoken, there would be no emotional release for the individual. The memory of a life becomes a built in portion of the soul after death but consciousness as a personality disintegrates in the process. This shift makes the entire experience of a life shrink into just a page of the great volume which is the soul's records. Then what was the unconscious mind during life takes over as consciousness. The loss of the conscious mind is related to the disintegration of the astral body, and many factors enter into this process. Individuals deeply attracted to loved ones, parents who have a strong desire to serve their children, political leaders who yearn to guide the people rightly; these may delay the loss of conscious memories because desire holds them in the astral after physical death. To experience rebirth there must be a release from the conscious connection with memories of former earth lives unless one is free from personal desires. Memories are not lost but filed away by the soul on microfilm you might say. The separation of the soul from its astral shell is related to the dispersion into nature of the elements of the physical body and for this reason it is helpful to cremate the body or feed it to the birds as certain religions taught. When one departs the physical body, he is no longer able to derive satisfaction from eating and drinking and bodily associations. Depending upon the development of his mind and the use he made of his opportunities in earth, he may find himself in a hell of burning desires from his earthy thinking or in a heaven of gratification of his longing to express beautiful ideals and serve mankind in a spirit of selfless devotion. You will learn that things are neither all black nor all white after death but an infinite number of shades of heaven and hell are possible. There is a progression in this interim state from the painful toward the better experiences that one has created by his thoughts during life. Thoughts must be relived after death and judged."

"Please, sir, you are taking me into deep water and I'm not sure how what you are saying is even related to meditation," I said.

"All that we are telling you now, David, you have experienced many times. We are preparing you to recognize what you will see when you move into the consciousness in which you may contact this information. Through meditation you may have access to the microfilm viewing equipment so that you may examine the records of your own past."

"What an exciting idea!" I exclaimed.

"It can be humiliating and painful to the extreme, David."

"Hmmm," I responded slowly. The two of us remained still while Rama Sandlob gave me a chance to think over the implications of his last words. Without my knowing when or how the thoughts were entering my mind, I began to understand what such a review of my past might bring. Times of silence with Rama Sandlob were, if anything, more educational to me than when his words came like conversation inside my head.

"How can I prepare myself to endure such an experience?" I finally asked with a new respect for the ordeal I had chosen to undergo.

"You have been in the process since your first came into contact with Dr. Karoll and his family, David. As you put the false I in its place, you will be able to bear seeing what pride, selfishness, and self-aggrandizement have led you to do."

CHAPTER 30

The Cruel Atlantean

"One thing that every aspirant to the mysteries should remember is that growth is gradual and relatively slow, is the method of every natural process and this soul unfoldment is, after all, but one of the great processes of nature. All that the aspirant has to do is to provide the right conditions. The growth then will take care of itself normally. Steady perseverance, patient endurance, the achievement of a little every day, are of more value to the aspirant than the violent rushing forward and enthusiastic endeavor of the emotional and temperamental person."
—The Life of the Soul
Alice A. Bailey

I had been following the routine laid out for me with a faithfulness that was out of character. Evidently, my sincerity somehow enabled the unseen entities around me to assist my wavering spirit to take charge of its house of clay. The exercise and liquid diet gave me a sensation of internal cleanliness and lightness. I was losing a little weight and my spine was noticeably more flexible. The icy water plunges twice a day gave me a feeling of aliveness that was worth the shock of the stinging cold. My memory was definitely improving and I found myself able to recite poetry that I had not repeated for years. "Hah," I thought to myself, "years AND years!"

"Good morning, David." Rama Sandlob's incoming presence brought a spirit of quiet solemnity like purple mountains outlined against a deepening orange sky at sunset and, at the same time, sparkling gaiety like sunrise in springtime.

"Good morning to you, sir," I said with enthusiasm. "May I tell you about a dream which I had last night?"

"You certainly may, David. We are glad you do not feel constrained to withhold from sharing it."

"Well," I said in surprise, "I was inclined to, but now I think that your mind reading assistants may have dissuaded me, all unbeknown to myself."

"Perhaps, they did," said Rama. I thought I heard a chuckle with that.

"Sir, if you know what I dreamed, it would be far easier for me to say no more about it."

"Oh, no, David. You should tell me all that you are able to remember of this experience. We did assist you to have the experience but it was your own past which you were seeing. It will help you to profit from it, if you will bring it out into the open."

"Then it was actually me who did these things and they were not just figments of an overstimulated imagination?" I asked in disbelief and yet with the feeling that I knew all along Rama Sandlob would say it was myself.

As he listened silently, I unfolded before him the details. I had seen the activities of a tall man with a long, narrow face and a cynical sneer. His face was that of one whose cruelty was untempered by concern for the possible reaction upon himself of his deeds. It was as utterly cruel a visage as I had ever beheld and yet it bore an unmistakable and startling resemblance to my own. As I looked at the face, I could read the character of the man behind it. There was no belief in him that there was life after death, no hope that the pursuit of virtue could be worthwhile, no fear that his evil deeds would react upon himself and a brilliant mind to carry out any diabolical plan he conceived.

Rama nodded his understanding and sympathy as I went on with my account. The ancient civilization he lived in was technically advanced far beyond what I had seen in America but its leadership had fallen into the abuse of their technology to subjugate the masses. The actions of the man I observed were a reflection of his disbelief in any form of survival of bodily death. He was one of a small group who had control over technical forces that could be used to renew the youth of a physical body. He had already lived several hundred years and had participated in a number of murders to help his group maintain control of the rejuvenating equipment.

The most shocking part of the activities of this man was his use of technology to enslave people. This ancient civilization had discovered a method for radio broadcasting in a range of vibrations shorter than light waves. It allowed an infinite number of individual frequency bands. Each slave had a tiny receiving set implanted in his skull with electrodes projecting into the pain centers of his brain. Using skills the society had developed, this nucleus of men created a horde of eagerly obedient slaves. At the slightest sign of resentment or disobedience, a slave would be subject to having a tiny electric current stimulate the pain center in his brain. The receiver in his skull which delivered this current was so designed that its removal by any method brought sure death to the slave. If the device was used to discipline a slave, his agony was such that he fell to the earth screaming and frothing at the mouth. It was seldom necessary to apply it more than once but the slaves were given reminders of its effect at the slightest provocation. The same device was used to establish a secret guard and police force. They were compelled to protect the group in power. If one of those whom the police guarded was killed, the units in the heads of the guards would automatically be stimulated by a preset signal to torment them until they committed suicide.

The life of this man was terminated as result of a massive uprising led by some heroic slaves. The key slaves who had the initiative to lead the others were former noblemen and political enemies of the group in power. Their head sets were of a different design from those of the common slaves, having the same fail-safe mechanism as those of the body guards. As a precaution, to prevent the rebellion of these capable men, their pain transmitters were battery operated. Death of the evil leaders and destruction of the nation's power stations would not stop their transmitters from the fail-safe action that would drive these men to suicide. Having full knowledge of this, great personal sacrifice was involved upon their part. These men could not have hoped to survive their successful planning and participation in the uprising that freed the slaves.

"That was quite a story, David. It would not have been possible for you to have this error of your past revealed to your conscious mind had you not had the experience in the air car with Dr. Karoll's family. Self condemnation would drive you mad if you did not understand that Divine Justice is the reality behind all appearance of cruelty and injustice. You have not finished righting the errors you committed in that far off time, but you have been working on it since you learned to live by the Law of Grace. You set your feet on this new path some ten thousand years before the birth of Jesus."

"Thank God for that!" I said with feeling.

"You have made many mistakes since that time, David, but your direction has never again been so distorted. You might say that you hit bottom in that life and have been slowly overcoming the defects in your thinking since then. In your striving to undo the error of enslaving others you have become the sworn enemy of all forms of slavery. You especially despise the enslaving of men's minds by any means. Thus you agonized over the enslavement of common peoples' minds in your day through misuse of the channels of communications, even though the people seemed to be physically free and free from material want."

"Yes, sir, that is true."

After a thoughtful pause, I asked, "I wonder if you can give me insight into a life experience during which I undid some of these knots that I have tied?"

"We could do that, David, but is not appropriate for us to do it. In due time, you will learn these things on your own as you develop in meditation. It is far better for you to obtain such information first hand. For you, nothing less than your own personal encounter with the records within your soul will ever suffice. We would not deprive you of the thrill of accomplishment that this will bring you, nor risk lessening your incentive to pursue the priceless pearl of self knowledge by revealing anything prematurely."

"Ah, sir," I said, after several minutes of deep thought, "you do know my true desire in this matter. Only the access to these records myself could ever bring me satisfaction. I would be skeptical on the one hand and feel deprived of my rights on the other, should anyone make the path easier for me, or open up a short cut that I had not earned the right to use."

"God bless you, David."

"Thank you, sir. May His blessings be with you."

Rama Sandlob's presence gradually faded from before me and I set about my exercises and studies for the remainder of the day.

CHAPTER 31

The Power of Animal Sacrifices

"And they shall build houses, and inhabit them; and they shall plant vineyards and eat the fruit of them. They shall not build and another inhabit; they shall not plant and another eat: for as the days of a tree are the days of my people, and mine elect shall long enjoy the work of their hands."
—The Book of Isaiah

Throughout the remainder of the day following Rama Sandlob's description of my personal involvement in the enslavement of people with electronic devices, I mused upon what we had said. As a disillusioned American, I had felt the need to express dissent with government policy. I objected to the mind stifling of youth by our system of public education and lamented our failure to establish any intelligent policy for regulating the use of channels of communication. Now I had to look at myself as a former Atlantean archcriminal. I was guilty of enslaving people by direct interference with the operation of their minds. What a humiliating experience this was!

I had thought of myself as one of the relatively few who were painfully aware that America was not the source of blessings to other nations that the news media said she was. I could see how our technology and productive capacity had been perverted to produce wholesale misery and fear among downtrodden peoples. We exploited the common people of backward nations by our trade policies. Our financial giants stole their natural resources. In the small countries where the common people were kept in poverty and ignorance, our financiers could deal with the rich land owners to purchase the oil or timber or mineral resources. Instead of alleviating the poverty of the masses in such nations, we encouraged American private interests to legally steal the wealth that should have been their heritage. When the common people of backward countries began to struggle for better distribution of their nation's wealth, they found that American private interests claimed they owned the wealth of their land. If a revolution unseated a corrupt dictatorship and the common people would try to regain their rightful heritage they found their efforts sabotaged and their leaders assassinated by the very nation that was founded on the ideal of freedom. An American Agency dedicated to the protection of private interests abroad was authorized and financed to freely use every tool available to undermine the political power of groups that were favorable to the interests of the common people. Bribery, murder, and the instigation of revolts were activities of that Agency. It had unlimited government funds at its disposal and freedom from supervision by representatives of the public. It operated in secrecy. Its policies were directly contrary to the ideals for which the American people thought their nation stood. It was furnished all that modern science could provide to carry on its cruel treason against human decency throughout the whole earth.

I thought about the murder of President Kennedy which took place shortly after his announced intention to disband that Agency. Many Americans like myself believed that his murder was part of a conspiracy by corrupt influences in our government. The Justice Department, the FBI and the American Medical Association joined hands to amass a report of the assassination that seemed an elaborate smoke screen. Truly, I thought to myself, the nation had fallen into the hands of ungodly men.

"David, you had best dwell upon your own sins rather than those of the nation," the words cut into my thoughts like a knife. "The errors of your past were the result of your disbelief in the laws which govern in the lives of all individuals. Should you be raised from infancy in the same kind of environment as those toward whom your thoughts were just now directed, you could possibly fall into the same kind of error that you once pursued so energetically as an Atlantean." One of Rama Sandlob's assistants was evidently monitoring my thoughts and had decided that it was time to interrupt them.

"I think you have a system that is more effective for eavesdropping than any of the electronic devices so effectively used by that Agency," I said with wry humor.

"We are simply trying to help you to learn to think correctly, David. It is going to require mental discipline upon your part to overcome the habits of wrong thinking acquired from your years in a confused and spiritually ignorant society. Remember, those who acknowledge only a single life and one physical body for each individual lived in a darkened half world of apparent injustice. Neither the causes for the vast differences in circumstances of individuals, nor the great inequities existing among races could be understood or intelligently explained in your times."

"You are saying all of the abuse of political power and the great injustices suffered by the common people were not the wrongs they appeared to be," I asked.

"Under no circumstances or conditions, David, may the natural laws which operate in the lives of individuals be violated. No force can bring to a soul an experience which was not created by the interaction of his own thoughts and deeds with his own physical, mental, and spiritual environment. There is no injustice in the assassination of presidents, in the use of hypnotised victims to commit such crimes, or the deception of the masses with false reports, and farcical jury trials. Your emotions, as you form judgement while thinking of these things, will generate forces that must compel you personally, to return in confusion in a future time to such a society as you just left, unless you discipline your mind to think about realities instead of appearances."

"God save me from such a fate!" I said with feeling. Then I thought about what had just been projected into my mind. I applied my powers of reasoning and argued with myself over the possibility that I was in deep sleep and must be still dreaming away in my first month of suspended animation back inside the lonely cave in the Appalachians.

"Oh, come now, David, if you don't think you're really here with us in this meditation tower, then go jump into the ice water tank down at the lower level and see what that does for you." The humorous twist of having this response to my private thoughts made me grin widely.

"All right," I said, "go ahead and work on me for my sins. I guess I deserve it."

"It's good that you put it that way, David, for it gives us a basis to discuss the science behind the religious terminology that you are familiar with."

"Well," I responded to this telepathic communication, "I know that I have much to learn in order to get my intellect to feel compatible toward the concepts and teachings of Christianity."

"David, meditation will enable you to verify directly, clarify or discard the concepts we present you, as you exercise and develop your own faculty for communication with the God-mind within. Your inner discernment alone must be the final test and only means of evaluation of all data which enters the consciousness through these senses. Sooner or later, all will come to the recognition that they, like Apostle Paul, must get their religion directly from Christ within, for no authority is higher than the 'Still Small Voice.'"

"If you mean that each person must decide for himself what he believes, there will be as many different religions as there are individuals," I said.

"To the contrary, David. All are offspring of the One Force and each will eventually become conscious of this Oneness and of their own place as an expression of a particular facet of Divine Mind."

"Perhaps, then, you will give me your explanation of the uniquely Christian concept among the world religions that God had to have a blood sacrifice by a perfect man in order to forgive the sins of the humans He had created?"

"There is nothing unique about blood sacrifices, David. These have been used since the most ancient times to produce psychic phenomena in connection with idol worship. The black magicians and witch doctors cast spells, caused crimes of violence, and engaged the services of discarnates with the energy released by the shedding of the blood of animals. The techniques for accomplishing such things were being rediscovered in your times. There was a widespread revival of the practice of the black arts."

"But the Israelites made blood sacrifices and said that it was God's instructions for them to do it," I said thoughtfully.

"Yes, David, this is true. Remember, also, how they often became sidetracked and made blood sacrifices to the idols of the peoples whom they had conquered or who lived in an adjacent territory. Some of the Israelites even sacrificed their own first born sons to make atonement for their sins. They felt that they should take what was most precious to them and destroy it as a sacrifice to please an angry god. Can you, David, imagine worshipping such a god?"

"How could the people become so deluded?" I asked.

"Easily, David. Their priests had learned how to produce phenomena that the people could see and hear and smell. They had developed the techniques which enabled them to manipulate natural forces to create powerful thought forms that became visible, and were even able to use them to win battles with their enemies."

"Do you mean that all of the Old Testament stories about God demanding sacrifices for the sins of the people or for worship were actually just accounts of how the priests maintained control of the people with the aid of psychic phenomena produced by the practice of black magic?"

"It's not that simple, David. You can't just roll all the various stories about blood sacrifices into a lump and discard them as error. It wasn't like that. In Homer's story of Odysseus, he describes how the shades were able to be given temporary consciousness and could make themselves visible after an ox was slain to furnish them fresh warm blood to drink. Homer was recording just one of many different kinds of psychic phenomena obtained by making blood sacrifices. Odysseus was thus enabled to talk to some spirits of deceased persons with whom he was familiar. These shades were the astral shadows of the dead who had fought with him in the siege of Troy. His deceased mother was there also, according to Homer's tale. This is one application of blood sacrifices. The discarnates did not drink the physical blood, of course, but absorbed its life energy, which enabled them to materialize for a short time. Neither were they the reality we call the soul but only a shadow of the personality, according to Homer."

"There is surely no relation between that story and the elaborate ritual of blood sacrifices set up by Moses?" I asked.

"That's a good question, David. As a matter of fact, there is an interesting parallel between them. The Lord God who led the people out of Egypt should not be thought of as The Infinite Creative Energy of the Universe. The demand that he should have been is only one example of the immature thinking and the self-centeredness of a primitive people who think they are the only inhabitants of the universe. The Lord was a member of a more advanced race whose people are serving God by acting as guardians to the evolving human race on earth. The individual soul who was in charge of the horizontal pillar-shaped cloud, the great celestial ship, was appropriately referred to as the Lord God of Israel by Moses. His celestial ship was spoken of as a pillar of a cloud for lack of other terminology. The Lord God protected the fleeing Children of Israel with the advanced understanding of Natural Law at his disposal.

"The sacrifices were the means to enable the materialization of his form into our level of vibrations. These advanced beings were invisible to the human eye because they exist in another level of material which is more refined and at a higher vibrational rate. Moses was a man who had purified his own nature in order to serve the people under the direction of the Lord. This means that Moses raised the level of vibrations of his body and developed his psychic faculties. This enabled him to communicate with more evolved beings quite directly. It was for the priests that would need contact through their senses that the blood was required by their Lord."

"Then you would say that, by means of the blood sacrifice, they held what scholars of the paranormal called a full materialization seance? The Lord needed ectoplasm from animal blood to enable himself to appear to the priests? The very mention of such an idea seems irreverent in the extreme," I said.

"Not one thousandth as irreverent as the suggestion that the Creator of Heaven and Earth had to be pacified with the blood sacrifice of a Perfect Man before He could forgive the mistakes of the human beings that He, Himself, brought into existence."

"There must be some strange distortion of meanings here. It would seem impossible to believe such a thing. Surely such a teaching as this has concealed the true purpose of the crucifixion," I said thoughtfully.

"Not really, David. Anyone who sincerely seeks to lose himself in service to others is not confused or disturbed by the perverted meanings that are generated in the minds of those who are not yet ready to lose themselves in Him."

"Please explain more about the blood sacrifices which Moses was ordered to establish," I said.

"If you will think back over the Old Testament story, you will remember that there were very elaborate instructions concerning the entire procedure. To carry out the ritual properly demanded objects made from various metals, colored cloth, selected wood overlaid with gold, designs embroidered in cloth, precious stones, special garments for the priests that included metal breastplates and stones inset in certain patterns. So far from being a product of a superstitious tribe, a primitive people, behind all of this was a profound science. All was related to the vibrational makeup of the human body and the proceedings were planned to enable it to withstand forces to which it was not accustomed. The blood sacrifice also provided energy to raise the vibrational level of the physical body of the priest and enable him to communicate with members of the advanced race guiding the

Israelites. The inner chamber, the meeting place for the priests and the Lord, was designed to protect the priest and exclude interference by discarnate beings of lower realms."

"Well," I said, "I see now that the sacrifices were not for the Lord's benefit but for the people's. This makes more sense to me. I never could follow the reasoning behind God wanting to smell the smoke of burning flesh. But why all of the other sacrifices...the first born male of every clean animal killed as a sacrifice, for example?"

"A nucleus of souls who had chosen to serve the race were being prepared to be instrumental in bringing evolutionary forces to raise the entire human race to a higher level. This, of course, was the real meaning of the chosen people. The purpose of the sacrifices was to provide the energy needed by the angelic influences to cause changes in the Israelites' physical-mental-spiritual bodies. After the refinements were brought about in the body patterns of the 'chosen' souls, they were to incarnate into other races. By this means, the entire human race was to be infiltrated with their upgrading influence. As soon as the work on their soul bodies was accomplished, the blood sacrifices were intended to be discontinued."

"Sir, you are giving me an entirely different slant on the whole Bible," I said.

"Remember, David, this science of an advanced race of guardians was far beyond the comprehension of the common people," Rama's assistant continued. "The application of the science was necessary to produce the changes in the ether body of this dedicated group of souls. The Bible provides a history of these events which stimulates and renews the dedication of the "Chosen People." It speaks to the unconscious mind of all but especially to that small group of Light Bearers who incarnate again and again with the same dedication to serve the race."

"Well, then," I asked, "did Moses have a personal, man to man kind of relationship with the Lord?"

"David, if you will carefully read the story of Moses, you will realize that he was dealing with a Celestial Being, who seemed to have somewhat human emotions. On occasion, Moses had to plead with the Lord to talk him out of annihilating the entire tribe of Israel. This doesn't quite sound like the All-Merciful Father of whom Jesus spoke, does it?"

"Do I understand, then, that such beings were needed to guide the race because the physical-spiritual mechanism of the people in those days was too poorly coordinated for them to have the inner consciousness of their real God-Self?" I asked.

"Yes, yes. Such had not always been so, but this was the condition into which mankind had deteriorated."

"Then the Israelites truly were a chosen people and became superior to others through the help they received from an advanced race visiting earth in space craft. Their religious rituals were based on scientific knowledge of natural laws and raised the sensitivity of all their faculties. While the Bible may not give a clear picture of the science involved, yet it was actually describing a constructive use of a little understood form of energy released by blood sacrifices?" I asked.

"Exactly, David."

"Then in all nations the most superior people, whether in government, or music, or in science, were likely to be former members of the tribe of Israel, no matter in what ethnic group they were born?" I asked.

"Right."

"Evidently, they frequently were born Jewish, too," I said, "for I remember how often the finest musicians and writers and scientists were of Hebrew blood."

"Yes, this is true, of course. However, all of us are inclined to set ourselves above others in the wrong way. The Israelites, who had chosen to enter into the earth to serve their fellow man, became confused during some of their incarnations and used their superiority to take advantage of others. The Jewish people, as a group, became identified with the 'Chosen Race,' but the term did not refer to an ethnic group. It was when they were the purest and most humanitarian that they were the nation to which the true Israelites were attracted. The nature of the children born into any family group, community, or nation is determined by the law that like attracts like in spiritual matters. Nations rise and fall according to the ideals they hold. When they are elevated, those who choose to serve the best interests of the race enter into them. The sons of Belial were recognized as such by King David when they revealed their readiness to take unfair advantage of those of his followers who were injured or exhausted when it was time to divide the spoils. He used every method he could to overcome the destructive influence they were having upon the ideals of the nation."

"Well," I said, "every nation must be a mixture of some Israelites, some sons of Belial and then the masses who are neither."

"Right, David. Jesus made reference to this situation in denying descendence from Abraham to those who oppressed Him. Although they were of the blood lineage of Abraham, yet He identified them as sons of Belial because of their actions."

"What has been the solution to the question of racial prejudice and minority groups," I asked.

"Very simple and obvious, David. Each person is evaluated as an individual. Each is given a truly equal opportunity to show how well he can serve in the great work of elevating the human race. Those who serve the race well to bring beauty in art, music, dance, to improve science and government, are our most loved and honored citizens. Blood lineage or color are not even considered to be a basis to have an opinion upon the merits of an individual. To express an opinion on such a basis would be an evidence of very low intelligence."

"You make this sound like just plain common sense," I said. "Can you tell me why that considerations of family, race, creed and color so dominated the lives of people in my time?"

"Easily, David."

"Then, why?"

"Because various facets of human nature needing refinement were being worked upon by an effective method to bring individual progress, that of group therapy. Each nation, each ethnic group, each minority, each family represented a particular set of human traits which needed to be brought into balance among the individuals incarnating into it. Individuals can best learn about themselves by meeting group destiny coinciding with their individual destiny. Of course, this means their thinking was similar and so there were parallels in their physical appearance."

"Then there is actually more individual responsibility when ethnic differences are not considered among men?" I asked.

"The progressive development of mankind, David, is marked by increased individual responsibility, increased recognition of the uniqueness and importance of the place of each individual in the overall scheme. As the evolution of consciousness progresses, the need for various ethnic groups, creeds, religions, and all that they represent disappears. To present the incoming soul with inequities is no longer a function of the circumstances of birth. Now each person is informed of his own strengths and weaknesses. He learns the purpose of life, is offered every assistance and chooses what he, himself, is willing to achieve through self-discipline and effort. No man relegates another to a class or group, but each man establishes his own position in society. There is no misunderstanding or injustice. We do have classes of human beings with vast differences. The superior are making personal progress by guiding and teaching and inspiring the lesser developed souls. There is no resentment upon the part of the lesser evolved souls but deep gratitude and humility in the presence of more God-like souls who are their servants and benefactors."

"Sounds like Utopia to me," I said.

"It is a Utopian society. This dream has always been in the consciousness of the great minds of the earth. The founding of America was a turning point in the history of the human race. The concept that all men should be born into a society that presented equal opportunity for them to develop and express their individuality was the ideal upon which it was founded. Those same epoch making leaders are in the earth today improving upon the work they began with the Declaration of Independence and the Constitution of the United States of America."

I fell into a thoughtful inner silence. The invisible entity who had broken into my consciousness by his powerful projection of thoughts bade me good wishes and departed.

CHAPTER 32

The Blood of Christ

"For as the body is one, and hath many members, and all the members of that one body, being many, are one body: so also is Christ. For by one Spirit are we all baptized into one body, whether we be Jews or Gentiles, whether we be bond or free; and have been all made to drink of one Spirit."
—First Epistle to the Corinthians
The New Testament

I awoke with a keen sense of having had an adventure in learning during the night but with no definite recollections. It was as though some subject which troubled me and caused mental conflicts had been cleared up for me and this had brought a release. I looked forward to having Rama Sandlob's insight into what had taken place.

After carefully making all the prescribed preparations for personal cleanliness and donning my meditation robe, I lit the incense burners and took my place on the low table in the center of the Meditation Dome. The heavy gold objects I now realized were a scientific method to aid my spiritual organs to function more as they normally should. To me the word 'normal' had an altered meaning. With regard to consciousness, it now referred to a vastly superior awareness which I had not experienced but had been informed should be the norm for human beings.

The diet and exercise had improved my sense of well-being. The promised increase in alertness and psychic sensitivity was plainly evident to me. This was to be my last day in the Meditation Dome with Rama Sandlob. Dr. Karoll and his family would arrive just after meditation.

As I sounded the last note of the meditation chant, the inner silence flowed through me. The awareness of myself as vibrations like pure music grew in this silence. I found myself conscious of different tones reverberating within all parts of my body. I was free of physical sensation, but felt like I was a sphere of intermingling vibrations, an infinitely complex symphonic chord. Through all was a pulsing sensation with changing minor beats reminding me of the rhythm

209

of music from India. Arising through me, like an upward breeze moving in from below and funnelling out the top of my head, was a pleasant sensation which I cannot think how to describe.

I directed my attention toward the breath while I inhaled slowly and deeply. What took place I can only give a hint toward describing but I am sure that anyone who has had the same experience will recognize it. As the air entered into my lungs, it seemed that the physical breath was only a small part of the real breathing process. My whole body was breathing, or rather I should say every atom of it was drawing in and sending out energy. It seemed to me that I was in the center of the universe and that every atom of my body had a counterpart which was represented by a star in the sky. A strand, perhaps made up by a single line of linked atoms, connected each minute element of my body to its particular counterpart in the starry heavens. The process of breathing seemed to be an alternate taking in and sending forth of energy by each atom of my body through its connecting strand to its coinciding star. I saw myself to be a tiny unit but was momentarily lifted in awareness to be conscious of my place in the Grand Scheme and of my body as a functioning miniature of the universe. My relationship to The Universe I knew was shared by every member of the human race. All humans were truly equal, each uniquely individual, indispensable to its functioning, equally precious to the Creator, and our individual welfare inextricably intertwined with that of each member. We all were parts of the Whole and, collectively, we made up the body of Christ, The Church.

"Now you know, David." It was Rama Sandlob projecting words into my consciousness. "Never can anyone take from you the peace that you may possess by being true to the vision you now have."

"Ah...sir, thank you for those words," I said. "Surely, this experience must be a constant influence upon my thinking."

In response to my thoughts Rama Sandlob was silent and waited until I allowed the experience I had just had to reverberate through my whole being. I wanted every detail of it to be etched into my consciousness for all time. At length, I spoke of my deep gratitude to Rama Sandlob for his part in creating the conditions which had enabled me to have such an experience.

Again we fell silent as we sat there facing each other in the Meditation Dome. An hour passed slowly while I continued to listen to the music-like vibrations from within. Eventually, I thought about the sensation that I had when I awoke that morning and my desire to question Rama Sandlob about it. Before I could frame the question he responded.

"You had an inner awakening during the night to truths that long posed a stumbling block to you, David."

"Can you tell me about this, sir?"

"No, David, but we can help you to go back through it consciously right now, if you will direct yourself to remember it in detail."

I half closed my eyes letting in enough light to prevent images and faces from distracting me as they often did when I closed them. I fixed my attention upon my sleep experience, restraining my thoughts and confining my mind into a point between my eyes. I began to breathe slowly and evenly, while listening with rapt attention to the Silence.

Soon I began to be aware of the content of my dream. I could not say how the information came, or when, but felt that I understood what the dream had done for me. The release was from an intellectual and emotional block I had with Christianity over the teaching that "the Blood of Christ washes away all sin."

"It may help to fix it firmly in your mind if you will try to explain to me what you learned," said Rama Sandlob, taking advantage of his free access to my thoughts.

"It is so simple and beautiful," I said, "and it now makes sense to me. It is no wonder that I felt relieved, since my mind has been long troubled over these points."

"Be specific, David, and do not assume that I know what you are trying to say," spoke Sandlob.

"The intellectual impasse which I had with Christianity, sir, concerned such sayings as, 'the Blood of Jesus Christ, His Son, cleanseth us from all sin,' or 'Behold the Lamb of God which taketh away the sin of the world,' or 'There is none other Name under heaven given among men whereby we must be saved.' My mind rebelled at a concept of God which required me to embrace these sayings as the Gospel Truth."

"What do you think of them now, David?"

"They are simple Gospel Truth but the words mean something altogether different than their literal meaning."

"What do they mean?"

211

"First, I think that I should explain my former views upon them."

"By all means."

"All right," I replied. "The idea that a man could consider himself freed from obligation to correct the wrongs he had committed by saying he believed that the 'Blood of Christ' washed his sins away seemed irrational and this disgusted me."

"Understandably, David."

"Next, the idea that the Protestant Christian faith was the only true religion seemed infantile. That all others would lead their followers into a state of eternal damnation was irreconcilable with my insistence that the God I would worship must appear to be perfectly just in dealing with all humans. Consequently, the God of the Christians appeared to me to be a figment of the imagination of a narrow minded and vindictive people."

"Strong words, David," said Rama.

"The idea of worshipping a God Whose Own Son had to be crucified in order to satisfy His demand that sins of the men He created in His Own image be punished was ridiculous."

"You are making the Christian God sound unGodly," commented Rama.

"Beside this, the idea of doing good to obtain a reward or avoiding evil to keep from being punished is childish. No man of character cares a whit for either reward or punishment."

"Now your coup de grace, David," said Rama with humor.

"Human beings come into the world in widely varied circumstances of birth. The extent to which one's birth determines the religious belief of an individual makes the injustice of an exclusive salvation for Christians incompatible with the simplest concept of fairness, much less of perfect justice."

"You sounded like a 'God is dead' advocate to your Christian friends, I suppose, David." I imagined there was a twinkle in his eye when he said that.

"Well, I think it would be correct to say that they felt me to be strongly opposed to Christianity. However, few of them could make intelligent conversation about the Christian faith because they knew almost nothing of what the Bible said. It was rare to find a church-going-Christian who had read it through once, much more rare to find one who read it through several times and pondered upon it as I had done myself."

"It is easy to see that you did have an intellectual impasse with Christian teachings. How has this been changed?"

"I have found that everything about the Christian faith is not only compatible with my intellect but deeply satisfying to it. The idioms which were such stumbling blocks now seem lucid and beautiful in meaning."

"How does the Blood of the Lamb take away the sin of the world, David?"

"Let me first tell what the dream experience last night seemed to show about the meaning of the terms."

"Surely, David."

"This seemed to me to be a personal experience lifted from a memory of when I was a member of the Tribe of Israel. It was a time when the Children of Israel were keepers of animals, lived in tents and moved from place to place to graze the flocks. The language I found myself speaking had many idioms associated with our way of life. They can only be understood when their source is adequately described. The key word 'blood' referred to the 'will.' This idiom lingers still in our language, for we refer to it by phrases such as 'hot blooded' or 'cold blooded.'" The term arose from the way an animal acted when it was about to be killed."

"How did that come about?"

"When a lamb was brought to be slaughtered, it sensed what was to take place and submissively knelt before the man who was to strike off its head. Under the same circumstances the hog is enraged and tries to kill its executioner."

"What does the 'Blood of the Lamb' mean?"

"In those times, the idiom for the 'will in the individual to follow the highest monitions of conscience,' was simply the 'blood of the lamb.' You might say that the phrases 'the will to do the will of God,' 'the Blood of the Lamb,' and conscience all mean the same thing. When a man decides to violate his conscience, it does not resist him but submits to his will."

"What kind of a personal experience gave you this interpretation?" asked Rama Sandlob.

"In my dream I found myself discussing an Israelite neighbor with a fellow Israelite and mutual friend. We were both concerned over his conduct in a situation involving a woman who was not his wife. I found myself shaking my head sadly and saying, 'old Zeb surely is shedding the blood of the lamb.' Now, I knew exactly what I was trying to express even though I used terms that would literally translate just as I said them. In plain language, I had simply said that old Zeb was certainly going against his good conscience."

"How did Jesus get His title 'The Lamb of God?'"

"The whole series of idioms related to the Blood of the Lamb opened up through this dream of the past. I found that we Israelites expected a superior Man to be reincarnated among us from time to time, who was the World Teacher. This Man had overcome human weaknesses and no longer shed the Blood of the Lamb like the rest of us. Because of this He was called the Lamb of God."

"How does this relate to the saying that 'without the shedding of blood is no remission?'" asked Rama.

"Very reasonably," I said. "In order for anyone to mature, he must have the opportunity to learn through meeting his own mistakes. In other words, he must have an opportunity to violate his conscience...shed the Blood of the Lamb...and have his errors come back to him as destiny from one life to the next. Thus, he will eventually accomplish the remission of his own sins; for every latent human weakness must be expressed, recognized, and the correction sent back, that is, remitted."

"Excellent, David," said Rama. "Now tell me why it was necessary to shed the Blood of Christ?"

"This is the beautiful part above all else. Truly every last soul has been saved from endless confusion and error...hell...whether in the body or out, by the death of the Christ Jesus."

"How can this be and how can you speak of it as though it were already accomplished, David?"

"He showed the Way each soul may overcome the errors of its past. Jesus was the first man that re-established his own relationship with his Oversoul, the Christ in Himself, and thus became the first begotten of the Father. He showed the relationship that each soul bears to his God-Self. He proved that all mankind could do what he had done and made His Own Consciousness available to each of us as our Guide, showing all the Way."

"You will have to clarify that, David. You sound almost like a preacher talking from his pulpit on Sunday morning. Surely, you can do better than that," Rama spoke thus with a tinge of humor. "Now just how does one get his sins washed away by the Blood of the Lamb?"

I was silent for a moment as I tried to coordinate these words with the concepts they expressed. Then I said slowly, "The Blood of the Lamb is the will within the individual to serve the good of the whole race. When a man allows the Blood of the Lamb to dominate his life, he actively seeks to serve all mankind. He seeks nothing for himself. He will have nothing at the expense of his brother's welfare."

"How does that wash away his sins, David?"

"All must balance the score they have with the Universe. When a man fully allows himself to be guided by the higher monitions of his conscience, then he creates no more indebtedness. At the same time, he is doing acts of service not required of him by any law, but the law of Love. The old law of Moses defined how one creates imbalances or indebtedness. With the Law of Moses approach, only one error in a lifetime would return one to a flesh body to meet his error. Mankind needed to recognize a more constructive approach and to be shown that it could be successful. Balancing the score, washing away the sin by practicing virtue, is accomplished by giving more than one receives from the society in which he lives. Jesus' Life was a demonstration of The Way. He showed how to overcome the negative aspect of the Law of Moses by practicing virtue, by doing good that was not required of Him, and by accepting injury without so much as a thought of giving injury in return. Instead, He blessed those who despitefully used Him. This was a perfect demonstration of the practice of the Law of Grace."

"Now hold everything a minute, David," said Rama Sandlob. "You have just made it sound like a man has to work at getting saved. What are you going to do with the words of Apostle Paul 'By grace are ye saved through faith...not of yourselves...not of works?'"

It stopped me short to have this scripture quoted. I was silent as I waited for the inner guidance to show me how to answer this contradiction. We had shifted to a different century when we spoke about Paul. The idioms of another period of time and a different way of life for the Jewish people entered into the writings of Apostle Paul. He had been given an opportunity to acquire the finest education available and studied in Jerusalem under an outstanding leader among the

Pharisees. Finally, I replied, "I'm afraid I can't give a good answer to that question. All that I can say is that I'm satisfied that I know the way things actually are."

"You'll have to do better than that, David, or you will not hold the attention of my intellect. Why not take a few minutes more for meditation?"

Placing Rama Sandlob's question before my mind, I restrained myself from thinking and listened intently for the 'Still Small Voice.'"

"Well," I said at length, "we seem to have an especially confusing set of idioms here combined with a word that is almost universally misunderstood. The meaning of the word 'grace' has been distorted beyond recognition."

"Can you explain what you mean by that, David?"

"I think so, sir. In the usage of the times of Paul, doing works meant keeping both the letter of the Law of Moses and a whole series of conventions. And so, this term referred also to following rituals and making sacrifices outlined by Jewish Law. As used in the scripture you quoted, the term 'works' referred to effort toward becoming perfect in God's sight by keeping the Law of Moses and all the conventions that became attached to it."

"Then what did he mean in saying 'by grace are ye saved, through faith?'" asked Rama.

"The fuller way of translating this would have been thus: By putting into operation the Law of Grace, having the incentive provided by faith that God will uphold from one appearance in the earth to the next the Law of Cause and Effect, each soul may gradually release itself from its bondage to flesh. You might say, drop by drop 'the Blood of the Lamb,' the choice to serve rather than be served, washes away each soul's debts to the race."

"What is the Law of Grace, David? Are you saying people don't get a free ride into heaven by the Grace of God? Sounds like heresy to me."

I had to smile at having Rama Sandlob take the position of a so-called fundamentalist Christian. However, his question stumped me and I became thoughtfully silent. When I did not answer, Sandlob began to elaborate on the question of the Law of Grace.

"What had been fundamentalism was rather anti-intellectualism. Since Paul was a keen intellect, these intellectually insecure 'fundamentalists' did not comprehend what was the basic fundamental of Paul's teaching. According to Paul, every individual soul must turn to Christ within and not lean on outer sources of guidance, including the Holy Scriptures. The impact on his thinking from his personal experience with Christ was such that Paul did not feel that he should confer with the Apostles or ask their opinions about it. Instead, he went off to be by himself for three years. Always, he insisted that his personal contact with Christ was the Source of the Gospel he preached and that everyone must accept no authority except that of the Christ within."

"But Paul's writings are full of Old Testament quotations as well as the teachings of Jesus," I objected.

"Yes, David, that is true. He came to recognize the truth in the scriptures he learned so well as a Pharisee. But the essence of the Gospel preached by Paul was that through the contemplation of the Christ, His birth, Life, death by crucifixion, His resurrection and appearances to the disciples, any man could re-awaken in himself a conscious relationship with the Christ within. Such an awakened individual recognizes that his relationship with his fellowman is his relationship with his Maker, that 'inasmuch as ye do it unto the least of these, ye do it unto Me.'

"The Pharisees believed in reincarnation and in cause and effect, Karma, from one life to the next. Paul was very familiar with this. Jesus, Himself, said He was bringing nothing new. But Jesus never spoke harshly or critically to any person or group, no matter how the New Testament may read. What Jesus pointed out to the Pharisees, in His gentle and compassionate way, was that they were not putting into practice what they taught. He did not call them hypocrites but in kindness explained to them that they were deceiving themselves. He told them that they could not draw closer to God by being served but only by serving others, no matter how carefully they followed the letter of the Law of Moses."

"Hmmm!" I said. "He did say He came to fulfill not abolish the Law. But you would say then that He added the concept that it was necessary to do more than just keep it?"

"The Law of Grace, David, is simply the good side of the Law of Karma, 'Whatsoever a man shall sow, that shall he also reap.' The true meaning of charity is to practice the Law of Grace. Eventually, each of us must choose to lose ourselves in service to others. This choice puts us in harmony with the whole race and thus with the Mind of the race, the Christ Mind. As you experienced, each of us is a cell in a vast body, the Body of Christ. Each of us will attain to the state of consciousness that was demonstrated by the Christ Jesus."

"Thank you, sir," I said. "I think I understand what you have said because of my dream, much more even but cannot put it into words very well."

"Try, if you will, David, to tell me what purpose was served by the Virgin Birth?"

"This historical event translated into terms able to be comprehended by the five senses a very important spiritual reality that had become submerged in the consciousness of the race. It presented the pattern of how each individual must give birth within himself and by himself of the Christ Child. Each must give birth and nurture the Babe within his own soul until it grows and matures so that self will is altogether replaced by the will of Christ."

"Now, David, you can see why the story of the Christ Child is so important to children. Their intuition grasps the meaning of the historical event while the adult mind has closed out the intuition and embraces an intellectual concept based on the material aspects of it."

We were silent again for a time, until Rama Sandlob asked me to explain how mankind could be saved once and for all by the drama enacted at Golgotha.

"Of course, this is a concept that I once rejected vigorously. Without an understanding of reincarnation it was impossible to make sense of such an idea," I said.

"Then tell me how you see it now, David. How can this one event awaken or 'save' every last soul?"

"Well," I began thoughtfully, "all the phenomena of the Universe may be just a projection of my imagination, so knowing what I know is an individual state of mind. I am conscious of Infinite Love surrounding me and protecting my consciousness from any influence within or without that would harm it. I know that every soul shall become conscious of having this same relationship with the Source of Life. The birth, the death, and resurrection of Christ has been imprinted on the Universal Mind of Man to show each of us his relationship with his Maker."

"You will have to clarify that, David," said Rama Sandlob. "How could the life of one man have this power?"

"This, sir, I now see as a great mystery that confounded my intellect because I was learned in the laws of the material world. As you have said, in small children we find the intuitive faculties naturally taking precedence over the intellect. So, in this sense, one must become as a little child to understand. Upon maturing, the intellect is given first place in the life of an individual, and then the story of Jesus becomes an incomprehensible mystery."

"Can you explain this mystery, David?"

"The once for all power of the Christ life to 'save' the race hinges upon the existence of a Collective Unconscious Mind. Like a great river flowing down through time, the Unconscious Mind of the race contains all the information that exists or has ever existed in the minds of men. Each individual has the latent faculties to draw upon this vast storehouse of information. When a human being is in a physical body, information must enter his consciousness through the senses or be interpreted to the mind in terms of the sense world if it concerns data coming from other levels of consciousness."

"What has that to do with Christ being the Saviour of the world, David?"

"His life provided the means for the conscious mind of each soul entity to comprehend its personal relationship with the Maker. Without such means, the intellect, which deals in data derived from sense experience, stood as a stumbling block between the world and its Creator. Now the relationship between each individual soul and its Maker can be understood, for it was portrayed symbolically by the drama of the Christ Life. Once this relationship was implanted accurately in the minds of people on earth in terms of the senses, then the act of redemption was complete. As more and more members of the human race are awakened by contemplating upon His Life, the pattern is growing stronger and clearer in the Collective Unconscious Mind of Man. All religions that teach the oneness of the race were founded by the Christ and all merge in the Life of Jesus of Nazareth. He said, 'If I be lifted up before the race, I will draw all men unto Me.'"

Suddenly the room was filled with radiant figures in robes of white and I experienced a sense of being surrounded with dearly beloved companions from out of the past. I felt myself to be the object of good will and blessings from them all. The experience was overwhelming in sweetness and beyond my powers to describe.

In another moment there was only Rama Sandlob before me again and our final parting time had arrived.

"We have successfully awakened your recollection of former knowledge, David. We have all gained through the opportunity given us to serve your need. Our consciousness and yours are forever knit together by our common goal to elevate the Christ in the Earth. Hold fast to what you have and build upon it." After a brief pause, he spoke aloud for the first time in a deep ringing Voice.

"God bless you, David."

"God bless you, sir, and all who have been with you. My deepest gratitude will always be with you."

CHAPTER 33

Metallic Helium

"Those men who frame general rules from the phenomena and afterwards derive the phenomena from those rules seem to consider signs rather than causes. A man may well understand natural signs without knowing their analogy, or being able to say by what rule a thing is so or so. And, as it is very possible to write improperly through too strict an observance of general grammar rules; so, in arguing from general laws of nature, it is not impossible we may extend the analogy too far, and by that means run into mistakes."
—From Concerning Human Knowledge
George Berkeley

I sat long in silence after the presence of Rama Sandlob faded from the Meditation Dome. The grandeur of the snow covered Himalayas spread before me as reminder of my insignificance from the standpoint of the physical shell that my consciousness inhabited. Even a few minutes of exposure to the air outside of the crystal clear dome would bring immediate death to my body. But now I felt that my existence was more real and more lasting than the great mountains of solid rock that surrounded me.

As I sat thus in the tower I became aware of an approaching speck high above in the eastern sky. I knew then that it would only be moments before the air car bringing Dr. Karoll and his family would be moored fast to the dome entrance. With a flood of emotions I arose from the meditation table and took a long last look about me before leaving the dome through the trap door. I knew that none of the family would enter the tower so I changed into the clothing in which I had arrived and waited at the exit chamber door. Within five minutes I was sitting in the air car with Dr. and Mrs. Karoll, Alice and her brother, James, headed for the Great Smokies.

As I looked from one to the other I realized that something had been added to my powers of observation. Not only were these people more beautiful than ever to me but I was seeing an aura of light enclosing each one of them. The light showed brightest particularly around the head and shoulders of each person. The colors varied; closest around the head and shoulders it was white, then hues of blue and lavender and sunshine yellow. Their auras radiated out so that they filled the whole compartment of our craft and intermingled with each other. It gave me a sensation like being in the midst of a lovely flower garden in full blossom.

Truly, I thought to myself, to be in the company of this family is as much heaven as I am able to comprehend.

"Oh, David, we are so glad to know that you feel like that," said Alice in her clear musical voice. "We are all delighted to have you back with us again."

Rama Sandlob and his assistants had made me accustomed to having my thoughts read, but when the answer came out loud and in a voice that I had not imagined was so dear to me, it had new impact.

"Ah," I said, "it is truly a pleasure to hear you speak. Possibly spoken words are unnecessary for human communication but I think that I would as soon have the birds stop their singing."

The whole family laughed at this and we began an interchange during which I described the high points of my two weeks in the Meditation Dome. All were intensely interested in the insights that came to me through the memories of earlier incarnations. My release from intellectual conflicts with Christianity especially pleased Alice, although I got the impression there was yet something which she had hoped that I would learn about. As soon as I let my mind dwell on this impression for a few moments, I realized she felt that we had a past experience together as companions. Nothing of this kind had been shown to me but I resolved to spend time in meditation with that question before me in the days to follow.

After a time our conversation took a scientific direction because of questions I asked about the operation of the air car. Dr. Karoll requested James to explain the anti-gravity unit to me more fully than Alice had done earlier.

"First," said James, "you must understand that gravity is a force that is present in all parts of our universe. You are aware that the difference between an ordinary bar of soft iron and a magnet of steel lies in the orientation of the molecules, individual magnetic particles exerting forces either at random or in one direction."

"Yes," I said. "Does that mean that gravity only exists as a directional force as a result of some action which the earth has upon random forces?"

"Precisely, Mr. Neuport," said James.

I raised my eyebrow at the scholarly way that I was being instructed by this sixteen year old.

"Then this is why all of the objects which our scientists were putting into orbit just stayed there. It really didn't matter how much they weighed or at what speed they orbited the earth but only that they were lifted high enough so that the forces of gravity were acting upon them at random instead of in one direction?" I asked.

"Yes, sir," said James.

"I think that there must have been many persons like myself who understood the original theory for putting an object into orbit about the earth. The steady gravitational pull upon the object in orbit was to be balanced by the equally steady centrifugal force obtained from its circular movement horizontal to the crust of the earth. The only result that could be hoped for was a temporary condition, an approximate balance that might have allowed the object either to slowly spiral inward or away. To hit a perfect balance between gravity and centrifugal force would have been like trying to balance a steel ball on a knife edge. When we learned that the hardware which put the first capsule into orbit also stayed up, then we knew that our theory of gravity was in error," I said. "These objects that were not given a carefully calculated horizontal acceleration continued to orbit the earth without falling back."

"There were many indications that your theory of gravity was in error. The forces which keep the moon and planets in their orbits never fitted into your gravitation of theory. The connection between the moon and the tides on earth indicates the same force is acting upon them both; not the moon's gravitational attraction for the sea," said James. "Astronomers had obvious signs that earth was not held in orbit by gravity from the sun. The stationary cloud of asteroids which the earth passes through once a year is an example. If the sun exerted a steady gravitational pull to keep the earth in orbit, then the asteroids would necessarily respond to that pull and be drawn toward the sun. They do not orbit around the sun, thus there is not an action opposing its gravitational pull by centrifugal force."

"It sounds like elementary reasoning when you put it like that," I said. "Now tell me why there seemed to be an attraction like gravity between the objects we put into orbit?"

"Oh, this is quite obvious. It gives a good illustration of how easily an inaccurate theory can be reinforced by faulty reasoning," said James. "Visualize that the force called gravity is force rays, subatomic particles radiated in all directions like light and coming from every star. Any object in space is exposed equally to these random units of directional energy. If you shielded one side of an object in the slightest way, the resulting unbalanced forces would cause its movement in the direction of the shielded side. Naturally, this effect verified a theory of mutual attraction between objects."

"How does this explain the anti-gravity unit in the air car being like a tank of air submerged in water?" I asked.

"The force around earth called gravity depends upon the existence of a liquid like media of more refined matter. It is all around the planet and permeates the elements of the earth itself. Its particles, which intercept the random force rays, are driven into a great spherical body with earth in the center. This sea of subatomic liquid, ether, pervades the earth to its core and reaches far into the stratosphere. It permeates all ordinary metals as easily as water moves through a sponge. The resistance to its flow through a given solid body is called density. The term 'density' designates how much directional energy a given element absorbs from the force rays. You can see from this illustration that gravity is a force pushing things inward, to all appearances, it manifests as an attraction or pull exerted by the earth."

"As I understood Alice," I said, "the unit which provides lift for the air car is a tank from which the ether is evacuated. How does this provide lift?"

"Why, it acts like a bubble under water," said James. "The same principle is involved but the forces are greater because of the pressure upon the ether which gives the effect of a liquid of great density."

"You have just said that the ether flowed through metals and the ease with which it did indicated their density," I said. "Now please tell me how do you make a container which excludes the ether?"

"This, of course, was the first necessity to be accomplished, once the principle had been surmised," said James. "The metal that was able to be developed from the condensation of helium by an alteration of the charges upon its atomic and accompanying subatomic particles gave us the needed metallic density. With this new metal we were able to construct a container capable of excluding the ether. Transportation by air of all goods, light or heavy, became a matter of course with the discovery of this principle."

"The principle appears beautifully simple," I said. "However, it required development by a society which had mastered a new metallurgical skill. Surely, the mechanism which could evacuate ether from a container must be fabricated from unusual materials also?" I asked.

"Well," James smiled at my question, "not exactly. The ether could have been evacuated from such a container in your time, Mr. Neuport."

"I don't see how that could possibly be," I said, in confusion.

"James," said Dr. Karoll, "I know that you are trying to stimulate David's reasoning powers, but you should not forget the personal element and the difference in your ages."

"No, sir," said James. "I am sorry."

I looked in wonder from one to the other. It was true that I found it a little humiliating to me to be instructed in question of physics by a mere boy. I wasn't sure whether I was grateful or not to have Dr. Karoll reveal what was troubling me. Just at that moment, the obvious answer as to how we could have evacuated the ether came to my mind. I looked at Alice to see if I could confirm what I suspected had just happened. All realized this at once and we burst out laughing together.

"Well, of course," I said. "I see what you mean. Alice painted me a picture. I'm afraid that I would not have reasoned it out. Our outdated idea of ether was that it permeated all space in the same concentration, or perhaps I should say in the same density. Now I see that the ether permeating our earth and its atmosphere differs as much from that in outer space as water and air are different. Had we the container, we could have sent it aloft into space to empty it."

With that Mrs. Karoll suggested we take some time for refreshments and listen to some music. I was grateful for the respite for the strain on my ever present ego was interfering with my receptivity toward James.

CHAPTER 34

Music

"Our birth is but a sleep and a forgetting.
The soul that rises with us, our life's star
Hath had elsewhere its setting,
and cometh from afar;
Not in entire forgetfulness,
And not in utter nakedness,
But trailing clouds of glory do we come
From God, Who is our home.
Heaven lies about us in our infancy."
Intimations of Immortality
—William Wordsworth

The music seemed to radiate from all sides instead of originating at a speaker or even at several speakers. When I asked about it later, I learned there was a ring of speakers encircling the compartment. The design and the materials used to make the speakers varied in order to best reproduce sound in several different ranges. The high range of audibility was extending upward with the refinement of the human bodies on the earth, and so I was not able to hear some passages of music with my less sensitive auditory system.

I asked if we might listen to some of the composers that I knew. Alice herself was a talented musician and played the violin with their community symphony orchestra. I had already learned she could discuss at length the music and composers familiar to me. She asked if I would like to know how children were taught to appreciate music. Enthusiastically, I answered that I would.

"First, David, we learned to begin their training in the cradle," said Alice. "Our understanding of the effect of music on physical-mental-spiritual health has been expanding with each passing year. You probably remember the early experimentation done with plants, showing that music had an effect upon their growth."

"Why, yes, I do, Alice," I said. "I seem to remember that even some popular music was better than no music, but classical music was best."

"As you may surmise, David, the effect of music upon the growth of small children was more apparent under controlled conditions than it was upon plants. The human body is a more intricate life form than any other upon earth, and thus, more responsive."

"Isn't tampering with the response to music of small children like brainwashing?" I questioned.

226

"There is more to a baby than a brain and a physical body. Other faculties which are developing need kinds of nourishment generally disregarded in your day. We discovered that music provided nourishment for the developing of psychic faculties and other spiritual attributes which the incoming soul strives to bring with it into materiality."

"But shouldn't each child have a right to develop its own particular taste in music? Surely you are creating a nation of musical stereotypes," I objected.

"Oh, David, didn't the study of nutrition establish certain standards for feeding babies and growing children? Did this create a nation of stereotyped eating habits?"

"Well, no, but food for the body plainly shows its value by the results it produced," I said.

"Do you think that this is not equally true of the nourishment provided by music for the developing intellectual and intuitive faculties of a child?" asked Alice gently. "Isn't it an obligation of society toward its children to see that none lacks proper nourishment through circumstances over which the infant has no control? The idea of condemning a child to malnutrition, poverty, ignorance and abuse because its parents are irresponsible or incompetent is unthinkable to us. It was just as unthinkable in your times except that the disciplines which your society needed to impose upon itself in order to correct these conditions were equally unthinkable. The incentive was lacking for society to fulfill its obligation to its incoming members. Once an understanding of the natural laws governing rebirth was established in the minds of the people, it became a sacred trust to themselves to make equal opportunity and care the birth right of every child. This requires self sacrifice and discipline on a national scale."

"What you say sounds so right, Alice," I answered. "I've been brainwashed to think of freedom as the absence of strictly enforced rules and disciplines. When you tell me of the application of your social discipline, I'm inclined to visualize a nation of automatons. After I think over what you say, I realize you are telling me how age old ideals and dreams are being put into practice and only their application startles me, for these are not new ideas. The fast vanishing freedom in America stemmed from our unwillingness to discipline our industry, our politicians, our entertainers, our food producers, our waste handling, our media of mass communication, our educational system, and our own appetites and desires."

"Shall we go back to a discussion of musical training for children?" Alice asked with a twinkle in her eyes. She did not conceal a trace of humor at my rebellion toward ideas which represented the fulfilling of my own ideals for the race in the first place.

I had to smile at myself when I thought about it. "Please do, Alice. Perhaps, I can listen to you without getting self righteous for a little while."

Alice smiled and began again. "After our experimentation with plants and animals had given us indications that musical rhythm and harmony affected growth and we learned that almost any kind of music was helpful, then we set out to learn how its rate of acceleration and its character would vary with the kind of music used. A marked difference resulted when the same music was used with different types of plants and animals. Eventually we were able to determine how to produce varied responses in different parts of the human body. We found that we could stimulate or retard the functioning of each of the endocrine glands with a particular type of musical vibration and that each individual had his own overall musical tone. Miracle-like healing techniques resulted. Our sound therapy causes the rapid knitting of bones, the disintegration of undesirable growths and the regeneration of lost limbs and organs. A system of classification according to individual tone response has been established in order to best minister to the musical needs of each person. The astrological signs, hand prints, and refinement or level of spiritual development are all related, and so is the type of music most conducive to the health and well being of any particular individual. We have seven general music classifications which embrace the full range of human evolutionary status in the world. It is needful to have both 'low brow' and 'high brow' music, just as we range from elementary arithmetic to calculus for different stages of one's educational development."

"Music to me is something mysterious in its power to affect human nature," I said. "In a way, I'm inclined to leave its beauty unanalyzed. Getting scientific about music seems like cutting up rose petals with a scissors."

"Oh, David, your thinking is out of date. This would have been true in your times. The shattering disharmony of your society with our precious and beautiful natural environment speaks for itself. In your time, the beauty of a river might well have been examined 'scientifically' and evaluated by how much industrial waste it was capable of carrying down to the sea." Alice spoke these words softly and without a note of criticism.

"I'm sorry, Alice. I surely did not intend to get pompous again. Your patience with me is a wonder. Let me try again to listen to you without bringing up my prejudices. I know that I can understand and learn far more if I will restrain myself from either agreeing or disagreeing and just listen with inner silence as Rama Sandlob instructed me. I have much self discipline to learn with regard to listening to others. Please go on about music."

"Music comes to us from higher realms of consciousness. The very Essence of Life is the Source of inspiring melodies and rhythms, but there is a science behind the mathematically harmonious vibrations in air which we call music. Should one understand why a particular piece of music is considered beautiful and why a melody touches the heart strings, he would have an insight into the Well Springs of Life." Alice said these words with such reverence that I was silent until she spoke again.

"We begin to awaken the soul of an infant to respond to its developing awareness of sound first with simple melodies in clear notes and a rhythm that is similar to a mother's heartbeat. Like their eyes, the ears of the infant must become coordinated. Music develops their ability to respond and gives the infant a sense of both security and joyous adventure. The music reminds the soul of higher realms of consciousness and helps to keep it aware that it is a soul rather than a baby. Heavenly music is nourishment which builds the connecting link between the physical and the spiritual body. It ennobles the mind and improves its capacity for the comprehension of any subject. Music has the power to generate moral courage and steadfastness, nobility of thought, and beauty of character. It provides a universal language which can sharply contrast impurity and weakness with the noble ideals of the race. A combination of music and fairy tales can have an impact upon the developing mind of an infant that will guide the soul entity while it is in a three dimensional state of consciousness." Alice paused with a smile to await my comments.

"You have stimulated my recollections about the power of music. How well I remember the way martial music caused a man to hold his head erect and determine in his heart to act courageously. I remember also how that all which was lovely in the relationship between man and woman was set aside by some of our popular music composers. You need not tell me that music is no longer permitted to be an unwholesome influence in the lives of youth," I said thoughtfully.

"If music could not be misused, it could have no power for good, David. It is a tool to channel the activity of the unconscious mind and thus a matter of exercising discipline and knowledge to insure its constructive use."

"What kind of music is generally good for everyone?"

"We have found that popular light music like Strauss waltzes, Hungarian dance music, folk music and Polkas is best to aid the forces in the body to establish normal health and growth. Such music has a life stimulating rhythm, does not demand concentration to be enjoyed, and produces a sense of well being. Other music which demands concentration from the listener can provide elevating spiritual experiences even to the point of producing a spiritual awakening. This type music is best reserved for such listening but to use it carelessly can be irritating and dulling to one's higher sensitivity."

"Do you teach all children to listen to symphonic music?"

"Only the youth who can respond to the more involved harmony and rhythm; and they first learn to concentrate for at least ten minutes," Alice answered. "We begin training in concentration by asking them to take a simple object like a stone or plant or seed and to keep all of their thoughts upon it. They may contemplate how it originated or what its chemical composition may be, just as long as they do not let their minds wander to another subject."

"That is more difficult than it sounds," I commented.

"Yes, this is true. It was more true in your times."

"What is the next step after they have mastered the training in concentration?" I asked.

"They are asked to listen to a well loved symphony, giving it their rapt attention and awaiting the sounding of each note with joyous anticipation. They are taught to notice what part of their body responds to each note of music and encouraged to see bursts of colors, sparks, as from an exploding rocket, or shimmering rainbow, as well as taking notice of the response in parts of their bodies. They learn that the music actually exists first in their own body and so they should listen with every cell of it rather than just their ears."

"Such an exhilarating experience as that a person could not possibly have while eating a meal or playing a card game or holding conversation," I offered.

"Music may open the doors to an awareness of the Divine Life within and prepare one's consciousness for entry into the Holy of Holies, the very presence of the Maker."

Alice said these words so reverently that I could sense she knew well the experience of which she spoke.

CHAPTER 35

Edgar Cayce Gravity Motor

"As to describing the manner of construction of the stone, we find it was a large cylindrical glass, as it would be termed today, cut with facets in such a manner that the capstone on top of same made for the centralizing of the power or force that concentrated between the end of the cylinder and the capstone itself."
—Description of the Atlantean Power Source
Edgar Cayce Readings

A fter a long silence that was filled with a warm feeling of human fellowship, Dr. Karoll turned to me and asked, "David, did you get your questions about our power sources answered during your meditation retreat?"

"Partly, sir, but I'm still not clear on the details. I did have a psychic experience which gave me the impression that the earth is immersed in a sea of energy which is flowing through it and radiating out from it. I did not see how this could be harnessed. I did see that to serve all man's trivial requirements would take but a minute quantity of the energy available."

"That question intrigued men for centuries, David."

"Many outstanding minds, including the world's greatest physicists and inventors, had given considerable thought to the possibility that power could be derived from our environment without the consumption of any fuel," I commented. "Such men as Nikola Tesla could not be deterred from thinking about self propelled power plants which would be driven by available energy from some yet unrecognized source. The most obvious directions for seeking to obtain power from nature without fuel consumption were from flowing water or sunshine or wind or tides that could be utilized to drive electrical generators. Nikola Tesla suggested that gravity might be like a force ray from outer space so that a heavy fly wheel could be driven by the force of gravity acting upon one side of the wheel."

"James may be glad to discuss these thoughts with you, David," spoke Dr. Karoll with a nod toward his son.

"Yes, I would like to," smiled James. "It would have been a great adventure to live in the times when crucial struggles to supply mankind's physical needs were being engaged upon."

"I don't know that it could be equal to the present adventure that you have in fellowship with extraterrestrial beings and in the realms of discovering spiritual science," I differed. "Besides, poverty and ignorance, or worse still, mind stifling propaganda, called education in my day, might have prevented the best of minds from being utilized in any fashion."

"You are forgetting the Immutable Laws of the universe now, David," interjected Dr. Karoll. "At no time may humankind be given powers which it should not have, nor can there be a withholding of scientific discoveries to which it must be exposed for either testing or its advancement."

"Thank you, sir. I know that you are correct. I must change my habitual thinking about injustice and confusion to embrace the concept that Law governs throughout our universe." I paused and went on, turning to James. "Was there a possibility that Nikola Tesla's theory was correct with regard to his energized power plant driven by the manipulation of the force of gravity?"

"Yes, and no! The force of gravity could not be shielded for it will freely pass through material of any density. All matter in the three dimensional world is pervious to these cosmic energy emanations. However, in the year 1928 there was a design of a gravity driven power plant that was given in dreams to a man influenced by the discarnate spirit of DeWitt Clinton. This discovery could have revolutionized the entire world with regard to the power available to the race. The question which was to determine if it should be released in human society hinged upon the use to which it would be put. Unfortunately, a turning away by the American people from the ideal of preserving world peace proposed by President Woodrow Wilson made our nation unworthy."

"Please, tell me how it worked," I asked with keen interest.

"The story of how this device was discovered was contained in microfilmed records of the Edgar Cayce Foundation, preserved for us in a Time Capsule buried at Virginia Beach. The capsule protected them during the period of devastation that he foretold would occur."

"You mean that I might have examined the information myself had I requested it from the Edgar Cayce Foundation?" I asked in unbelief.

"Possibly it would not have been as simple as that. Some of the psychic readings which made reference to it were freely available.

The key information was not, for reasons already given. Not that individuals were intentionally withholding a great boon to society, but rather that it was not yet in society's best interest for Divine Mind to release it."

James spoke as his father might, in acknowledging the place of Higher Wisdom in such a matter.

"Can you give me any kind of description that I would be able to understand?" I asked.

"It was primarily an eccentrically mounted drum. The proportions of the model described in Edgar Cayce's readings were: Diameter, eleven inches; length, thirty four inches; eccentricity, several inches; with leads in the form of sprangles sufficient for proper action in the cams in each end of the drum. The following was given by Edgar Cayce as the wording for the patent application: 'Means of generating power within self by virtue of a relationship of liquid to some other substance, either contained or uncontained, that has the less specific gravity than the liquid.' The ideal combination probably would have been mercury and air in those times."

"You mean that the idea of manipulating gravity by some mechanical device to derive power is a possibility?" I asked, delighted at the thought.

"Not just possible, but relatively simple and exceedingly practical. There is hardly any limit to the size and output for power plants of this type. They can produce more than one horsepower per pound when designed efficiently. Such engines could have driven the world's generators, powered the aircraft, ships, trucks, automobiles or any other vehicles in your own times. Once started, their output of energy would require only the maintenance of the bearing surfaces of the moving parts and no fuel of any kind."

"Are they in use now?" I asked.

"Oh, yes. They are useful for many things and may run indefinitely without attention."

"This is not the way that electrical power is developed, is it?" I asked remembering something about a great crystal in an earlier discussion.

"They are often used in connection with generators but this is not the principal source of energy for the world. Great crystals which gather the cosmic energy and transform it to high frequency electrical emanations are the chief source of power. This energy is broadcast somewhat as Nikola Tesla proposed and may be tuned in at any point on the globe. These crystals were used in the Atlantean Times, some eleven thousand years before the birth of Christ. They were redis-covered when a once submerged portion of Atlantis arose. Such a crystal was housed in a temple-like structure upon the land mass that came to the surface. This event was predicted by Edgar Cayce and a description given by him of the crystal itself."

"Thank you, James. I shall be looking forward to visiting a cos-mic energy power plant when the opportunity arrives." James and Dr. Karoll agreed that they would both accompany me on such a trip one day.

CHAPTER 36

Farming and Restoration of the Natural Environment

"In all ages the man whose determinations are swayed by reference to distant ends has been held to possess the higher intelligence. The tramp who lives from hour to hour; the bohemian whose engagements are from day to day; the bachelor who builds but for a single life; the father who acts for another generation; the patriot who thinks of a whole community and many generations; and finally, the philosopher and saint whose cares are for humanity and for eternity…t hese range themselves in an unbroken hierarchy, wherein each successive grade results from an increased manifestation of the special form of action by which the cerebral centers are distinguished from all below them."
—Principles of Psychology
William James

Far below I could see that there was great expanse of land under cultivation. We were just beginning to pass over the westward parts of America so this land was what was formerly the central plains. Remembering how terribly America had abused her soil from the early days of cotton and tobacco down to the times of chemical fertilizers and hard pesticides, I asked the means employed to restore its fertility.

"Many natural forces at man's disposal wait only for him to manage them properly, David," spoke Dr. Karoll. "One of mankind's great benefactors is the spiritual being that manifests itself in the physical world through the lowly earthworm. When we decided to cooperate with this willing servant of mankind, we were able to improve the quality of worn out soil until it became superior to its condition when first plowed."

"How did you accomplish this?"

"It was rather a matter of providing suitable conditions to let the earthworms accomplish it. We used sea weed to replenish the lost elements and trace minerals and created ideal conditions for earthworms with a ten inch covering of straw mulch. This retained the moisture and provided them the needed environment to multiply. Now organic materials are properly returned to the soil. Crops are planted through the mulch and plowing is done only at intervals of several years when the soil may require some special attention to maintain the proper chemical balance or improve conditions. Annual churning up of fields is a thing of the past."

"What about weeds and insects? Why, farming had reached a point in America that one would not even have a crop without using both poisons to kill insects and chemical fertilizers to make plants grow," I wondered.

"Your system for farming was as shortsighted as your banking system. You cannot continue to get more than you give. Nature demands to be cooperated with; no life forms that have existed for ages may be crushed without a reaction. Each specie of insect has its place in preserving the natural balance. The common house fly should never have been regarded as a pest but as a friend and conscientious servant. After all, the fly is Nature's means for converting decaying matter into life which otherwise would cause an excess of harmful microscopic organisms to contaminate the air. The fly is one of Nature's most effective scavengers and should be deeply appreciated. It is only evidence of man's improper treatment of waste when they are over abundant. Instead of correcting conditions, man viciously attacked such helpful creatures and seriously disturbed the insect balance."

"But there were lots of problems with insects before the widespread use of poisons began. The devastation of crops by the insects is what created the demand for poison sprays in the first place," I countered.

"Of course, David. However, it does not require any great reasoning power to understand this. Suppose you visualize the diversity of Nature and contemplate how She arranges for the balance to be maintained between one life form and another. Then visualize a great acreage of a particular crop that provides the ideal food for a specific type of insect but provides no cover or conditions for the reproduction of its natural enemies. The answer to your question is obvious. How very elementary the thinking is which enables man to organize the production of food in harmony with Nature!"

"Then you are saying that we should have given more thought to living in harmony with the natural order of our environment instead of opposing with force the plant and animal and insect life that interfered with our food supply?" I responded.

"It was pride and ignorance and rebellion against natural order which first inspired the use of poison to control any life form. In the final analysis, the reaction to the abuse naturally could be expected to result in man's own body becoming contaminated with these poisons. They took their effect upon his sensitivity to delicate spiritual forces, leaving him even more benumbed and apathetic toward his misuse of the discoveries of science."

"Does this mean that a great variety of plants are now cultivated side by side on the same field?" I asked.

"Yes, it does. It also means that some of the plants are not grown for human food but to serve the needs of the creatures whose cooperation is required, or to repel certain other creatures which would normally feed upon neighboring plants. The science of agriculture is now one of cooperation with the various life forms in our environment. Depleted crop lands in all parts of the globe are being restored with the help of earthworms, the use of organic matter from the sea, mulching to hold the moisture and control the growth of undesirable plants and crop rotation. Our streams run clear as crystal and contain an abundance of fish for we have no run off water that carries top soil or chemicals."

"I know that all of these principles were understood in my own times," I sighed.

"They have been known since ancient times, David. Only because of his ignorance was man destroying the environment which he would himself inherit by rebirth. With a belief in only one life on earth, each man was inclined to think lightly of the injury he was doing himself by his abuse of Nature."

"Well," I said, "I can see that we have been hard on our best friends. I'm glad that the earthworms and flies don't hold grudges. I suppose the humble snail is one of our good friends, also."

"A very good friend. His place in maintaining the balance is partly to provide food for various predatory creatures that need him in their diet. Without the enforced discipline of Nature, you can easily see that no species could continue to exist. These lower life forms depend upon their natural enemies for their own existence. The classic example in America was the disappearance of the beautiful mountain goats after the bounty hunters killed off the mountain lions. Very shortly, the goats over populated their habitat and starved themselves into extinction. Almost overnight, an abundant and lovely form of wild life was destroyed because its only enemy was killed off."

"Dr. Karoll, it looks like we had so many destructive plans to engage our educated minds that Nature had no way to give us the lessons we needed except by giving up and dying," I said in sad recollection of the dying birds and fishes, the blights, the dead soil, and the disappearing wild bees."

"Things are never what they seem. The reality is not visible to the one sided view of material minded man, David," said Dr. Karoll gently. "The crucifixion of Mother Nature by man to whom She gave of Herself to sustain is a parallel to the crucifixion of the Inner Man by the ego. Only through exercising his opportunity to abuse Nature does man learn that, as a race, he must meet what he sows in relation to his environment. The great opportunity was to work with Nature to create a beautiful environment. The opportunity to work with living forms, guiding them into useful and exquisite expressions of life by the science of horticulture, was a gift to man by his Maker. The choice between right-use-ness, life and beauty or unright-use-ness, death and ugliness, had to be presented to man, both individually and collectively, or else he could not learn to know himself through meeting the consequences of sin, misuse of his powers."

"With the delayed reaction between exploiting Nature and suffering the consequences, mankind could not learn better. Unless there was a scientifically established understanding of rebirth, man could become extinct," I commented. "The power to destroy his environment in disregard for posterity and the knowledge of reincarnation stand as opposing forces. The tools to establish the science of reincarnation and disseminate knowledge of it throughout the earth were developed simultaneously with the means to destroy all life."

"Not quite, David. You lived in the time of testing of the race. First came the capacity to destroy or bless the entire race by scientific discoveries and then, after the choice was clear, came the knowledge of rebirth to human society."

"The public was aware of the power to destroy first, I'm sure," I answered. "The test you refer to reminds me of a story told me by a Sunday school teacher. It was about two brothers, the first rich through application of his talents to serve others, the second poor and resentful. To help his poorer brother in a constructive way, the rich one asked him to be his contractor to build a home. He gave him the plans for the construction of a beautiful house on a fine building lot. He asked his brother to build it of the best materials and insist on the highest quality of workmanship, and allowed him to think the house was for the rich brother's family. He trusted his brother to spend money carefully and to supervise the work properly. When the work was completed, the second brother brought the keys to the first. In the process of building the house he had taken every advantage of the situation to prosper himself. He bought shoddy material and showed on the records the price of the best. He falsified the record of hours and wages so as to draw more money than was required to pay the labor. The finished home was excessively expensive and of poor quality throughout. When the rich brother received the keys, he took them with a smile. Telling his brother that he trusted he had done a good job and that he was not even going to look over the house, he handed them back to him. The house that the second brother had been furnished all he needed to build was actually a gift to himself from the start."

"Your story draws parallels, David," spoke Dr. Karoll, "but by the grace of God there is a heartening difference to be taken into account. Man is given another chance to do better after each failure. This is the very purpose of his earth experience. Down through the centuries mankind has revered those who serve it well and forgotten those who hinder. This is true of ourselves with regard to individual incarnations. Only good lives on."

"A heartening difference," I agreed.

CHAPTER 37

Returned from the Tower

"Returning to himself, let man consider what he is in comparison with all existence; let him regard himself as lost in this remote corner of nature; and from the little cell in which he finds himself lodged, I mean the universe, let him estimate at their true value the earth, kingdoms, cities and himself. What is a man in the Infinite?"

Pensees
Blaise Pascal

D r. Karoll set the controls for our descent and in moments the ship was settling down in front of its enclosure beside the garden. It had been a long day for his family for they had been in the air for twenty-four hours. Alice and her mother had served the evening meal before we descended and all were ready to make preparations to retire.

I had no more than just drifted off to sleep with the perfume of the cool mountain air stirring up visions of my last trek through the woods when I felt someone vigorously rubbing my wrists and calling, "Dave, Dave, wake up!"

Startled I opened my eyes to see who it could be.

"Darch! Bill Darch! How did you get here? Where am I? How, in the name of God, did I get here in this cave?"

"Take it easy, Dave. It's all right. I had to wake you a month early."

"Wake me a month early! What do you mean wake me a month early! I've been awake for six months and you've been dead a hundred years," I screamed.

"Easy, Dave, easy, you're fine...blood pressure's coming up...temperature's almost normal...you've done it Dave, you've done it!"

"Oh, my God, my God, Darch! You don't mean that I've only been asleep for two months? Oh, no, no! It just can't be," I moaned.

Professor Darch didn't say anything more but just kept working on my wrists as I lay there. I looked around at the newly chipped stone ceiling. The days came to mind when we had worked together with air tools to enlarge this natural cavern about a hundred feet in from the cave's mouth. I tried to sit up.

"Easy, Dave! Don't try to move for a little bit. Wait until the blood circulation is a little better." Then he said with enthusiasm, "You made it, old man, you made it!...two months of suspended animation and you're still alive. I've been working over you for three hours to bring you out."

I was stunned. The smell of the cool air in the cave, the details of its interior, the equipment in the chamber and Bill Darch massaging my wrists...what was the use to try to deceive myself...everything was just as it was when I had laid myself down there. Instead of being grateful to be alive and back in the world that I knew, I just wished that I could have died during my hallucinations of Utopia in 2103.

"That's right, Dave, just lie there and relax. Inside of another hour you ought to be able to sit up. I'll explain why I had to wake you up early a little later. It will be best for us not to discuss that just now."

Professor Darch's effort to sound soothing was not altogether successful. I detected a note of anxiety which set me wondering. I studied his face as I lay silently while he massaged my wrists and ankles. Time went by slowly as my mind was racing madly through the dream experiences I had just been through. It had all been so logical and now I had a whole set of intensely personal memories to assign into the category of hallucinations. I wasn't sure that I was willing to do this. Maybe, I thought, I would prefer to hang onto them and be called mad.

"You can try to sit up now, Dave."

I was so engrossed in my thoughts that I didn't take notice.

"Dave, Dave, try to sit up, please," Professor Darch insisted.

"Uh...all right."

I painfully pulled myself up and started to black out and let myself back down again. The professor worked with me for two or three more hours as I tried to sit up from time to time. When he finally got me onto my feet so that I could walk to his cabin, he was worn out. He stretched out on a couch to rest and was soon in a deep slumber. In the meantime, I found myself gaining strength with each passing hour.

There was no thrill of achievement because of my success. There was no joy over having proven a theory to the scientific world. I was filled only with burning memories of Alice and the Doctor's family and the way of life that I had observed and participated in for more than six months. So real were the impressions that I could not conceive that it was only an elaborate creation of my own imagination.

I began to think about the situation in America and of the terrible financial collapse which I dreamed had devastated the land. Had I had a prophetic dream which foretold events that would transpire in the near future, I wondered? If my dream was a true vision of future events, then the great collapse had just taken place and this was the reason Professor Darch had felt he should awaken me early. This thought set my mind to racing in another direction. I began going over all the news events I remembered from just prior to my entry into the trance state. By some strange manipulation of the unconscious mind I now found that they fitted the picture described in my dream by Dr. Karoll. As it does with a dream that incorporates into a sleeper's visions a cause for the sound of a passing truck, possibly, I thought to myself, my sixth sense had interwoven real current events into my dream of the future.

Evening was well upon us by the time that Professor Darch had led me from the cave to his cabin. The strain upon him was evidently more tiring than I realized. He had worked over me for about six hours, I estimated. When he had lain down to rest, I covered him with a blanket to keep him from getting a chill. As the night wore on, I realized that he was going to sleep through until morning. All thought of sleep was out of the question for me as I sat out on the porch in the cool night air and reviewed the many questions I had. The moon was almost full, the night cloudless, and feeling the need to stimulate my blood circulation, as well as to quiet my nerves, I decided to walk down the winding dirt road in front of Bill's cabin. The dusty picturesque little road followed a brook until it led into a paved county road about two miles farther down.

Ordinarily, such a walk in the moonlight would have been a deeply satisfying time of communion with Nature for me. Now it was a time of frenzied thinking. I made a special effort to breathe slowly and very deeply to help my body adjust itself. The breathing soothed my nerves and helped me think. Almost before I realized any time had passed I found myself standing at the edge of the county road. Not wanting to go back to the cabin quite yet, I decided to walk on in the direction of Asheville.

It was possibly around one o'clock in the morning. The road I was on had no traffic at that hour for it served only the people of a few scattered mountain communities thereabouts. I had been walking along for about ten minutes when I heard the unexpected sound of an approaching vehicle. An old Chevrolet pick-up truck rattled up from behind and stopped beside me.

"Need a ride into Asheville?"

"No, I'm just out for a walk."

"Do you know what's gone wrong with the 'lectricity and the phones up here, mister?"

"What do you mean?"

"They're all dead. I got to get somebody to help my wife or take her into the hospital in Asheville but I can't get a call through to nobody."

"You're coming right back from Asheville?"

"Yeah! Got to get back to her quick."

"I'd like to ride with you."

"Get in."

It was too noisy to talk without half shouting and we were both too occupied with our own thoughts to care about trying. The road twisted and turned as we rolled through the sleeping unincorporated villages beside it. When we arrived at the approach to the freeway, the lean, drawn face of the young mountaineer beside me was outlined for a moment by the headlights of an oncoming vehicle.

"That's funny," he puzzled.

"What?"

"No lights on the freeway and hardly no traffic."

I sat bolt upright and looked both ways down the four lane divided highway.

"Ah never seen that before," he drawled.

"When did everything go dead?" I asked quickly.

"'Bout three days ago."

He pulled onto the highway and accelerated up to sixty-five. We rattled along that way for about five minutes without passing another car. Then we reached a crest in the highway which gave us a view over the outskirts of the city.

"Holy cow! The lights are all out." He was startled.

I had guessed by now why he was so anxious about his wife.

"You had best turn back and get one of your neighbors' women folk to stay with your wife," I said in his vernacular. "That town's got bad troubles and there's no chance of your getting her into a hospital or getting a doctor."

Without a word he turned around, crossing the divider strip in his haste. Before more than two or three minutes, we saw three men standing in the highway blocking the way and waving.

"Don't stop," I said quickly, remembering my vision of the chaos after the money collapse.

"Why not?" He slowed down as he spoke.

"They may want your truck," I said.

"I don't pass nobody needin' help."

"All right; have you got a pistol?"

"Loaded forty-five."

"Give it to me. I'll put it under my jacket and pretend to be asleep."

"Okay."

The pick-up slid to a stop on the gravel shoulder.

"Get out, kid." There was no mistaking the speaker's intentions.

I was observing the situation through almost closed eyelids. One of the men had stepped up and raised a twenty-two rifle just as we stopped. He was pointing it in the driver's face.

"Look, mister, my wife's expectin' and she needs help. Why don't you stop the next car." The boy had courage.

"Get out kid or she won't have you. Move quick!" There was cold blooded murder in his voice.

The boy had his wits about him. "Awright, this truck ain't worth much, no how." He drawled this out like he didn't care too much about the whole thing and didn't want any more trouble than he already had.

He opened the door as wide as it would go and climbed out, moving straight toward the man holding the rifle in his face. He moved slowly. The man with the gun backed away from him. Then the boy stepped toward the front of the truck. Holding the door wide with his left hand so that I would get an unobstructed view, he lifted his right hand up over his head like a man in a hold-up.

The gunman now perceived me sitting slouched back against the right side of the truck with my eyes closed.

"You there, get out!"

I didn't stir. I was sick with disgust over what was apparently my obligation now. I wished that I had not decided to try to protect the boy and his truck.

"You! Get out!" He knew I couldn't sleep through his shouted command.

I stirred a little, like I was just waking up and then opened my eyes wide so that I would be able to see clearly. Then I saw the man's face in the moonlight and I knew that I hadn't any choice in the matter. I had just meant to play it safe in asking for the forty-five but now I was going to be forced to take advantage of my ruse.

"Get out!" This was shouted by the man like he was losing his self control.

The forty-five was a regular issue World War II automatic. I knew the piece well. Still under my jacket, I slipped it from single shot to automatic and squeezed off three rounds point blank into his upper body. The impact of the heavy slugs knocked him back several feet. I jumped out with the gun pointed in the direction of the other two men.

"Don't shoot," one of them screamed, as they both threw their arms up over their heads so that I would know that they were unarmed.

"Pick up the rifle, son," I said, then, turning to the two men, "Start running!" I fired one shot over their heads when they were about fifty feet away. Then I motioned toward the man on the ground. "Leave him. I'll be responsible if there are any questions."

We rode back in silence. After the incident I suddenly felt exhausted almost to the point of passing out. I realized that I had misjudged how much energy I had. I asked the boy to drive me up to Professor Darch's cabin. He helped me up onto the porch and into an old deck chair. As he left, he spoke one word with feeling, "Thanks."

The cool night air helped some to refresh me. Exhausted though I was, there was no feeling of sleepiness. I had never suffered from insomnia but I guessed that I was experiencing what it felt like. Tense, wide awake, nervous and exhausted, I sat there mulling over the events of the evening.

It was just beginning to get light when Professor Darch pushed the screen door to the porch open and stepped out rubbing his eyes.

"Didn't mean to sleep so long, Dave. How are you feeling now?"

I looked over at Bill Darch's familiar form for a long moment and forgetting his inquiry asked, "When did the Europeans refuse our currency?"

"It'll be two weeks tomorrow," then in amazement, "but how did you learn that?"

"When I was in the cave, Bill, I had some kind of dream...vision... experience. I saw it all...saw why it happened...devastated the big cities...the whole government was gone...cannibals...the city people went wild...they were starving...roamed the country in packs like wolves."

"Wait a minute, Dave, that hasn't happened yet. Things look pretty bad but not cannibals!"

"This is the reason that you woke me up a month early, isn't it?" I already knew the answer.

"Well, yes, of course. I didn't know what might happen. Everything in the way of communications has broken down. No one is selling goods. You can't even get a gallon of gasoline. I didn't want to stop the experiment before time but there was no telling what might happen. We actually may not be safe here. There is no law enforcement of any kind."

"This is the way I saw it all, Bill."

"You must have been having some kind of psychic experience."

"Yes, I guess that's what it was," I said, still unwilling to believe that I had awakened a month early instead of having overslept a hundred and twenty years.

"How do you feel now?" asked Professor Darch, changing the subject.

"Well, I'm pretty weak. I thought I was stronger and took a walk down to the county road last night. Rode part way into Asheville with a young fellow looking for help for his wife. We turned back when we saw that the lights were out in the city. Figured that meant things were pretty bad. Got stopped by three men who wanted to take the boy's truck. I killed the one carrying a gun with the boy's automatic. Left the body by the road...figured that my dream of how things were must be accurate. Been up all night thinking about it."

"Great God, man!"

We both fell silent for a time. Professor Darch went inside and began to prepare some breakfast. He was out of groceries and had little more than flour, cooking oil, salt and baking soda to work with. He was a pretty good hand at making biscuits and I had begun to feel like I could take some nourishment. In a little bit he had set out breakfast...a cup of instant coffee and biscuits made with bleached flour.

I sipped the hot coffee very slowly. The biscuits smelled delicious to me. The two of us sat silently thinking. The idea of several years of anarchy in America was standing before me like a specter.

"We had better see if we can get a group of people together that can help each other and share what they have. It's going to take some clear thinking just to survive for the next few months. Winter will be here before this thing gets straightened out."

"You are probably right, Dave. You are probably just about right."

"No farther than we are from Asheville, we could be in serious danger right now," I commented thoughtfully. "Do you have a gun, Bill?"

"I turned mine in when they began enforcing the gun control laws. Most people around here wouldn't do it, but I did. I had no occasion to use it. I only had it for protection. I assumed police would eventually pick up all the weapons. I never had used it and I don't hunt."

"I'm sorry to hear that. I guess that we couldn't get one for love or money now...much less get any ammunition."

"You are surely correct about that, Dave."

"What do you know about edible wild plants, Bill?"

"That subject never held any interest for me. I'm afraid that I know very little." He thought for a moment. "As a matter of fact, I don't know any edible wild plants except blackberries and plums. They are always too sour for me, even when they are ripe."

We were silent again for several minutes as we thought about the situation at hand.

"The city people must already be pretty desperate," I commented. I looked over at the biscuits. "Your cooking gas won't last long."

Professor Darch nodded at a wood heating stove over in the corner. "I cooked those on top of the wood stove in an iron skillet with a lid on it."

"Hmmm," I said thoughtfully, "that might have been a mistake."

"What do you mean, Dave?"

"Smoke."

We spent the next hour talking over how we should get started with the community idea and what steps we should be taking to make needed provision for ourselves for the next few days. Both of us had forgotten about the smoke and the possibility of danger from intruders when we heard a sound like some rocks thrown on the roof.

Professor Darch got up immediately and started for the front door. I was right behind him when I stopped and decided to hide in the closet just in case there was danger. Without a second thought, Bill stepped out on the porch to look around.

"Up with your hands, Mister."

The voice was soft and pained. The speaker was plainly troubled and doing something that went against his conscience.

"Go through the house, son, and see if he's got any canned milk, specially. Don't take all his food but get some shells for this gun, if he's got 'em."

He turned back to Professor Darch. "Sorry to do you this way, Mister, but nobody's been willin' to help us by askin' 'em."

The man sounded like a millhand. I pictured him as a humble, conscientious employee who had just been able to provide a meager living for his family on his income but had served faithfully over the years. I deeply sympathized with him. The request for canned milk made me guess that he had a wife and a hungry baby somewhere about. It was hard to decide how to cope with the situation. The boy would probably be looking in the closet I was in before he got through. I didn't have a plan in mind.

The man evidently decided to come in after the boy. The three of them, the boy first, Darch, and the man shuffled down the hall. I watched them through the crack at the edge of the almost closed door. I decided to bluff from my vantage point in the darkened hall closet. I cracked the door about two inches and stayed back out of view.

"Stop where you are!" I said calmly. "I have you covered with a twelve gauge. Set that gun on the table and raise your hands."

The boy and the man were stunned. I told Bill to pick up the gun and cover them and then I stepped out of the closet into the room.

The boy took one look at me and shouted. "He ain't got no gun, Dad."

They both dropped their arms and lunged for us. The boy was about seventeen and overgrown. He grabbed the skillet off the stove and started for me.

Professor Darch didn't realize what had happened. He stood look-ing dazed as the man grabbed the rifle barrel with calloused hands and jerked it toward himself with the muzzle pointed toward his own groin.

We were no match for the two of them. I fended off a blow from the skillet aimed at my head. I hadn't guessed that my bluff would backfire. By this time the unloaded gun had changed hands and I heard a dull thud as Bill Darch caught a blow in the side of the head from the butt. I ducked another blow aimed at my head by the boy. The man started toward me as Bill slouched to the floor.

A brilliant flash of sparkling light filled my consciousness for an instant and I sagged to the floor with darkness closing in fast.

CHAPTER 38

Conclusion

"Mind is the builder."
—Edgar Cayce

“Don't you think that we should wake him; he's groaning so.”

“No, dear; he may be having an important dream experience.”

I was just half conscious as I heard those familiar voices. I struggled to wake up quickly. It was early dawn and both Alice and her mother were standing beside my bed in their robes. I shook my head and braced myself up on one elbow. Blinking my eyes hard to focus them, I stared at Alice and Mrs. Karoll uncomprehendingly.

“What were you dreaming, David?”

“Dreaming?” I repeated in a dazed manner. Then, “Dreaming? Yes, of course, I must have been dreaming,” I almost shouted. “What a dream! Oh, what a dream!” I reached one hand back to feel if the place where the rifle butt struck me was sore and then I let out a long sigh of relief.

By this time Dr. Karoll had entered the room and was standing by quietly. He spoke his cheerful, “Good morning, David,” with a smile and asked if I should like to tell the family about my dream. I was still wondering if I knew what was real and what wasn't, and so I didn't answer for a moment. Mrs. Karoll took this silence to indicate that I needed some time to gather my thoughts together. She suggested that we dress and enjoy a hot drink before breakfast while I told the family about my dream.

It was about twenty minutes later when we gathered in the family room for an herb tea with a little wild honey and lemon. The dream had not faded from my consciousness and as I described it to the family the details stood out even more sharply. They listened spellbound while I gave minute details with vivid recall. I re-experienced the emotions that had shaken me so during the dream while retelling it.

After I had finished my account, Dr. Karoll suggested that we should all remain quiet to have fifteen minutes of meditation upon the meaning of the incident.

The meditation was closed with a simple prayer and we began discussing the implications of the dream.

"How do you feel about your dream now, David?" asked Dr. Karoll.

"The experience still seems so real to me that I am having difficulty thinking of it as a dream. I wonder if the dream experience was possibly the way things would have fallen out if Professor Darch had wakened me a month early."

"Well," spoke Dr. Karoll seriously, "we know that all major events in a person's life are first previewed in dream experience. The individual makes choices and decisions on a soul level before he meets these situations in normal consciousness. It is possible that your dream was an accurate portrayal of the sequence of events that would have ensued, had you made the inner choice to be awakened at that time."

"That is an intriguing thought," I mused. "Perhaps the choice presented to me was between the uncertainty of my future after an indefinitely extended time in the cave and the immediate hardship of violence of my dream. I'm certain that in any case I would have gone to great lengths to avoid the incident on the highway."

"There is a distinct possibility that you made such a choice, David," Dr. Karoll nodded thoughtfully.

"Our family is glad for the choice that brought you into our home. You have won our respect and our love." Alice sounded a little unnatural to me. It was as though the words she spoke had more emotion behind them than she was free to display. I looked full into her lovely eyes for an instant and, as once before, I experienced an emotion of such power and impact that it almost left me dizzy. I turned away for fear that I would embarrass everyone should my deep feelings toward Alice become noticed. No one appeared to see this but I could not help remembering how often a member of the family had spoken aloud to answer my unvoiced thoughts.

I was grateful that I had been working at acquiring the control of my thoughts for several months and felt I had made much progress. My respect for Dr. Karoll's family and all the people I met gave me the incentive to pursue this difficult task. I wanted my every thought to be so in harmony with my ideals that they could always be exposed to public view. In Dr. Karoll's household, I was not sure but that my thoughts were constantly like an open book.

At that moment, Dr. Karoll stood up and suggested that we should have breakfast. I was grateful to have this distraction just then. After breakfast was over, he said that he wanted to discuss some things with me which concerned my further preparation to take a place in society as an active citizen. After all, he commented, it was going to be necessary for me to earn the right to vote and to take my part in society as a responsible individual.

"I know that you have been giving this question a lot of thought, David," he commented.

"Yes, sir, Dr. Karoll, I have been looking forward to the challenge, as well as the opportunity to acquire the education to become an active citizen like yourself. The privilege of being with your family is a blessing beyond description but it is altogether out of character for me to be in the roll of a dependent."

"You have high aspirations for yourself, David, and we admire you for this. It would not be fair to have you think we are unaware of your feelings toward Alice. Memories out of the far distant past cause you both to be drawn to each other. But there is much work that you must accomplish upon your own self before such an association could be taken up again. Hardly could you choose a higher goal than to desire to make yourself worthy of Alice. You must become physically, mentally, and spiritually her equal for such a union to be approved by the Centuria."

"I should have known that everyone in the family knew, sir, and yet I felt too sensitive to admit this to myself. It is quite a shock to realize that I am in the midst of a situation that compels forthrightness in my every thought. I think that it is beyond my present ability to achieve this."

"One can train himself to be straight forward in his thinking just as he might train for an athletic event. These are times when we know how to bring a person's intuition, his intellect, and his will power into harmonious cooperations. The real decision you face is between giving up all personal ambition to dedicate your life to service to the race or to put off such a sacrifice to another time, possibly another life. Alice has made the highest choice. If you would wish to have her stand by your side, then you must choose the same path."

"Your words are music to my ears, sir. It is my single desire to serve the race. The story of King Arthur and his Knights of the Round Table stirred this ideal in my heart when I was a child. That I might pursue such a course and, in addition, become worthy of Alice is a goal beyond my most fanciful dreams; I can conceive of no more joyous a challenge."

Dr. Karoll outlined the tentative program for my training; the development of my physical body, of my mind, of my psychic faculties, of my will power and character. I would select a specific branch of learning in which to make practical application in service to others. I might choose one of the many fields in medicine, science, or engineering. I would develop a highly organized mind in the process of mastering my educational requirements. The evaluation that had been made of my potential assured that I could achieve the goal set before me. The choice to discipline my body and mind was for me to make and to renew daily.

"To achieve the status that will enable you to ask Alice to become your companion will require several years," Dr. Karoll informed me solemnly. "You will regain the physical health and stamina of youth and learn to maintain this youth for whatever length of time you choose to spend on earth in a physical body."

"Sir, do you think that your beautiful daughter might wait, possibly for years, while I am striving to become qualified to ask for her hand?" I asked, hardly daring to hope for an affirmative answer.

"If she loves you, David, she will wait as long as necessary."

"How can I hope that she might love a person so inferior to her as myself?"

"She has memories of you when you set an example for manliness that is still remembered and honored. Alice does not feel you are inferior. If you and she were associated in the past, then she may know you better than you know yourself. The questions you are asking should be taken up with her."

"After my dream experience of last night, I am hardly sure whether or not I'm dreaming now, but the challenge set before me is irresistible. The hope and aspiration set before me to achieve citizenship in your society, and to serve it with Alice as my companion, exceeds any dream of heaven that I have ever entertained."

"Dreams are realized through effort and discipline, David. You have everything before you, if you are willing to pay the price."

I stood up and walked over to the window thoughtfully. The example set for me by Dr. Karoll included two years as a Noble-Contender, and I already had more than an inkling of what this could mean. As I was turning these thoughts over in my mind, I saw Alice through the window which overlooked the garden. She and her mother were starting toward the tennis court with rackets over their shoulders. Alice turned as though she felt my glance and waved with a smile. In that instant I could see there was only one path that I could choose and for me the future was as sure as the will of a man could make it.

Acknowledgements

There are so many who are contributors to our life experiences, to the development and maturing of our ideals, and to any honors we achieve, that there is hardly a way to give acknowledgements. The following are only a few:

To my wife, Mary, who patiently typed and retyped the manuscript—all the while giving sorely needed encouragement.

To Laurie Douglas, whose talent and expertise as graphic artist could not be bought any more than could her friendship.

To Rudolph Steiner, whose guidance through his book, *Knowledge of the Higher Worlds and Its Attainment,* was instrumental in the awakening of the psychic faculties given voice in this work.

To Harold Waldwin Percival, whose book, *Thinking and Destiny,* described and, to me, confirmed my personal experiences (in other levels of consciousness)—especially the hypothesis that the individual— the soul entity—reappears again and again in a physical body which is ordinarily almost alike from life to life because its configurations and makeup represent the character of the slowly evolving inner man.

To the Association for Research and Enlightenment in Virginia Beach, Virginia, for the preservation of transcripts of the words spoken by the entranced seer Edgar Cayce which confirm the accuracy of my personal memories of ancient Atlantis and the building of the great pyramid of Egypt and presenting the story of the Birth, the Life, the Death and Resurrection of Jesus Christ in the most elevating and inspiring manner this author has ever experienced.

About the Author

Joseph R. Myers, P.E., has practiced as a freelance registered professional engineer in North Carolina for many years to support himself and his wife, Mary, in their work with psychical research and in their efforts to promote greater understanding of the teachings of Eastern Religions, of reincarnation and of the relationship these teachings have with Christianity. He has written seven one-hour radio documentaries that have been broadcast by National Public Radio. He has also spoken about reincarnation, the Bible and related subjects on radio and television programs, at universities, colleges and high schools, to various civic clubs such as Rotarians and Civitans, and to many church groups.

During World War II, he was an aircraft maintenance engineering officer and attained the rank of captain with a superior rating as an officer. He obtained an FAA rating as an aircraft airframe mechanic and power plant mechanic—the A and P licenses.

He is the original inventor of the stressed skin-compression rib tent design featured as best on the market in the March 1980 issue of *Popular Science*.

The following documentaries are on 60-minute cassettes and may be purchased by writing to the address below:

The Edgar Cayce Story	Asaph Community
The Flying Saucer Story	P.O. Box 1416
Outer Space Communications	Lexington, NC 27293
Hypnotism	
Lost Atlantis	
Spiritual Healing	
Psychedelic Drugs	

1958-1998
Testing Period of the Great Tribulation

The questions and answers given here are from A Commentary on the Book of Revelation, *published by The Association for Research and Enlightenment, Virginia Beach, Virginia.*

Q. Is this the period of the great tribulation spoken of in Revelation, or just the beginning, and if so just how can we help ourselves and others to walk more closely with God?

A. The great tribulation and periods of tribulation, as given, are the experiences of every soul, every entity. They arise from the influences created by man through activity in the sphere of any sojourn. Man may become, with the people of the universe, ruler of any of the various spheres through which the soul passes in its experiences. Hence, as the cycles pass, as the cycles are passing, when there *is* come a time, a period of readjusting in the spheres, (as well as in the little earth, the little soul) — seek , then, as known, to present self spotless before that throne; even as *all* are commanded to be circumspect, in thought, in act, to that which is held by self as that necessary for the closer walk with Him. In that manner only may each atom (as man is an atom, or corpuscle, in the body of the Father) become a helpmeet with Him in bringing that to pass that all may be one with Him.

—Edgar Cayce (1877-1945)
Edgar Cayce psychic reading
given March 13, 1933
at Norfolk, Virginia